MW00577936

One Cops Journey

One Cops Journey

DETROITS DEADLY SEVENTIES

A. W. Boudreau

Copyright © 2016 A. W. Boudreau

All rights reserved. No part of this book shall be reproduced or transmitted in any form or by any means, electronic, mechanical, magnetic, photograph including photocopying, recording or by any information storage and retrieval system, without prior written permission of the publisher. No patent liability is assumed with respect to the use of the information contained herein. Although every precaution has been taken in the preparation of this book, the publisher and author assume no responsibility for errors or omissions. Neither is any liability assumed for damages resulting from the use of the information contained herein.

ISBN: 0692760946
ISBN 13: 9780692760949
Library of Congress Control Number: 2016912459
A. W. Boudreau, St. Clair Shores, MI

Contents

Acknowledgements

I WOULD LIKE TO ACKNOWLEDGE all of the first responders of Police Departments everywhere. These men and women do an unselfish job that no one can ever understand unless they walk in the same shoes. They do it because they care. They care about the people they serve unconditionally and believe all people deserve to live a good life in peace in neighborhoods where they can live free from crime or fear. My wife always says my identity has always been as a proud police officer. The memories compiled in this book are the good, bad and some of the ridicules moments that I experienced with the many characters inside and outside of the Detroit Police Department. This book of memories could not have been possible without the support of my family who got me through many ups and downs during the job and beyond. I would like to thank all those officers that I worked with during my time with the Department, my family, my wife of 35 years together (amazing women), and my children who will never understand how much they mean to me because words just never seem enough. My appreciation to dear friends, Lieutenant Patrick Jordan, Retired DPD, and Nancy Jordan who assisted in the editing process and offered their invaluable advice and insight and to Donna Ernst, who I have never met but very much appreciate her independent review and comments as I was in the final stages of this book. I especially want to acknowledge the families of the Officers who also paid a price for our protecting and serving.

Prolog

THIS IS A TRUE STORY as I remember it of my time as a Detroit Police Officer. I have purposely left names out, but the officers and co-workers know who they are and can remain anonymous if they like. I started this book because I wanted people to know what a young naïve inner City police officer goes through to make or break him, or her. Some make it to retirement and some don't, but all are completely changed.

I am trying to give the reader a true inside view of actually being on the job. I want them to see the good, bad, and the ugly of the inner City and how it affected and changed cops during the 1970's. In the decade of the 1970's, historically the most violent, Detroit was truly the murder capital with up to 700 plus homicides a year which is more than twice the amount of today's. Detroit is still usually leading the nation in violent crimes and called the Murder City. There was four times the number of officers killed each year in the 70's as opposed to now. The times have changed but it is still a dangerous job that takes a toll on those that serve.

In the 70's and early 80's, it was like combat with constant danger on Detroit's streets without any let up. We had it worse and better than cops before or after us. Worse because the daily violence was over 3 times as much as now and better because standards and qualifications pre-1975 where much higher from top to bottom and everybody was held accountable.

In my opinion, the mid 70's were the rapid start of the departments downhill slide due to affirmative action (reverse discrimination), lowered qualifications and standards (oral boards instead of investigations), testing (the Otis test dropped), training (Academy lost its certification) and the rapid extreme outreach employing some unqualified people. Most of us, who really wanted to make a difference, didn't realize that politics could and would be such a negative force from the mid 70's and on. That made it very difficult to do the job and caused an exodus of Detroit's citizens. There are still good people and good cops but, unfortunately, there are less of them. Detroit not only looks like a war zone, it was and still is as dangerous as one.

CHAPTER 1

The Beginning

1968

In 1968 I was working as a draftsman at Chrysler Corporation, Highland Park Engineering. The day after Martin Luther King's assassination our supervisors sent everyone home because of rioting in Detroit. While leaving the Design Center, there was a tank sitting in the parking lot and Detroit cops directing traffic off of Oakland Avenue to east bound McNichols. It caused me to take notice.

It was the first time I felt real fear and anger as I watched people breaking out windows, looting and running into the streets, stopping traffic and scaring the heck out of everyone trying to get out of the area. Through my rearview mirror I saw a young girl driving behind me who looked scared to death as she watched the rioters running up to cars trying to intimidate people. I waived for her to follow me and turned off McNichols to take side streets to 8 Mile Road. There were people everywhere and even in the streets, but we finally made it out of the City. She waived with a look of relief as we hit 8 Mile Road and then went in different directions out of the City. I felt disgust toward the unruly mobs but a sense of satisfaction that I was able to help someone who was in total panic and fear.

Becoming a Cop

When I heard that the Detroit Police Department lowered their height requirement to 5'8", I decided to apply. I wanted to make a change in the City and help those that couldn't help themselves from the violent predators. Even as a young boy growing up I felt very protective toward someone who was being bullied or picked on and would step up to help, when I could.

In the next few months, I was investigated and tested mentally and physically. We were given what was called an "Otis" test that was 3 to 4 hours long. It was a very hard test that measured general intelligence, similar to a college SAT exam. There was a general test that was a shorter version that we called "The Idiot Test" that all City employees had to take. There were also different psychological tests and interviews to determine mental status. The physical fitness part included a broad jump, chin ups, push-ups and a running dash to show that we were physically fit. In the end, there were only a few that were slightly overweight but they had passed all the tests, no exceptions! Those that didn't were sent on their way.

1300 Beaubien

In 1968 the medical section was at 1300 Beaubien Street on the 5th floor. As a young naïve suburban kid everything was exciting and new to me. I entered into the front lobby and the first thing I saw was a marble wall with hundreds of names of officers who had been killed in the line of duty. The building was busy with uniform officers, detectives and a lot of strange looking people going in different directions. I found the elevator and took it up to the 5th floor. When the door opened, I took my paperwork through the door marked Medical Section where there was a group of new recruits, just like me, all about my age standing in line.

We spent most of the day in our socks and underwear being examined physically and mentally like a bunch of sheep. I don't know why, maybe because it was a long strange experience for me, but as they were doing blood work on me, I watched the blood going through the tube and at the same time saw an officer playing with a switch blade knife, which gave me a strange feeling about what I was doing.

After a long day going through all the required testing for the physical including blood test, we were taken to another room and told, not asked, that we had to donate blood. As I was giving blood I started feeling odd but didn't say anything because I thought it was normal when giving blood. All of a sudden the attendant opened a window, turned on a fan and checked my pulse. She looked concerned because I had turned white and nearly passed out. I was given orange juice and a cookie and started to feel better. As I was leaving one of the nurses suggested that I might not want to give blood again. What a day it was.

Second Thoughts

My friends and family were investigated along with me and I passed. When giving notice to my drafting job, I was promoted and given a large salary increase. So, I decided to stay with my employer. My family was relieved. They weren't thrilled with me becoming a cop especially after the 1967 and 1968 riots, or the fact that I would be taking a large pay cut.

That decision continued to haunt me. As a kid I always stood up to bully's and tried to protect the weak and innocent so, early in 1970, when drafting work slowed I reapplied and was accepted. There was one minor problem, when I first applied in 1968 I was too short to meet the height requirement of 5'8" by almost 2". Lucky for me my uncle was a body guard for the Mayor of Detroit (Cavanaugh) at that time and he had friends in recruiting. So after the first failed height test the Lieutenant in charge had me stand against the wall with the height board on my head and surprisingly punched me in the stomach which made me jump. He then pointed to the board and asked me to tell him what it said, and I replied, 5'8" and he simply said, "You passed." With that, I was ready to be the smallest cop at the academy.

Just before entering the police academy, my wife and I separated. This would be one of many separations before finally divorcing in early 1973. Most of my police career was as a single man who was living life with the attitude that I might not be here tomorrow. Whatever needed to be done my motto was always "Just do it." That's how I lived my life and career.

My friends at the time didn't understand my decision to become a cop. During the 70's there was a strong anti-military, anti-cop attitude. Some of my friends hated cops and asked me why I wanted to be a pig. My usual answer to them was to ask, "What did we use to do on a Saturday night?" Their reply would be, "Go looking for some excitement." I replied that as a cop, I would have a radio to tell me where it was happening. Then they understood and accepted me becoming a cop. The real reason was that I really did want to help people and do something really important with my life. I was also told by some not to do it because it would change me. They were right, it did.

Uncle Chet Stabbed

There were no cops, fireman or first responders in my family history that I knew of while growing up. So I had no knowledge, or close contact with any police officers until my Aunt Pauline married her second husband who was a Detroit Police Officer. I remember when I was about 12 years old being curious about my Uncle Chet. He was a quiet, pleasant man who smoked a pipe and drank a lot of coffee (no alcohol) at family functions. One day I heard my relatives talking about how he had been stabbed by a prostitute while on the job, but he was ok. At my young age that kind of excitement was a "WOW." It was right up there with the hero worship of my two Uncles, Frank and Jim Bridgewater who both won Bronze & Silver Stars, Purple Hearts and numerous awards in WWII. All three of them were quiet, humble men. I think that could have been the beginning of my quest to be at the center of what was happening and to be involved and not just listen to second hand stories. I just knew my quiet hero uncles had seen and done a lot in their lives and careers that they rarely spoke about.

As a young cop I spent a few days with my Uncle Chet as he worked on his retirement home that he was building with some of my other uncles. I understood then why he was quiet and didn't talk shop while civilians were around. We had a special connection of seeing hell on earth that they would never understand. He became my hero even more as I spent time with him.

Mind Over Matter

I pretty much kept in shape by weight lifting and working out at the gym mostly for strength, not bulk. I weighed around 150 lbs. and could bench press 240 lbs. I was always the smallest on the football and baseball teams I played on and still played football with my much larger buddies. So going into a profession that was historically for large tough men didn't intimidate me as I really didn't realize that I was any smaller than my peers. Mentally, I had been taught to play over pain and "Just do it." My grandfather was a boxer and my dad a hockey player; both were easy going, confident, tough men who taught me mind over matter and playing by the rules.

I was born left handed, but immediately switched to right by my parents. In those days everything was set up for right-handers and being left handed was considered a real disability. Being ambidextrous gave me an advantage later because police officers had to be able to use their weak hand just as well as their strong hand in case one hand was injured during a confrontation. I came in with an advantage in shooting (sharp shooter), boxing, and other physical areas.

Another Marriage Statistic

I was married in 1965 at 18 years old, before the Vietnam War had ramped up, and had 3 children by 1968. My draft status was 3A which meant I wasn't going to be drafted. I still had thoughts of enlisting like a lot of my friends, but my ex-wife wouldn't have put up with that. Marines would have been my choice as it made no sense to me to go into the military unless you had the best of training and saw combat.

It was during one of the many separations with my wife, that I joined the Detroit Police Department. We continued to try to work things out and one of my thoughts was, unlike the military, as a police officer I could come home every night oppose to being away from home for long periods of time. Like a lot of people in the 60's and 70's she didn't like cops. On top of that, the pay was much less than I was making in design work which didn't go over well. I didn't know then that 70% of existing police marriages didn't make it and I was to be included in that statistic.

Pre-Academy Headquarters

After being accepted, I was offered the opportunity to start on April 13, 1970 or wait for the class of 70-H to start on May 1, 1970. I decided to start right away as that would give me two week's extra seniority.

I was separated from my ex-wife at the time and left our only car with her and the kids. That meant walking to a bus stop with new shoes (blisters) and taking a couple of buses downtown while wearing my student patrolman khakis in an environment that was hostile to cops. I knew nothing of downtown buses or the hustle and bustle of the big City. As it turned out, my career was almost over before it even began as I got off of the Gratiot bus at Detroit Police Headquarter on my first day. I was like a naive farmer who was seeing the big City for the first time, as the bus pulled off, I started to cross Gratiot Avenue while looking around in awe when the guy next to me grabbed me and jerked me back in mid step as another bus flew by just inches away. That was close. I thanked him and went on my way to the Pawn Shop Bureau to help the clerical staff for the next two weeks.

My supervisor was an old salty Sergeant who was way past retirement and told me it was ok and probably a good idea to roam around headquarters on my breaks. I did exactly that and saw lineups, dispatch, and various bureaus like homicide, robbery, armed robbery, property section, sex crimes, vice, etc., etc. It seemed everyone knew my Sergeant and they let me check things out. It was an education in itself and kind of sad but exciting when I had to leave for the Academy.

The Academy – Class of 70-H

We were given a list of items to purchase and told where to get them: khaki's, black belt, shoes, snap on ties, gym shorts and t-shirts with Detroit Police Academy printed on them. I reported to the Academy on May 1st at Palmer Park for 13 weeks of training and 2 weeks of advanced street training in either the Tactical Mobile Unit or the Precinct Support Unit which was the elite of the elite at that time.

First Impressions

My first impression was that this group of men was very different than people I had known in my civilian life. We were drilled until we marched as one unit. We had to square our corners. We ran until we were out of breath; some were vomiting. We exercised until exhausted and we were screamed at by our TAC officers while saluting everyone in a blue shirt and calling them sir loudly. We also had to have our long hair cut short with white walls around our ears; mustaches and facial hair was also shaved. I was glad I wasn't overweight because those that where had to wear sweats in the 80-90 degree heat. Before graduation, all of them had lost enough weight to lose the sweats and enjoy shorts and tee shirts.

I once touched my cap bill while saluting and had to stand in front of the flag saluting for an hour and also received demerit points. I quickly learned to do everything as best as I could and keep a low profile and let the screw-ups attract the attention of the training officers. Keeping a low profile wasn't easy as everyone was taller than me. I knew any attention I received had to be for excellence.

The first 13 weeks consisted of extensive training in the following classes:

Sociology
Basic Psychology
Human Relations
Race Relations
Officer-Violator Relationships
Civil Rights
Police Ethics & Morals
Changing Role of Police Officers
Criminal Law-Liquor Law-Traffic Law
Court Procedure
Rules & Regulations
Misc. City Ordinances
Advanced First Aid
Patrol Techniques
Field Inquiry
Report Writing
Collection & Preservation of Evidence
Firearms
Physical Training with Aikido, Boxing

Training Continues

We had to sit straight with our hats placed on the tables next to us, at attention, in a room with no air conditioning with temperatures around 80 degrees. As uncomfortable as it was, as a group, no one wanted to be the first one to break or quit. Staying awake and attentive wasn't easy especially after lunch during our law classes.

We trained for riot control, were tear-gassed and we learned how to safely use and handle multiple types of weapons. For thirteen weeks we were broken down and then rebuilt. Evenings and weekends were for homework and studying. They critiqued the mistakes in detail that previous officers killed in the line of duty made. That upset most of us until we realized they were doing it to save us and not belittle the officers. That is when I really realized that this was not just a job, but a very dangerous career. I then started to understand why these people seemed different than the average civilian coworkers; most of them were combat veterans from specialized units in Vietnam.

Rouge Range

Firearms and riot training was held at Rouge Range. It was a large hole in the ground on the banks of River Rouge with a couple of old buildings for class room training and a large area set up with targets that could be automatically turned and a PA system to give us our directions.

In the summer of 1970 it was stifling hot and muggy without a breeze as we were surrounded by high hills, forest and swarms of bugs. It was not a very pleasant place to be, but we had been waiting weeks for this and everyone was excited to learn about and fire the weapons.

Our training officers were tough and professional just like the ones at the Academy and all with plenty of experience. Most of the student officers were fresh out of the military and combat vets from Vietnam. Some had been given early outs with pay if joining the police department. A few, like me, had never fired or even held a weapon. We were told it would be easier to train us because we had no bad habits to break. That might have been true as I always shot sharpshooter throughout the academy and my career. I wasn't into guns and never practiced on my own, but shot sharpshooter every 6-month's as continual training was required. It was mentioned a few times about training for the pistol team, but I just wasn't into it.

My first weapon issued at the range was a 38 cal. 5" barrel Smith & Wesson revolver. After the excitement of receiving my weapon, we were told to open the cylinder and make sure it was empty. As I opened it, the cylinder slid right down the length of the barrel and with a loud clunk, hit the wooden floor. The range officer came over, picked it up and to my astonishment said, "These pieces of shit are all over 35 years old."

A few of us had to be re-issued different, but just as old, weapons and then we went on with our classroom training. I wasn't gun savvy and I was a little worried about it exploding or not working when needed and wasn't alone in my concern. I just assumed a big City like Detroit would have new or at least good equipment for their new officers. I was finding out we sure weren't a priority for anything. First time on the firing line after firing numerous rounds we were told to reload our weapons with regular ammo, holster them and return to the classroom. As we were walking a shot rang out. We all ducked and started looking around except for one trainee who was standing with his weapon in his hand. He was taken into the office for a while and then he joined us in the class room.

When class was over the instructor asked if we had any questions. The student who fired the shot raised his hand and we all looked at him in amazement. He asked the training officer, "What is the proper way to change hands with your gun?" You could see the training officer turning colors as he loudly stated, "One thing is you don't pull the fucking trigger." We tried not to laugh, but everyone had to put their heads down so they couldn't be seen cracking up. I heard he didn't make his first year on the department which didn't surprise me.

We shot M1 carbines and trained a lot on the 12 gage riot shot guns. As we fired them, we soon realized they had a lot of kick and you needed to tuck tight and lean into them. Standing and firing was easier than walking along a line with officers in front and back of you when they turned the silhouettes and you had to turn, take the safety off, fire one round, re-rack it, put the safety back on, then continue to the next target and do it all over again and again. When we were done I noticed a few student officers had bloody mouths. Apparently they didn't hold their weapons correctly and got slapped in the mouth. That kept me paying attention to my body position when firing.

During training we would be allowed smoke breaks usually one in the morning and one in the afternoon in an area where they had a couple of butt buckets. At the end of the day they lined us up across the range and we walked from back to front picking up anything that was on the ground that wasn't supposed to be there. Our training officers would supposedly find one to four cigarette butts that we missed and we were told to run a lap for each one. It didn't take long to figure out they were finding butts where nobody smoked and there was nothing we could do about it but suck it up and run.

Riot Training

The first time we had riot training, we were put in 8 man squads that were formed in a 'V'. We proceeded to practice moving a crowd while stepping in unison, yelling, "Move, Move, Move" while thrusting with our nightsticks. After a while, we were pretty organized and professional looking, even when smoke canisters were being tossed so that we could hardly see. All of a sudden we realized that one of those canisters wasn't just smoke, it was tear gas. It felt like I had been hit in the face with a board. My eyes, nose and mouth were burning as I gagged, almost throwing up and couldn't breathe, see, or stop the fluids from running from my nose, eyes, and mouth. I was told later by the ex-military guys in our class, that it was more potent than military grade. This part of the training was done to us without the benefit of gas masks. So much for our perfect formation; everyone started running in different directions. One student even ran into a tree and temporarily knocked himself out. We were told we were going to be gassed again the next week, but with masks. Without showers, we just cleaned up the best we could and headed home with the tear gas smell stuck to our sweat and clothes. The next time we were gassed, I was very apprehensive to breathe in after the first experience, but finally had to and happily found out the mask worked fine. The ride home still wasn't fun as the gas was in our clothes and smelled strong.

It was pretty clear whether they handcuffed us and jerked us around or gassed us without masks, that they wanted us to experience the equipment that we were going to use so we didn't overuse it on citizens. In the 1970's, we didn't have mace or tasers, just night sticks and black jacks to counter the unwilling and I am glad they didn't make us experience those too.

Autopsy

We were taken to the medical examiner's office to watch Dr. Warner Spitz do an autopsy. Apparently it was to expose us to gory things that we would be dealing with almost daily in a big City. Without going into much detail, that is exactly what happened. Thankfully, one of the student officers gave me some Vicks to put under my nose. He said the smells are worse than the sights and he was right. We saw deceased babies laying on large gurneys and watched human organs being removed one by one as Dr. Spitz explained the stages of disease and cause of death. As Dr. Spitz removed a green and yellow liver from a 30 something pregnant alcoholic woman, he swung it and splashed some of the student officers. One officer almost passed out, another threw up and most of us were gagging. I was very relieved that the Vicks masked some of the smell and helped get me through it. Dr. Spitz seemed to enjoy our discomfort. I learned I had to be tough enough to handle anything. I was slowly being conditioned to do what normal citizens couldn't, or would never want to do. My old life was becoming distant and I was starting to understand what was to come in my new chosen life.

County Jail

We spent a couple of days working on 4 hour shifts in different sections of the Wayne County jail to learn how to handle real prisoners. We ate the same food as the prisoners and it was good. My first shift was in the intake section and we had to fight with a large bald violent nut case trying to make him comply with the procedures. Days later, on my last four-hour shift, I was to relieve a regular deputy in the maximum security section. He explained the procedures and told me he had been on the job for 8 weeks; that was less time than I already had in the academy which surprised me and he hadn't even started his academy. Before he left, he told me that everyone was secured and only his trustee was out to sweep. After he left, I went into the back to check on the prisoners; without going into detail about what they were doing, I will say, I was shocked. At the end of the long corridor, I saw the trustee sweeping. To my utter surprise, it was the very same violent prisoner we had to fight before. Now I was locked in, unarmed and alone. The prisoner was totally different this time, but I kept a nervous eye on him, as he was twice my size. My world was becoming crazier every day and I liked it.

Freedom Festival

In late June 1970, we were authorized to carry our weapons early to work the freedom festival fireworks. We were assigned an area on the river front and told to keep some change in our pockets because there weren't enough portable radio's (preps) available. We were in our khakis and stood out like a sore thumb in the crowd. Regular uniform officers would stop by to check on us as we had no way to communicate and our areas were huge. While talking to the officers, we could hear on their radios officers being sent to fights, attempted rapes, and armed robberies. So much for what the news media put out about how safe it was at the festival. I quickly learned that the media always has an agenda and not to trust them or what they report.

We did have a couple of goof-ups that didn't make it through the training and were let go. One claimed a goose attacked him at the Palmer Park duck pond during his lunch break, so he shot it and a few more were dropped or quit without explanation. One, who I went to high school with and had won the scholastic trophy, quit the day before graduation telling me he had to get out now or he never could. I was already completely hooked.

Part of our training was advanced first aid which included delivering babies. After book and class room training, they showed us a movie of a police officer delivering a baby in the back seat of a car. We watched, sitting at attention as usual (everything we did was treated seriously without any humor throughout training). The officer, in the training film, was leaning into the vehicle with his hands in the proper position to receive the baby when, all of a sudden, the woman's water broke and almost blew the officers hat off. It was hilarious, but we didn't know what to do, laugh or not. Then we saw the staff officers watching us and laughing their asses off. It turned out that it was a doctor in uniform and a nurse actually having the baby for a training film that went wrong and they decided to use it as it was technically correct and a stress breaker for the trainees. We definitely remembered how to deliver a baby after that. During my time on the job, I was there for two births, one lived and one didn't. Life was rough in the big City and I was to learn that quickly. It was time to get real serious.

Palmer Park

One night in the woods at Palmer Park, I was on security and armed with an M1 carbine because of a bomb threat to the Police Academy. I heard a person in the dark going "psst, psst." I racked my carbine and ordered, in a loud menacing voice, for them to halt and show themselves. As I shined my flashlight in the pitch black darkness, there was a man, who seemed scared to death, waving his arms in a frantic girlish manner. I told him the park closed at 10pm and to leave immediately to which he did, quickly. I was nervous looking for bombers and he was looking for a lover. That kind of took the edge off of being out in the dark woods alone with a little humor. From then on, I started laughing at things and situations that I would have been scared to death of before. I was entering a whole new world and learned that the dark was my friend and an advantage if used correctly. If I ever was afraid of the dark before, I wasn't anymore.

In Service Training

The last four Fridays in the academy we had our normal 8 hours of class then were assigned to ride with regular officers for 4 hour shifts at night on the streets of Detroit. We made arrests, and were introduced to the violence of a big City. I saw my first innocent victims of homicide, rape, robbery, and traffic accidents. We went on high speed pursuits and foot chases through the neighborhoods. I was sold. I felt it was my calling to help and protect the weak and innocent. I knew I was born for this and there were no second thoughts. I could hardly wait for my next Friday night ride along. I liked the adrenaline rushes and the group of people who I was becoming a part of. I was all in for the ride of a lifetime and to be the best of the best and not here to just get by.

At the end of our classes at the academy and some extremely tough tests, we were assigned to either the Precinct Support Unit (PSU) or the Tactical Mobile Unit (TMU) for 2 weeks advance training with regular officers. I was happily sent to PSU which were the elite of the elite working only on felonies and serious crimes in progress. TMU was for riot control, traffic enforcement and flooding areas of high crimes at that time. I was glad to be sent to the PSU unit that later was turned into the STRESS (decoy) unit. I learned how to hunt violent criminals by who they associated with and generally was influenced by officers who were there to do what had to be done. They lived cop 24-7 and I fell right in. It was here that I learned to put together what they called "Want Books" that contained mug shots of wanted felons and where and who they were arrested with or hung around with. Names, addresses and any helpful information were recorded in the Books. We didn't have computers in those days so our "Want Books" were usually done off duty at home at our kitchen tables. If they or one of their cohorts were arrested, while others got away, we usually had a good idea who was with them and where to find them. Worked Great!

P.S.U. – In-Service Training

During my In-service advanced two-week training at the Precinct Support Unit (PSU) the crew I was riding with met with an informant with information on a man wanted on a homicide warrant. The informant told them what room number he was in at the Cabana motel at Harper and Conner. They had a Journal with his picture, physical description, the warrant number and other information about him. This was a learning experience that I would use my whole career. We went to the front office of the motel, confirmed the room number he was in and threatened the clerk not to notify the room. We then sat across from the room door in an alley until he came back. Then we quietly snuck up and unlocked his door with the extra office key and entered loud and fast yelling "Police". He was totally caught off guard by the speed and noise that he just froze and we had no trouble with his arrest. Every night for my two weeks I worked with different crews and saw what a crew can get done when given time and freedom to work.

One night one of the crews took me downtown to check on a wanted person and one partner told the driver, "Go ahead and show the kid the bull." They then drove slowly in the right lane of one of the main streets when all of a sudden something hit us in the rear bumper. It made the scout car lurch forward a little and then it happened again and again until they stopped the scout car. A midget on a fat tired motor scooter like the old 1950's Cushman Eagles passed us on our left giving us the finger. It was crazy; he had a fur covered helmet on with large horns on it and a monkey hair vest. The driver immediately turned on the siren and roof lights and started chasing him as he turned down the first alley going like a bat out of hell. The crew was cracking up and only chased him down the alley a little way then turned off the lights and siren telling me while laughing that I had just met the "Bull". They said he had been doing that for years and if he could get some rookies to chase him for a while or get their vehicle damaged, he was happy. Most cars in the area just ignored him unless showing him off to new rookies. It was after midnight and most of downtown was closed and quiet. We then started to head back out of the downtown area and saw a bum type woman standing in the mouth of an alley and the driver slowed to take a look and see if anything was out of the ordinary. I had never seen anything like the "Bull" or a bum lady before, so I was totally shocked when she said to us, "What the fuck are you looking at?" and then squatted right there and took a dump on the side walk like a dog. As we drove off, both officers were just laughing. I could only think how disgusting that was going to be in the morning when the streets were busy with the morning rush.

The Academy Then & After

In the mid 1970's after Coleman Young was elected the 3-4 hour "Otis" intelligent test was dropped with a lot of the other higher requirements of physical, mental and background investigations because minorities were only averaging 44% on the test. The new agenda was affirmative action (reverse discrimination) even at the expense of the quality of the officers dropping; which it did. The student officers that I graduated with, including minorities, were required to meet a much higher standard and were a lot more motivated to get involved and protect and serve with confidence in their follow officers. Many of the minority officers that I knew and worked with weren't happy with how the new Administration was hiring and promoting. It was just as unfair to the minority officers that trained and worked hard and earned their jobs and promotions at a higher set of standards. I am not belittling today's officers as most of them would have qualified in my day too. Affirmative Action brought not only more minorities, but also less qualified non–minorities and some were only there for a paycheck and not to provide a service. Lowering standards did not prove to be good for the City.

Crime more than doubled in the mid 70's and the officers that were doing most of the work were getting injured or killed and were openly criticized. Some others who shouldn't have even been hired were double and triple promoted as the City instituted separate promotion list and for each white male promoted, 1 minority was promoted. In essence and it happened, a white male who wrote 90% on the test wasn't promoted, but a black male or female could write a 70%, not even passing, and would get promoted. That was affirmative action Detroit style. Indians, Arabs, Hispanics, etc., etc., were not considered minorities in Detroit. Not to mention political promotions skyrocketed too, without even considering their lower test scores.

When they shortened the Academy to only 8 weeks instead of the 13 weeks, plus 2 weeks extended training in specialized units that we had, the Academy lost it accreditation. It was tough in my day, but we had a solid foundation and weren't allowed to just repeat the academy over and over with pay if we failed the first time like they did later. Then if you couldn't make it, you were out. The dead-beats were eliminated in the early 70's. Only those that made it through the 13-15 weeks and passed the tests with higher standards, made it on the street. They fought hard to be there for the right reasons; the same with promotions in the early 1970's.

Academy - Badges & Gear

A few days before graduation, we went as a group to the uniform section at headquarters where we were issued our badges, ID cards, uniforms, etc. We were all curious about who had the badge number before and what happened to the officer as they were not new but re-issued over and over. I received #2209 and the previous holder had been retired early on a disability. I didn't take that as a good sign, but at least he wasn't killed on the job. We all had hoped that the previous owners had not been killed, disabled or fired, but retired after a long career.

When we were issued our uniforms naturally they didn't have pants short enough for me and mine had to be tailored at my own expense. The riot gear consisted of a very heavy old steel WWII helmet painted blue, with a large plastic shield bolted on it. The blue riot coveralls zipped up the front and had 'Detroit Police' stitched on them. They were too hot for summer and not warm enough for winter. I never saw anybody wear them even when I was on riot duty during the Bolton Bar disturbance on Livernois in 1975. Unlike all the equipment they have today, all we had was a gas mask, helmet and a longer night stick used for riot control.

Surprise Neighbor

Around this time period while I was renting an upper flat with a lifelong friend who was also separated from his wife, I had met a good looking, wild girl at a local suburban bar. As it turned out she was married to a rather large guy who was a butcher with anger and drinking problems. Unknown to me our flat in Detroit was right around the corner from her house. Her husband would come home from work drunk and fall asleep on the couch and then she would walk around the corner to visit me. The day that I was issued my gun my roommate was ecstatic and he told me he was worried that her husband was going to follow her and kill us all. After a while we both reunited with our wives and moved out of the flat. A couple of years later while working undercover vice and separated again, I ran into her at a go-go bar where she was dancing for a Detroit Motor Cycle Club. My new roommate, who was working uniform, took a liking to her, until he drove her home one night in his uniform and was shot at by the bikers. Those guys don't like anybody messing with their money makers and she was still a wild one.

Graduation Day

Graduation Day turned out to be hard for me with many mixed emotions. Paul Begins widow sat right behind me; her husband was being honored (Posthumously) with the Medal of Valor and her teary eyes choked me up.

I went from extreme pride of making it through the toughest time of my life and to the other end of the emotional roller coaster of feeling for the hurt of a widow, her orphans and for a young Detroit Police Officer killed while trying to help others. As I returned to my seat with my diploma, I saw the young widow looking with pride, and sadness, at me and the rest of us rookies who were there; all of us ready to go into harm's way like her husband.

I later found out that Officer Begin was shot in the back of the head while allowing a prisoner's girlfriend to ride into the station with the prisoner. At that time, we weren't allowed to search females and no female officers worked the street. Being too nice could get you killed in this City. This was the second time his young wife became a widow as I was told her first husband had been killed in Vietnam.

CHAPTER 2

The Rookie Year

Rookie – The 7th Precinct

After successfully graduating the academy, I was officially a new probationary rookie and full of confidence that I was one of the best trained officers in the country. Detroit's academy was rated one of the best in 1970. We were told to call the academy the morning after graduation to find out where we would be assigned. I hoped to be sent to one of the east side Precincts even though they were known as the roughest.

I was excited and scared when I was told to report to the 7th Precinct the next day. The 7th was one of the most dangerous in Detroit but that was what I signed on for and didn't want a suburban type area. I wanted action and that's exactly what I got.

I, along with seven other rookies, reported to the 7th and was surprised that most of the officers looked very young but had a hard distant look and personalities. I later found out when they attained seniority a lot of the officers transferred out leaving mostly young officers working together. While we were waiting to be assigned to our shifts, I noticed a wall with a lot of pictures of officers in uniform. I asked an officer, "What did they do, win an award of some kind?" thinking maybe police officer of the year. He replied, "They're all dead, kid" and walked away. I was shocked that so many officers in one Precinct had been killed in the line of duty. I was not feeling so cocky anymore and started to know why these guys were so close to each other and distant to anyone who didn't know their friends on that wall. I could clearly see we weren't just going to be accepted; we would have to earn their respect. I was assigned to the afternoon shift with two other rookies and the other rookies were placed on other shifts.

State Fair – 7th Precinct

After reporting to the 7th Precinct after graduation, we were advised that all new rookies were to report to the police command at the State Fair for duty. We were assigned to security and traffic control at the main exit on State Fair Street. I quickly learned to hate directing traffic as there were always some jerks that just wouldn't follow directions. We had two officers hit by cars and one was seriously injured; another officer threw his 3 cell Kel-lite through a car's rear window. It was a hot, dusty and frustrating duty, but there was one benefit in the early 1970's that we didn't mind. During that time, women's lib brought many young women to go braless and the style for some was to go braless with semi see-through blouses. The girls would hang around us cops and bring us cold drinks and friendly smiles. Not everybody hated cops.

The Beat & My Grandpa

The first few afternoons after the fair duty, I walked a beat on Gratiot and Mt. Elliott. To my great surprise, my grandfather, who lived with me most of my life and was extremely proud of me, showed up on my beat in a rough area and told me and my partner to let him know if anyone bothered us. My partner was touched to see a little old white man in the area; let alone trying to protect us. That was my grandpa, still tough and scared of nothing. I gave him the end braid button of my police cap that had Detroit Police stamped on it that he wore on his suit coat all the time. He would always listen to a police scanner radio and at one point as I began getting into more dangerous situations it had to be taken away from him. It wasn't good for his failing heart to get excited or worry about what was happening. He was a WWI Horse Calvary Veteran who won the boxing championship in the Philippines and taught me how to protect myself, but never to bully anyone. He was buried with that button on his jacket the day after Christmas in 1973. He was a good man who taught me a lot and I sorely miss him.

Scout Car Duty

One day during my first weeks, I was assigned to a shift in a scout car with an officer who had just been confirmed (1 year including the academy). We handled our calls barely knowing what we were doing or where we were at most of the time. Somehow we made it through our shift. When our vehicle was inspected at off duty roll call, our Sergeant asked us where we took fire. We looked at each other, both turning pale, as we realized that what we thought was a stone that hit our car was a bullet. I didn't even know I was being shot at the first time and there would be many more times to come.

Before roll call some of the officers played cards or talked to each other, but no one talked to, or even acknowledged us rookies. We mostly walked beats and occasionally were happily assigned to a scout car for a shift.

When in a scout car, we weren't allowed to drive, but had to do all of the reports, direct traffic and sit with dead bodies or anything unpleasant that needed to be done. Every so often our senior partner would yell to us, "Where are you?" and we had to know our exact location at that moment. During that time, we had to watch for snipers and learn the streets and addresses of our Precinct. Still it was exciting to work a squad car instead of walking a beat. I quickly learned about the groupies who would pick us up after our beats and we would go to Belle Isle and party with them. It seems some girls hated cops and others liked being around the danger and fast pace of living life with a cop in a big City. I was already learning to live one day at a time to its fullest because there was a chance that there wouldn't be a tomorrow with this job.

The Beat and the Good People

On the beat the store owners loved having us around and tried to give us anything we needed and wouldn't let us pay for anything. While walking by party stores the owners would run out and ask us in broken English, "What you smoke?" He then went back in and grabbed a hand full of cigarette packs for each of us telling us to stop in and have a pop. Being rookies, we asked our Sergeant what we should do with all the cigarettes. He told us don't ask for anything, but if you are offered cigarettes, pop and non-expensive things, it's ok, but don't get greedy. He explained that they want us around and are showing their appreciation, so let them; it's also good PR. Later I found out the cop discounts or freebie went way back in police history from when cops didn't make much money and it was strongly frowned on if abused. We were there to take care of, not use our local business people. We became pretty good friends with them by stopping and having a pop or bag of Fritos periodically. We learned their ways and they asked about ours as some were fairly new to our country.

At lunch one day while sitting at the counter, the waitress dipped a napkin in a glass of water and proceeded to clean dirt off my forehead just like my mother used to do when I was a little boy. I was caught between mixed emotions of trying to be a protector and being treated like a young son. These were the people that I would die for if needed; as quite a few officers already had and more were going to. I mostly walked the Chene-Ferry Market beat and at the end of the 12-8pm shift, when the market closed, the Farmers would try to give me bushel baskets of vegetables, fruit and even live chickens and ducks instead of hauling it all back to their farms. I was astonished as we were loved or hated with not much in between.

As we were walking in the alley on Chene Street just after dark, about a week after being shot at the first time, two men exited the rear of the Tic-Toc Bar and fired a shot at us and escaped through the front door. Yes, the 7th Precinct could be very hostile and you had to be alert all the time. In the early 1970's time period, there was talk about combat type pay as certain Precincts, like the 7th were more dangerous than others. Officers transferred out of these Precincts as soon as possible leaving them staffed by younger officers with less experience. There was a big need for older officers to teach us younger ones how to do our jobs and stay alive. I had already been shot at on two separate occasions. The Sergeant interviewed the bar patrons and without our being able to identify anybody or prove the shots were aimed directly at us it was dropped.

Acceptance

A few months into my time at #7 it was my turn to work a regular scout car shift again. At the start of the 4pm to 12am shifts roll call, the regular officers were still not paying any more attention to us rookies than they had to. During that shift, we received a radio run, "Hold up in progress with shots fired." As we pulled into the alley we found a deceased black male sitting in his vehicle shot in the chest numerous times. The paperwork, statements and preserving of the scene taught me a lot that would be used many times in my career. Still I couldn't help but stare at the poor old guy who was just parked reading his newspaper and bothering no one. I can still see him when I think about it.

The next day I was assigned to a regular scout car and at roll call one of the hardened vets of #7 (most were Vietnam combat vets) said, "Hey kid you want to play cards?" I was about to burst with excitement as I was being accepted and shown some respect. My beat walking days were over, but I was still a rookie and had a lot to learn and prove to myself and co-workers. My arrest a few days later wasn't as exciting but garnered a lot of attention. I arrested Reggie Harding a 7-foot tall ex-Detroit Piston (basketball player) for disorderly conduct.

As I walked Reggie into the Police Station, with him at 7 feet tall to my almost 5'7" and the smallest cop in Detroit, I had to reach up to his waist level to hold onto my hand cuffs that were on him. Before I knew it, word spread and most of the station had come to take a look at David & Goliath with a lot of humor to Reggie's embarrassment. Years later, I arrested another Detroit Piston, Terry Thomas, for assaulting a police officer. This one was quite violent and he went to the hospital instead of the lockup. Street talk was that the same guy who took a few shots at me later on in my career had killed Reggie Harding in a drive by shooting in 1972 and he got away with both.

Another award for acceptance by the guys was when they showed me how to get into the Altas Brewery on Mack & Hurlbut. When we got off our shift at midnight, a lot of the east side officers met at the Brewery to talk and drink fresh cold beer right out of the tap without having to change out of uniform. That was when I learned that cops where not usually charged for drinks. Bars, party stores, and clubs all wanted cops to hang around as long as possible for two reasons: 1) Security in rough neighborhoods, 2) Vice left them alone if they weren't big violators.

Ziggy's Bar

Every Precinct had a main bar where cops hung out and cashed their paychecks every two weeks. Ziggy's was #7's and they had a back room where on duty officers could eat lunch in peace with good homemade food. Most of the bars that the cops hung around on paydays would usually have good looking groupies, nurses, waitresses and females who were not anti-cop. Just the opposite, they loved cops. It was usually frowned on if someone brought a wife or regular girlfriend to the bar, but not unheard of.

The payday bars were usually packed. A couple of times I saw two cops arguing, both armed, go outside to square off with half the bar following to watch. I quickly learned you didn't touch your weapon even when losing because that wasn't manly and against the unwritten code of macho. Yes, these were my kind of people, settle your differences fairly, win or lose, and forgive and forget. That is exactly what my grandfather and father had taught me. No sucker punching or fighting with someone who didn't want to. A copper bar was safer, fun, and very entertaining unlike any bar that I had been in before.

There was another bar some of us younger officers went to sometimes called The Sewer. It was located in an old industrial area on Atwater on the river side of Jefferson. It was in a dark area with no street lights and there was nothing else open in that area. The Sewer was a folk music bar and a perfect location for hippie types to handout. It had pretty good live entertainment and good looking young females. The females didn't want anything to do with someone with short hair who had to be a soldier, a cop or an ex-con which made you very unpopular with this group of people. Some of the guys grew their hair long and then wore short haired wigs for work. The rest of us ignored the dirty looks and enjoyed the music. So much for the hippy motif, "Love your neighbor."

There was a Go-Go bar with some older dancers that one of my partners took me to that didn't charge cops. After an hour or so of free drinks and dancers sitting with us, the owner asked us for help as one of his patrons was outside getting beat up. I was a rookie but, I knew nothing was for free and besides I liked the excitement. My partner, who later became a good friend and roommate, didn't like excitement and didn't want to get involved; he just liked the free stuff. The owner and the waitresses were all jumping around the side door yelling, "They're killing him." My partner wanted to leave by the other door and stay out of it, as we were off duty. I talked him into helping because of how good the owner was to us. He reluctantly went out the side door to help and immediately got knocked down. I pulled my revolver and put all 4 perpetrators against the wall as two scout cars roared up. The victim was all bloody and I assumed he was stabbed, but he wasn't. He didn't want to prosecute as they all knew each other and were drunk.

That was the first and last time my partner and roommate listened to me about getting involved in off duty battles. Over the years when we were in bars or situations, he would leave laughing and shaking his head, knowing that I would be in the middle of it and enjoying every minute.

Hit by Car

We responded to a radio call at Federals Department Store at Van Dyke & Harper, "They're trying to hold one for assault." As we pulled up, there was a large 250+ lb. violent women chasing the manager. As my partner stepped in between them she tossed him aside. I then tried to grab her and she threw me into on-coming traffic where I bounced off of a passing car that flattened my cap. She then took a large bite out of my partner's forearm. I got bruised, battered and was surprised by her violence. I had been taught by my parents, under no circumstances do you hit a woman. Well I had to pound her head against the trunk of a parked car until she stopped fighting long enough to handcuff her (no tasers or mace in those days, just brute force and black jacks). After we were all treated at Detroit General Hospital for numerous injuries and my partner was doing our report, I was called into the Sergeant's office. I was scared that, as a probationary officer (Rookie), I could be fired for almost any reason. I thought that I was in big trouble for her injuries. I went in and as the Sergeant closed the door he proceeded to chew me out shouting, "The next time two of my officers are injured like this, the defendant better be hospitalized; now get your ass out of here."

I learned three things: 1) Women can be just as dangerous as men, 2) You had to meet force with more force without being excessive, 3) You didn't have to be a punching bag. I also learned we had to make our arrest and leave the area as soon as possible. Any delay could and would usually cause a hostile crowd to form and you could lose your prisoner while being attacked.

Dangerous New World

I was aware of the dangers to Detroit Police Officers before starting the academy. Too many officers were seriously assaulted and killed in the early 1970's. Including P.O. Richard P. Woyshner, William Slappey and Joseph Soulliere who were killed and their partners seriously wounded. I felt for them, their families and their co-workers.

We were taught to not only closely watch street levels, but second floors and above for snipers when on patrol. Almost every day we received numerous calls of shootings or shots fired with a lot of them phony just to get us there quicker. Sometimes they were real shootings, stabbings, or serious assaults and we had to take all of them extremely seriously. Our adrenaline would be up and down all day long. One thing I did notice was with the constant fear, excitement, and adrenaline rushes, you really felt alive.

Some of us were called "lily whites from the suburbs" because we came from a completely different type of world. This new world sometimes seemed like a third world country, full of hate, violence and sudden death. We had the Republic of New Africa, Black Panthers, SDS, Weathermen and Black Muslims which turned into the National of Islam. They all hated the white officers and would ambush us at any time if they could. I was having a hard time understanding why. I only wanted to help and protect those that needed or wanted it, even if it meant injury or death to me. It didn't take too long to understand that there were a lot of good people who did want and need us. They had to keep a low profile around the aggressive ones because we couldn't always be around. We even started to pick up the street language enough to understand the street talk. There was still a lot to learn, but we weren't quite as naïve as we had been. This new world was coming into focus and maybe we could help and survive, too.

Drunk Driving Arrest

While driving south on Gratiot Avenue toward downtown, I observed and old Ford Sedan straddling lanes and driving very slow so I pulled it over. I could smell an odor of alcohol on the driver's breath; he was slow talking and had a little stager in his walk when out of the car. In the 70's we didn't have hand held breathalyzers' or give street tests, we just had to use our best judgment as to whether someone had too much to drink to drive.

As a new rookie this was my first drunk driving arrest and he was cooperative and blew a .015 which was the minimum for driving under the influence of liquor (D.U.I.L.), but higher than impaired driving which was .012 - .014, it was borderline, but a legal arrest and I thought he would learn a lesson as he seemed to be reasonable and knew what he did.

A couple of hours later a beat up newer Cadillac passed and cut us off while changing lanes almost hitting us. I put on my siren and lights and she kept going for about a quarter mile before she finally pulled over while bouncing off of the curb. I immediately exited our scout car as she apparently put her car in reverse instead of park and it backed into my car, luckily she hit our push bars. As I walked up to her driver's door she opened it and fell out into the street breaking her pint of whiskey that was in her hand while yelling and MF'ing me loudly. It was a wrestling match to get her up, handcuffed and placed in the back of our scout car and then again trying to get her into the station. This was totally the opposite of my first arrest as she was uncooperative, violent and totally drunk and unable to control her vehicle. She blew .031 which was at the top level of intoxication and at .032 she would have been taken to the hospital instead of arrested. The ice was broken and I now knew how to process drunk drivers and I also learned there were totally different levels. Now I was about to learn, for the first time, just how unfair Detroit's court system was.

I had both suspects' court cases in front of the same referee at traffic court one right after the other. The first case was the working suburban family man without a record or traffic violations who had barely failed the breathalyzer test at .015 which was close enough that there could have been a tolerance error and probably should have been lowered to impaired. I was surprised when they basically threw the book at him with a large fine, loss of driver's license and refusal of a limited license to and from his employment. Wow, I thought when you pled guilty to save the court a hearing they usually gave you a break, but this was one tough referee. Next they called the lady who was combative and blew .031 and who hit the scout car and had open alcohol in her possession. I thought this referee would probably really throw the book at her since she had a long traffic record and was driving on a suspended license without insurance.

Usually when choosing to have a hearing rather than pleading guilty in front of a referee it would result in a stiffer sentence. The referee found her guilty and now the big surprise, she was placed on probation, her driver's license suspension increased by one year and there was no jail time or fine given to her. I later asked the court officer what it was all about and he told me she was on assistance (Re: no fine), had children (Re: no jail time), and lived in Detroit. The man was a suburbanite, worked (Re: the fine), and that was how the judges and referees balanced their conviction rates to breaks given instead of the situations whenever possible. I was still a rookie, but still had a little rebel in me and knew what was right and wrong. This was totally wrong as she had no business driving and justice was supposed to be blind and not prejudice for or against. I guess I was still naive. They were my first two arrests for drunk driving and my last. I basically didn't work traffic, but if I ran across someone who shouldn't be driving I would lock their keys in their trunk and either drive them home or drop them off at the all night Clock restaurant. They had to be taken off the street, but habitual violators were the ones killing people and this system was totally upside down.

The Meat Wagon

In the early 1970's Detroit didn't have EMS units and very few private ambulance services for two reasons: 1) It was too dangerous in the high crime areas, 2) They didn't usually get paid for their services. Each Precinct had at least one black Ford or Plymouth station wagon with two stretchers in it. Usually two uniform officers with low seniority had to work it.

It was also called, "The Meat Wagon", because as fast as you took someone to the hospital, and washed the blood off of the rubber stretcher, you were on your way to another serious injury - shootings, stabbings or assaults mostly. Sometimes, after conveying a victim, you would get a call to go to the homicide section because the victim had died. We could usually tell who wasn't going to make it, but we always played it down as to not excite them and many times they died in route. The harsh reality was at least we could get a description or ID of the perp which EMS crews wouldn't get.

As a young, lily white cop from suburbia, I was seeing a lot of death and learned that no one went easy. I still don't know if lying to the victims in their last few moments was right or not. They trusted and believed us at that moment, so to ease their mind, we told them, "You're not hit too bad, you'll be ok", when we knew otherwise. On the other hand, when we were injured, we didn't believe it when told it would be ok, because we had said it so often to victims when it wasn't true.

Nobody usually wanted to work the wagons. So we rookies often caught the assignment. We cared and we tried our best usually pushing those fast as hell Fords until the brakes got heated up so much we could hardly stop them. There were times when the station wagon was busy and there was another serious injury we would have to put a stretcher in the big auto which was the prisoner van to haul the injured.

At first I couldn't figure out why regular officers carried black leather gloves in the summer. I soon found out as we had a call to convey an elderly woman who was dying and unknown to me, as we placed her on the stretcher all her bodily functions had let loose and my bare hands were full of body waste and it was too late to let go. The next day I had leather gloves too and it also helped when you had to fight, which was quite often. If you had a weak stomach or were afraid of "icky" you better get used to it fast, or do something else as it was a daily thing. In the winter we would cut a small slice out of our glove on our shooting hand so we could put our index finger on the trigger, while still wearing our gloves.

Another call on a hot day was to a 4th floor apartment where a large woman was having a heart attack. The stairway was circular and tight with no room for a stretcher. So we had to squat down facing each other and grasp each other's hands with her sitting between us to get her down the curving steps. We then put her on the stretcher and rushed her to the emergency room at St. Joe's on East Grand Blvd. My partner and I were sweating and exhausted. As we put her on a gurney, we were told by the admitting nurse loudly, "We're not taking her." As we looked at each other in total shock, the nurse explained to us that she did this a couple of times a month. We tried to explain to the lady that we only had one station wagon and someone seriously sick or injured couldn't be helped while we were trying to help her with a non-emergency. We felt bad for her and understood she was lonely and did this for attention but we were too busy handling life threatening calls. We immediately called back in service and left for our next call.

We had a lady suicide jumper jump off of the Belle Isle bridge right in front of us as we were crossing the bridge. Luckily for her we called it in immediately and the police boat docked near the bridge picked her up and we had her on the way to the hospital in minutes. She was very upset that we saved her and said that she was going to kill all her kids. All I could do was put that in the report and wonder if we did the right thing by saving her and maybe putting others at risk. I'll never know, but I hoped not.

The Ear

One day while working the wagon, we got a call on a knife fight in progress. When we got there one guy was bleeding from the side of his head. His right ear was gone with just a stub left where his ear should have been and he was looking around on the ground for his ear. My senior partner was asking him for a description and name of who did it so he could put it out over the radio. Our victim wasn't co-operating and was refusing to give us any info about the perp. One of the neighbors gave me a small bath towel to put against his ear to stop the bleeding as we carried no medical equipment in those days. As a new rookie I didn't say anything, but I could see my senior partner was getting aggravated with him not answering our questions, like his name, address, age, etc. etc. Like normal, from what I had seen so far, he didn't carry any identification. It seemed like no one in Detroit's inner city carried identification and everybody walked slowly in the middle of the street refusing to move for cars with an air of arrogance until they got hit which happened often. I searched him and put him in the back seat, while putting the towel on his ear and told him to hold it tight and then sat next to him, unsure if my partner was going to convey him because he was so uncooperative.

We started off toward Detroit Receiving Hospital where we conveyed those who didn't have insurance and he then asked my partner, "Aren't you're going to find my ear?" To that, my partner asked him if he was going to prosecute, to which he replied, "Hell no, he's my friend." My partner then said, "Tell your fucking friend to find it," and off we went. Yep, I was in a tough crowd.

Driving

After weeks of riding shotgun and doing all the reports without driving, I got very excited when my senior partner, who was a large guy, said, "Hey kid, you wanna drive?" That was a sign that he thought I was ready and knew the area well enough. Usually the driver drives 4 hours then rides shotgun 4 hours doing the reports with the tasks shared equally. As I got behind the steering wheel and started to pull the bench seat forward so I could reach the pedals, he let me know that was not going to happen. So I had to drive while sitting on the front edge of the seat to reach the wheel and pedals. The big guys weren't going to be cramped so it was up to me to adapt until the cars came out with split bench seats or I worked with some of the newer, smaller officers. Unfortunately for me, everyone was a lot bigger.

Burnouts

There was one officer that acted strange that I was assigned to scout car duty with. A lot of the other rookies were snickering at me when they read the next day's assignment sheet. He seemed nice enough, but kind of off into another world. About halfway through our shift, we found a stolen car at Mack and Concord. As I was getting the VIN# and other information, my partner, told me to stay with the vehicle while he went to the station to pick up PCR's (Preliminary Crime Reports). I waited for what seemed like a long time, without a radio and with a lot of strange, hostile looks from the locals. I was starting to get nervous when another scout car crew came by and asked me, "What the hell are you doing out here alone?" As they were taking me into the station I was told Mack & Concord was a Delta One area because of snipers from a Black Panthers group house and any calls there were handled by at least 2 cars and a supervisor. When asked, I told them who I was and why I was left there. They just shook their heads and warned me to be careful and pay attention to everything and everybody. I got chills and realized I better learn quickly if I wanted to survive in this world. When I found my partner he was just sitting in the report room staring straight ahead. When he saw me he just said, "Oh, hey I forgot you." Now I knew that not all of my co-workers were completely dependable and some of them were really burnt out. Another one who worked a one-man report car carried 5 guns and stayed away from anything serious. One officer told me he kept his money in his shoe and if anything happened to him to get it because he said all of the medical examiners assistants were thieves and I should watch out for them.

We had another officer that knew most of the stray dogs in the Precinct. He would drive to different locations, stop and call a stray over by name and it would come over to his window and get petted then go on its way. He did this 7 or 8 times. These wild dogs were mean and not normally friendly to people. I was amazed. I saw a stray on the sidewalk and jokingly asked him, "What's his name?" He seriously replied, "Never met him." Like he required an introduction; then drove on.

One of the other rookies pointed out an officer who had accidently shot off one of his toes practicing quick draws in the report room. Afterwards that story was confirmed by other officers. I was meeting some of the legends of the Police Department that I didn't even know existed. There was another officer who had his weapon taken from him when off duty. Numerous officers pointed this out as we were to never give up our guns under any circumstances. We were also told that if we were held hostage, when backup arrived they were going to go right at the perp and to take cover as best as possible. Later in my career at #11 that is exactly what happened. An officer, who was being held at gun point, got shot in the cheek as responding officers exited their vehicles firing at and shooting the perp. Lucky for the officer, he turned his head causing an angled shot by the perp instead of a straight on head shot. I don't know if that was an actual Department policy, but that was the understanding everywhere I worked. You don't give up your gun and if used as a hostage, your co-workers are coming in shooting. There were very few but there were some pretty strange officers that I was learning to avoid and at the same time, I kind of felt bad for them as they had started off healthy, but now were broken.

Backup Gun

Most of the guys carried a backup gun. Usually an off duty weapon in a shoulder or pop up holster and a larger holstered weapon. A 12 gage riot shotgun and a M1 carbine were checked out daily. My Mother and Grandfather bought me a .38 cal., 5 shot, 2-inch barrel off duty weapon that was easier to conceal. I started carrying it on duty as well. I wasn't about to let myself be disarmed without a fight. We knew if we were disarmed or wounded, we would most likely be assassinated with our own weapon, whether on or off duty.

In these days of snipers, angry citizens and lawlessness, even the police stations weren't a safe place. There was an officer assigned to the front of the building and one assigned to the rear as station security. I was assigned to the rear and the garage where officers entered to unload prisoners. I was told nobody not in uniform was to be allowed through the back. Others were to be advised to enter through the front door no matter who they were, with or without police ID. Well of course a plain clothed Deputy Chief tried to enter, showing me his ID. He got pretty upset when I physically would not let him enter. He was embarrassed and had to go to the front. He soon calmed down and acknowledged that I was doing what the desk Sergeant had instructed me to do. We had pretty good bosses then who didn't try to place the blame on someone else and he quickly stated he gave me that order.

Another time a women came running through the parking lot with multiple stab wounds with her boyfriend still armed with a large butcher knife chasing her. Lucky for me a scout car crew had just pulled in. They tackled him and then conveyed her to the hospital.

On New Year's Eve, 15 minutes before and 15 minutes after midnight all the scout cars were called in to the station and all the outer office lights were shut off. Station security was ordered to stay in the building. It turned out the locals firing their guns at midnight liked to aim at the station or scout cars instead of up in the air. In Detroit, shots were fired instead of fireworks. Later on while working at the 10th Precinct, as times got worse they closed their shades and shut off the outer office lights after dark every night. Station security wasn't even safe. Kind of like the movie "Fort Apache the Bronx", but worse and very real. You could drive down the street of any Precinct station that I worked, the 7th, 10th or 11th, at night and wouldn't even know it was there in the mid 70's because they would be blacked out because of snipers and angry citizens.

One time, a scout car was unloading a prisoner when another car could only get half way into the garage when someone pushed the button to close the large overhead door. The door apparently didn't have a safety stop. As the door closed on the second cars roof beanie light it exploded in a loud bang causing a half dozen cops to duck and draw their weapons. It didn't take long before I was just as gun shy and jumpy as they were.

During the 70's, I had shots fired in my direction at least ten different times and don't remember how many times I had a weapon pointed at me or heard shots nearby.

Time off

We knew better than to even ask for weekends or holidays off. Seniority was experience and responsibility and meant a lot, street decisions, assignments, days off, shifts and pay-grades, etc., etc. It was alright with me because I liked working nights and weekends. That was the busiest time with a better chance to make good arrests. Later, when I had the seniority to work or not, I still would usually work nights, weekends and holidays, which made me very popular with my partners who had less time on the job. I liked locking up the bad guys, but hated going to court on my off time. My partners liked going to court and the paid time and a half, so I only went to court for the trials when necessary. It worked out well for all of us.

Christmas day was the only holiday I took off as that was the day my ex-wife agreed to let me have my 4 children and some Sundays for visitation. At the time, I thought, right or wrong, it was better for my kids to be in a stable family in the suburbs with their Mom who had moved out of Detroit. I was living through a violent, hostile, and dangerous time in my life and didn't want them to have to experience that.

I was rapidly turning into an ex-suburbanite and to a street warrior. No 9 to 5 job for me anymore; I didn't even like days or midnights as it was too slow.

Shot, Not Shot

It didn't take long for my larger coworkers to figure out little Al could, and would, go into places they couldn't. It happened at every Precinct and unit I worked at and before I knew it, they were taking off my Sam Brown (gun & equipment belt) and putting me feet first in basement windows, holes in roofs, or any small opening. They would then hand me my gun and Kel-lite to either search the location or open a door for them. It was scary at first in the dark alone with no immediate help available, but after a few arrests, my confidence soared and I welcomed the challenge of it. I also liked it when other officers saw there were positives to having me around and I felt more accepted. Years later, during one super-hot summer night, we were called by another car to what was thought to be a burglary suspect trapped in a dairy queen. As usual, off came my equipment and in I went through a small service window. After a thorough search, I found no one in the building. So, being hot and sweaty, I made an ice cream cone. The hot officers outside were begging me to give them one to which I replied, "You can't fit, you don't get," while teasing and laughing at them. As they left, I heard a few of them laughing and someone yelled back to me, saying, "Boudreau, when you come out we're going to kick your ass." Back at the station, there was a lot of teasing going on and that broke up the evening.

In January 1971 with approximately 5 month's street experience, I received my <u>1st Commendation/Citation Award</u> for "The Arrest of two subjects for B&E business (Burglary)." That arrest solved over 60 open cases. We received a radio run, "B&E in progress, shots fired." As we pulled up as quietly as possible, with our lights out, I saw a male standing by the double overhead garage doors armed with a handgun. I drew my weapon and ordered him to "drop it," which he did. I then saw a broken out panel in the door. We secured the subject and then entered the building and arrested 2 more suspects. We found one of the suspects had been shot in the leg. After investigating the male who had the gun, with one round missing, it was clear he shot through the window and hit the one subject in the leg and was in no real danger at that time. The shooter confirmed that he lived next door and saw the break in. When we asked the perp who was shot what happened, he had quite the attitude and said, "What gas station? I wasn't in no fucking gas station." I was amazed that he would lie even when shot and caught in the building, red handed. No wonder he already had gotten away with more than sixty B&E's. I was to learn a lot of people could and would lie even when caught in the act.

The next thing amazed me too and showed me a side of street justice that would be repeated often as I learned how bad the court system was. My partner said to him, "Well, I suppose if you weren't in that building then you're probably not shot either, are you?" To which the perp responded, "Fuck no, I'm not shot." My partner then released the guy who had the gun and gave it back to him empty. He advised him that the court system would prosecute him for attempted murder and to get the hell out of there and never say anything about this or he could be in big trouble. We then took the two B&E subjects to the lock up without saying anything about anyone being shot. We did our paperwork, and then went back on patrol.

My partner told me if he didn't want aid and was claiming he wasn't there and wasn't shot, that it wasn't our problem. Well, it was a little our problem. We were called into the station and our guns were checked to see if they had been fired. The subject had passed out in the print room; still claiming that he wasn't shot. I don't know if my partner had anymore explaining to do, but I heard no more about it until I received my Commendation for "In recognition of efficient and valuable service," signed by the District Inspector.

Apparently there was a lot of street justice happening out there and many things and people weren't so easy to figure out. I was into a whole new violent world that my instant decisions would affect people in many ways. I was here trying to help those that needed it and remove those that deserved it, but hadn't thought about the heavy responsibility of actually doing it. The nice thing about receiving awards was you were given an extra day off with pay. During roll call months after the incident, I was asked to step forward. I didn't know what my shift Lieutenant and Sergeant were doing until the Lieutenant read the Commendation, congratulated me and shook my hand while the rest of the shift applauded. I was caught off guard, embarrassed, but also pleased that I was being accepted. I never got over the embarrassment of being singled out, but loved those extra paid days off. I received 14 Citations/Commendations and 7 letters of excellence during my career.

Elmwood Cemetery/Choir Practice

I knew I was totally accepted when I was invited to my first choir practice. In 1970 it wasn't yet called choir practice as Joseph Wambaugh's best seller, "The Choir Boys", hadn't come out yet. It was a way to wind down after a busy shift and have a couple of beers. Kind of like a macho way to get out emotions with people who were experiencing the same daily violence, death and cruelty. This was our way to vent what we were witnessing in a community that we were trying to serve and protect. Elmwood Cemetery was a historic cemetery located in the 7th Precinct and was one of the oldest in the country. It was a quiet safe place in the middle of a war zone that had civil war veterans, famous names and head stones from the 1800's. Everybody pitched in and brought beer and snacks. To my surprise, there was quite a group of uniform officers from my shift there. I was handed a beer and introduced to the headstone of an officer who had been killed and had worked with this group of guys. The guys talked about their arrests, battles, and the gruesome details that occurred on their shifts and every once in a while someone would pour a little beer on the grave while talking to him as if he were there. I was told later that he had requested that his buddies have a beer with him if he had gotten killed on the job. That was exactly what they did. It was new and amazing to me to see and feel their closeness. At that point, I hadn't lost a close co-worker, but that was going to happen all too soon and often in the future.

New Commissioner, New Rules

In January of 1971, we got a new police commissioner, John Nichols. With the new commissioner, came changes in the department; some changes were good and some not so good. The not so good was that he was very military oriented and roll call inspections were stricter with shined shoes, pressed shirts and gun inspections often. John Nichols started changing things right away and let everybody know to shape up or pay a price. It didn't bother those of us that were fresh out of the academy, but the seasoned troops who had been working in a war zone bitched like hell. Everybody was issued new Sam Browne leather belts with handcuff covers and holster flaps which made it harder to get your cuffs out or draw your weapon. We were told the changes were because the public was offended by the sight of our guns and handcuffs. When riding passenger in your vehicle your weapon hung between the seat and the door sometimes and it was almost impossible to pull the flap up and get your weapon out quickly. With officers being ambushed in their vehicles regularly, this policy could make them sitting ducks with any delay accessing their weapon. Other rules included, no smoking, and hats on all the time even in extremely hot vehicles (no air conditioning). Supervisors were ordered to write up anybody that did not follow the new rules, no matter the circumstances.

Working in fast paced, violent, dirty, dangerous combat type of situations, we knew it wasn't suburbia, but it seemed like they thought it was. We realized we were a semi-military organization and should look good at all times, but the honor guard dress rules were a bit much.

S.T.R.E.S.S.

The Police Commissioner and Mayor Gribbs started the STRESS unit (Stop The Robberies Enjoy Safe Streets). We all knew it was a good idea and what the City needed, but the press and politicians, demagogued them for starting the unit. They took the Precinct Support Unit (PSU) that I had worked at as extended training right out of the Academy, and converted it to STRESS and made it voluntary. They were the best of the best that worked strictly felonies.

The STRESS unit became a plain clothes decoy unit in high crime areas. It doesn't get any more dangerous than letting an armed, violent felon rob you and then attempt to make an arrest in a high crime neighborhood. Before Mayor Coleman Young disbanded STRESS for political reasons, it had caused violent crime to drastically drop. With bad press causing citizen uproar, 65% of the black community was against STRESS, but 78% of whites and 85% of the black businesses were for it. In that time period 26% of Detroit's population was black and responsible for 65% of the serious crime. Race was raising its ugly head. Politicians and the media were using race instead of real facts to the detriment of a unit that was making a large drop in crime in black communities under siege by violent predators. As time went on the violent crime rate doubled without STRESS Units. I was there to see it all.

I was adjusting to my new environment which was a dangerous and sometimes hostile work place. I thought I had seen and handled most situations pretty well. Some of the officers, and rightly so, were not keen on going into harm's way with unproven rookies and would rather be with their regular experienced partners. Every day, every shift, there were numerous shootings, hold ups and B&E's dispatched by radio calls. Some calls were real and some were to try to get a priority response faster because of a shortage of response units. Some of the senior officers were pretty good about taking us rookies and teaching us the dangers of the street while putting themselves in even more dangerous situations.

Daniel G. Ellis

One officer, patrolman Danny Ellis, was the most willing to take us on patrol and teach us. Danny was patient and a good, honest, hardworking officer who had a lot of experience to share with us and was always willing to do so. He was my first mentor.

After working a shift with Danny, I had the next day off and was watching the news during dinner when they announced a police officer was killed at Mother Waddles Perpetual Mission and then went to commercial. That was MY Precinct. I had been on the job while several officers that I didn't know were killed and that had bothered me immensely. When the news came back on they reported that Daniel G. Ellis of the 7th Precinct was shot to death today, February 3rd, 1971. My mouth went dry, the pit of my stomach felt empty and my eyes watered. I was feeling total and complete shock. This couldn't be happening. We worked together yesterday; he was a good guy, a smart, caring cop, well-liked and respected, a family man with a wife and kids. I know him; I knew him. I just couldn't believe it. For some dumb reason I didn't think about this happening. Only those that were living it knew the hurt. Danny was the ninth officer killed since I first sat in front of Paul Begins widow at my graduation exercises; less than a year before.

Danny Ellis was killed by Willie Green a paroled convicted murderer who beat his wife to death. Danny as usual was working with one of my academy classmates. They were responding to a disturbance at Mother Waddles Perpetual Mission on Gratiot Ave. near Mt. Elliott St. As they entered the Mission they were confronted by Mr. Green who was armed with a hand gun.

Danny shoved his rookie partner out of the line of fire, but couldn't return fire because of a pregnant woman who was behind the shooter. Danny took three rounds in the chest. Danny's co-workers and friends on the force conveyed him to the hospital, but he died before they got there.

There was always angry talk that the flap holster cover put the officers at a disadvantage. Shortly after Danny's shooting, we were told we could purchase and use our own private holsters if they had quick release straps and I went back to mine immediately. When reporting for duty the next day I was handed a new elastic black ribbon to wear on my badge. The old cloth ribbon seemed worn out as I had worn it nearly my entire short career. This time was different, it was for Danny. Before and after our shifts, individually and in small groups, we stopped at the funeral home to pay our respects. On the day of the funeral the Tactical Mobile Unit worked our Precinct so all of the 7th Precinct officers could attend. Never being in the military or at a police funeral, I was on an emotional roller coaster between holding back tears and standing straight, tough and tall. Still my heart hurt and tears trickled down while I choked back sobs while seeing the senior heavy experienced veterans doing the same as our shift was placed at attention in line across from the honor guard.

A 21-gun salute, taps, folding of the flag with it presented to his widow was beautiful, but emotional; almost unbearable. I just learned what the Blue family really was all about. I was to lose friends, partners and attend too many funerals of dedicated young men who died violently while protecting others during my career. They risked everything and gave their all, while being demagogued, spat upon and treated harshly by some.

It's been over 45 years since Daniel G. Ellis was killed and this is the first time that I have been able to let myself completely go there and I still choke up, my eyes get wet remembering his mentoring me, and a lot of young officers, which most likely kept us alive. I still remember how adamant he was about the uncomfortable handcuff holders that were on your kidneys and how unsafe the flap holster covers were. There were no bullet proof vests, shields, seat belts, or air bags in those days.

Looking back, I think that was a big turning point of my moving away from civilian life and my marriage breaking up. I moved back in with my ex a few more times, but each time she was more anti-cop and I was more pro-cop. I kept going back and trying to work things out because of the kids, but finally realized it was better for the kids not to be put through separation after separation. We were finally divorced in 1973.

In 1970 and 1971 we had ten officers killed, numerous others shot and many more shot at, including me. I was in a war zone that my family and civilian friends didn't understand or even knew existed. We had close to 300 officers killed nationwide with most happening in the inner cities. Officers seriously assaulted and injured was over 300% higher in the 1970's opposed to now. Detroit today is usually still leading the nation in murders, rapes, robberies and serious crime, but Detroit really was the murder capital back then. With less than a year on the job, I had experienced more than most suburban and some Detroit Officers had in their entire careers. I had quickly changed from a lily white from the suburbs, to a street hardened cop without much in common with my old life and suburban friends. There are almost 60 thousand officers seriously assaulted each year nationally now and more back then. During the 70's, over 2,600 officers received treatments from our Medical Section a year out of a 5,000 man force. That is approximately 50% receiving some kind of injury during the year.

Firemen Attacked

I was amazed that when a fire truck was dispatched a police unit was also dispatched to protect the fireman and their equipment. I just couldn't believe that there was so much anger and hate toward first responders, especially fireman and medics, but there was and it only got more violent as time went on. I saw crowds at fires cheer when a fireman was carried out on a stretcher when seriously injured while trying to protect their property. At another large building fire, they had to dispatch numerous cars because of a large unruly crowd.

One time I got hit in the head with a transistor radio that someone threw at me or the firemen while I was standing crowd control so the firemen could save some of their homes. Another time while on patrol, a small crowd of people pointed out a closed Bar-B-Q Restaurant and were pointing and yelling "Fire" and screaming that there were babies upstairs. As my partner was calling in the fire, I went upstairs and crawled on the floor so I could breathe while calling out for the children. The next thing I knew, two firemen were carrying me out and sat me on the curb. As I was coughing and getting my breath back, I could see the people in the crowd who were yelling about babies now laughing. After I got my breath back I lit a cigarette. The firemen just shook their heads and laughed. They told me the upper flat was, and had been, vacant for years and everybody knew it. This rookie had just fallen for a dangerous joke.

I was still learning and not as smart or experienced as I thought. Now I knew why the senior cops were a little more cautions before running into a situation. You couldn't believe everything the people on the street were telling you. Many of them didn't like cops, or firemen, and didn't care if you made it or not. I learned it was up to me to stay alive.

Belle Isle Bridge

I was told the inspector wanted me in his office at 10am. Our Inspector, who was in charge of the whole Precinct, was a gruff and scary old salt who swore and yelled a lot at everyone. Our group of 8 rookies was being evaluated because we were getting close to one year on the job and we were to be confirmed as duly certified police officers, if we were acceptable. Nothing was guaranteed, but I wasn't worried to much as I made a lot of good arrest stayed out of trouble and had even been awarded a commendation for excellent work.

As I entered his office after loudly asking "Permission to enter sir," he pointed to a chair and said "Sit." As he read over my file I thought he might be pleased and lighten up a bit, but no, he curtly asked me if I believed in traffic enforcement. I replied, "Yes sir, I do." He then asked why I didn't write more tickets. I told him if you look at all the traffic stops I've made and the verbal warnings given to those that understood their mistakes, you could see I stopped more vehicles than most. To which he replied loudly, "I don't care about warnings, you're not writing enough tickets." I then made another big, big mistake. Rather than complying with his order with a "yes sir," I innocently asked, what was the normal quota of tickets per month? Big mistake.

His face turned red with his eyes bulging out and I knew I just screwed up big time with the word "quota." He jumped up and came toward me while yelling, "Get the fuck out of here." I left as fast as my feet could carry me, while the desk officers were smiling and enjoying the entertainment.

A Sergeant took me aside and told me 10-15 tickets a month with other arrest would get me by and that the inspector was a fair guy and would give me a chance without holding a grudge. When I came to work the next day everybody was kind of snickering at me. I looked at the daily assignment sheet and saw I was assigned to beat 55-A. I asked the Sergeant where was beat 55-A because I had never seen it listed before. He told me while laughing, it was the Belle Isle Bridge and that he was told to make sure I was on it and walking all the time except for my lunch break. I was shocked as the temperature was below freezing. It was a very strong message not to use the word quota and to write more tickets; which I did. It was a miserable day, but the street Sergeants who were checking on me stopped with hot coffee and let me sit in their cars every once in a while. They were right about the inspector; he didn't hold a grudge and gave me a good rating for my confirmation.

Confirmation 4/13/71

For the first 12 months on the police force you are a probationary officer (rookie) and subject to be let go for almost any reason, i.e., not up to standards, bad behavior, unacceptable performance, physical and mental health problems, etc. So I was happy to learn my commanding officers report, the medical sections re-examination, and personnel section reports were all good. That is until they checked my height and exclaimed, "How in the hell did you get on the job, you're too short!" My heart dropped as Mayor Cavanaugh was gone and my uncle's friend was no longer in charge of the Personnel section. I had put in my all and was no longer a civilian. I was already a cop 24/7. This couldn't be happening to me. I was good at it. I lost friends, I helped people, and I paid my dues.

I was then asked to wait in the outer officer. A few minutes later, I was called back in and told I had a good record and they handed me my Confirmation Certificate of Appointment signed by the Police Commissioner, John Nichols and congratulated me as a new confirmed Detroit Police Officer. I left knowing that I had received the best training and more experience than most police officers nationwide in the last year. I loved this job, but I have never experienced more highs and lows or adrenaline rushes in my life and this was one big one.

Coal Cars

Well not being a rookie anymore and on probation, I was curious as to why some of the scout car crews were manned by all black crews and only a few mixed. I was told by the black officers that they were the coal cars and each car had 3 officers with 2 working and one off each day it was in service. Most crews were allowed to pick their own partners and they had more in common with each other, but worked other (mixed) cars when all 3 were working and only 2 could work their car. I didn't see or notice any prejudice between the crews or supervisors. We all bled blue and a lot of people out there wanted our blood, black or white. Ten officers were killed in 1970 and 1971 and the next two killed in the summer of 1971 right after my mentor Danny Ellis, were black officers, Ulysses Brown, and Frederick Hunter, Jr. In those days, when we heard a call of "officer in trouble" or "need a backup," there was no hesitation because of color. In fact, we were all quite close even though we had different backgrounds, we all went through the same experiences and training.

Dispatch

In the early 70's dispatch was manned by experienced street officers who had been on the street and knew what it was like out there. When you were in trouble or a little shaky with a situation like a chase, they were calming experienced voices that were very welcomed and would calm you down immediately. On the other side of the wall were the 911 operators. In those days 911 operators were also experienced officers who were mostly light duty officers. The walking wounded who were temporarily assigned to answer incoming calls while healing up to return to the street or be retired on a disability. They also knew the street and what to ask incoming callers to eliminate phony calls, and get real information that the dispatchers could relay to the responding crews.

Civilian operators asked callers a lot of questions but important information was never relayed to the responding crews. The civilians wasted time when time could mean life or death for someone. Later I got into the habit of asking the citizens, what time they called so I would know if I was in service and how close I was at that time. When it took a long time for the police run to be dispatched and we found out they had waited an unreasonable and unnecessary amount of time, they were advised to file a complaint. I told them when I got the call and where I was and that I would rather be locking up the perpetrator instead of making a report after the fact. I was here to work and not run around all night making after the fact reports for an insurance claim. You could really see the difference before the mid 70's, when the changes were made from officers to inexperienced civilians.

Well back in the good old #7 days when I was new and learned what was not taught in the academy, we were busy doing a report when my senior partner stopped at a party store and picked up a case of beer and two large pizzas' and headed downtown. There was a separate private elevator that was in the police garage and next to the door was a regular old shopping cart. He put the beer and pizza in the shopping cart, threw a rag over it and up we went to dispatch. I was very nervous knowing this was not normal procedure, but as a rookie, I just followed my senior partners lead. There were about 20 cops up in dispatch so they got one beer and a slice of pizza each. I knew we could get into some trouble if caught, but one beer for each shouldn't cause a problem and the senior officer was always in charge. He introduced me around to them as his new partner on 7-4 and everybody was friendly. On the way back to our scout car area he told me every once in a while he drops off some beer and pizza and if he needs extra time out of service to attempt an arrest or legitimate reason they would give it to him if nothing serious was pending.

Third Man - Rotating Shifts 7-4

No longer a rookie and with new rookies coming to #7, I was assigned to scout car crew 7-4 as a 3rd man on rotating shifts, midnight, afternoons & days. When both of my senior partners were working I was assigned to another car or put together with a rookie or another 3rd man whose senior partners were together. That made for a lot of bouncing around with us younger officers who were a little more adventurist when together.

Foot Chase B&E Man

On midnights some of the older officers would park to catch a nap after the bars closed or let us younger officers drive, with the understanding we wouldn't get into anything serious. While driving along in the parking lane on Chene St. and checking the store fronts while my partner was sound asleep, suddenly I made eye contact with a black male yanking on a cash register in a closed bakery. I slammed on the brakes, bailed out and gave foot chase. My partner later, after chewing me out said he heard dispatch calling 7-4 mobile do you have 7-4 prep (officer on foot) in sight? He said he sleepily looked over to the driver's seat and saw I was gone and he went into full panic.

I had chased the B&E man for two blocks and then, after a brief struggle, hand cuffed him. I gave out my location and my partner pulled up just before other backup units arrived. In a different time and place, this arrest could get you a Commendation, but at that time, it was just a normal arrest.

I didn't say anything about him sleeping and I realized I should have woken him up. The driver wasn't the one who usually gets into the foot chase, the passenger does. It was another example of what I was learning day to day.

Knowing when to shut up, as minor mistakes were made, earned trust from your senior partners. As we all were human and hopefully learned not to make them again, a mistake could and sometimes did cost lives. We all knew the difference between mistakes and bad behavior. We learned how to give a look or brief comment to the cop getting close to crossing the line. Those officers who would get braver and pushy when they saw back up coming, soon found out back-up could put it in slow motion with lights and sirens on while driving 5mph. We knew who they were pretty quick. We had plenty of physical confrontations that were necessary, and we didn't appreciate getting into one that wasn't necessary. Dispatch figured out who those few officers were and who to give the rotten runs to. They wouldn't get back-up unless it was a situation that truly required it. Eventually most of those cops transferred to jobs off the street. The street wasn't for everyone and if they couldn't handle it, they shouldn't be there.

First Drug Raid

One of the first drug raids I went on was in a high crime area on a hot summer night. Our job was to secure the perimeter and convey the prisoners. I was amazed at how organized and smooth it went. Just like street arrest, you obtain your evidence, secured and searched your prisoners and got the hell out of the area as soon as possible.

There were no cell phones or social media, but the street telegraph could produce a dangerous hostile crowd in minutes. My senior partner wasn't happy working with a rookie and had been riding me all day long. When it was time to leave, he told me to grab those three prisoners as he pointed at 3 handcuffed men leaning against a wall. I attempted to explain to him that we might want to take 3 different ones and he cut me off and said in an angry voice, "I told you what to do, now put them in the car." I did what I was ordered to do and put all three in the back seat and then got in and stuck my head out the passenger window. In those days there wasn't a shield separating us from the prisoners. As we were heading into the station, the stench started drifting into the front seat. My hard to please partner started yelling, "who shit, who shit?"

I had my head out the window and I was trying really hard not to laugh because he was suffering. He was asking me why I didn't tell him that one of them shit his pants. I didn't need to remind him that he made me take that particular prisoner when I tried to take different ones. Still, I couldn't help but laugh.

It was another good lesson for me. Most of the lessons I was learning were how to protect, serve and stay alive. This taught me about the smell test when I had a choice of which prisoners to convey. Earlier, I had learned the touch test while working the wagon without leather gloves. I was getting there, and learning a new lesson every day.

Mailman & Dogs

While patrolling I noticed a white mailman delivering mail in a black high crime area with a pack of wild, vicious dogs following him every day. I got curious and had to ask him if he ever had any problems. He told me this had been his route for over 10 years and as the neighborhood deteriorated with wild dogs, he started carrying dog yummies and slowly made friends with a couple of them. The couple turned into a pack. As one left or died another would join the pack. It was amazing to watch the dogs walk behind him and sit or stand still as he entered a business with the mail. As far as I know he was never robbed, assaulted or attacked by man or beast. His continuing pack of wild dogs met him at the start of his route every morning. I didn't recall seeing many cats, but I did see rats and rodents that were at least the size of cats and with the wild dogs they probably didn't have much of a chance.

Dog Tails

An officer I had worked with accidently ran over a dog on Field Street and Jefferson and felt so bad for the kid that owned the dog that he bought a puppy, leash, collar and dog food for him. About a week later when I was working with him, we stopped to see how the kid and dog were doing. The kid said in a matter of fact way, that the dog had run away. He didn't seem to care much about it and wasn't even very friendly or appreciate what the officer tried to do for him. This was a tough crowd.

Crime went up during the holidays as those that had where victimized by those that wanted. While working one Christmas Eve., we had a call of a "B&E, occupied dwelling." As we were getting information from the victims about what was damaged and missing we heard whimpering. To my shock, I looked toward the empty present boxes around the Christmas tree and saw an 8-12 week old puppy with an extension cord tied around its neck and a 12 inch butcher knife entering its neck going all through the length of its body. As an animal lover, I was disgusted and angry with the perpetrators and the victims. They were not even concerned; when I tried to get permission to take and aid the puppy, they replied, "He will die soon," and he did. My senior partner advised me that it was their dog and their decision, not ours.

He said we were too busy with backed up serious calls and I will soon learn that life here, even animals lives, was seen differently than other places. Was I really in a third world country? Could people be that hard and uncaring to the death of people or animals? If I was to mentally survive, I had better toughen up. To this very day I remember that Christmas Eve on Lucky Place Street. It was a horrible sight that strangely kept popping back into my head even though I saw a lot worse.

Shot Gun Stuck

One afternoon I was assigned to work with an officer who it turned out had dated my cousin. He was an ex-Marine who saw combat in Vietnam like a lot of the guys on the job. As we were turning onto East Grand Blvd. from Agnes Street near Belle Isle, a volley of shots rang out and people near us on the street scattered. This was the 3rd time I was apparently under fire.

I reached to get the shot gun out and it was jammed in the rack. As I was ducking and yanking on it my partner called in "shots fired at Agnes & the Blvd." He was calm and I was freaking out as he drove toward the sound of the gun fire. I jumped at the second volley of shots and he was still calm. I gave up on the shotgun and drew my backup gun since my service revolver, with its new flap holster, was between the seat and the passenger door and I couldn't get to the flap fast enough. Just about that time a STRESS unit backup officer entered a foot chase with the suspect who got away. I was then given some of the best advice that I ever received to keep me alive and give me an advantage against someone shooting at me. My partner taught me the sounds of gun fire as he learned from Vietnam combat. He explained that: 1) A "Loud Boom" was close, but not in your immediate direction so stay calm, don't panic and try to spot the shooter, 2) A louder "Crack Sound" was in your direction, get down and try to spot the shooter, 3) A loud "Snapping Sound", get down it's close and 4) You don't hear the one that hits you. The bottom line was not to panic, stay calm and go and eliminate the threat, if you can. This was advice that I used many, many times to my advantage and to which some officers thought I was a little nut's later on in my career. Most everyone ducked and it is a strong instinct to duck at the "Boom" sound, but I would go up instead of down to get the drop on the shooter and it worked. We became good friends and roommates and ended up working at another Precinct together years later. He worked uniform accident prevention and always teased me because I had enough seniority to take a position with a little less danger, but didn't.

I hated writing tickets and the changing of shifts, but found out if you make a lot of felony arrests or work undercover in Special Operations you didn't have to write tickets, or do traffic enforcement. So, that's what I did throughout my career. I worked undercover, felony units, and mostly the 7pm to 3am Precinct Special Ops shift with the gung-ho type guys. My assignments included Morality (vice), Gambling Conspiracy (organized crime), Bravo Units (felony car) 80-Series (felony car) and Precinct Cruiser (Big Four) hunting felons.

Corporals / Signs of Burnout

I wouldn't be honest if I didn't include some of the stories of senior burnt out officers. Most of them were good, honest, hardworking street officers, but apparently in the field too long and under too much constant pressure. One afternoon, I was assigned as a Corporal, that is when a regular officer drives a Sergeant around for a shift. I soon learned to try to avoid getting that assignment whenever possible.

On this particular call there was a Mounted Division horse tied up outside a bar on Jefferson and Van Dyke that was a popular rock & roll joint with lots of girls. As we pulled up I couldn't believe my eyes, a Mounted Police horse really was tied up in the front of the bar standing there calm as could be. The Sergeant requested a mounted supervisor or a horse trailer to convey the horse back to Belle Isle which was the closest horse barn, but still pretty far away. We entered the bar and to my second shock and amazement, in the middle of a wild dancing crowd, there was a fully uniformed mounted officer in complete dress regale, hat, boots and riding pants, dancing with a group of girls and having one hell of a good time. We took the officer into the 7th Precinct lock up; he was laughing and drunk as hell. I never found out or asked what happened to him and I really didn't want to know. Usually any officer not committing a crime is taken to what is called a trail board of Senior Command Executives. Most likely he would be sent to Brighton Hospital for 30 days without pay or suspended. Unlike most job suspensions when you are suspended for say 5 days off it's like a vacation. On the police department, if you're suspended for 5 days by the Trial Board, it means you work your 5 days off without pay (no vacation) and nobody wants that. With just about a year on the job and now knowing what these guys went through, I felt sorry for him and the others who got somewhat goofy. Still I must have already started getting a little goofy myself as I found these situations funny. My sense of humor had changed from civilian to cop.

Another time I got stuck working as a Corporal was even worse. A Sergeant unit's radio call signs were in the 70's, like car 7-70 or 7-71, etc., and Lieutenant unit's were in the 60's (7-60, 7-61). I was working 7-71 and we were dispatched to a motel on Jefferson and the Mt. Elliott area to meet Unit 7-60. As it turned out the guys from my shift were having a bachelor party and I really didn't want to be involved in this call. I wasn't in the military, but this must have been like a ship's crew on liberty with every one drunk. Apparently an idiot attempted to hold up a couple of the off duty cops in the parking lot. The cops took his gun, kicked his ass and sent him packing. Then they went inside the party and auctioned off the gun to raise money for the bride and groom. Crazy as it sounds the holdup man went into the 7th Precinct to file charges that his illegal gun was stolen by two men at the hotel. What a mess. Both officers were suspended indefinitely and quite a few received days off without pay. The world I was in was totally bazaar. I found it funny at times, but sad too, seeing good cops self-destructing. I was still naïve to the drinking, suicide, and isolation they used to deal with what they were experiencing every day.

I wasn't there for this incident, but the situation was an officer working a one-man report car was at his brother in laws bar on Jefferson and had a few to many beers at lunch. One of the regular patrons came in telling everyone about his new motorcycle. Somehow the officer talked the guy into letting him take the motorcycle for a ride saying he was experienced driving bikes. He started it, put it in gear, and flew through the parking lot out onto Jefferson hitting a car, wrecking the bike and breaking his arm so bad a bone was protruding out of it. That's the funny part. The crazy part was he showed up for off duty roll call as if nothing happened. He had made a deal with the bike's owner to pay for the repairs and minor damage on the car. The car was old and the driver did not have insurance or proper plates and just wanted to get out of there. The deal fell apart when the bikes owner had second thoughts and showed up at the station to make a report. The cop was suspended. I transferred out shortly after that not knowing what happened to him. This environment made some people, some cops, a little strange and I was starting to understand it.

I was lucky enough to have a day off when, for some reason, a bunch of the guys got drunk on Belle Isle and commandeered the Harbor Master Police boat. They supposedly put the crew off & took it for a ride. I did hear from some of the younger officers that a bunch of them showed up for off duty roll call drunk wearing large straw Mexican sombrero's they took from a vendor. More suspensions and time off was given. Every incident I was seeing kept surprising me because out on the street these same guys were doing their jobs and then they would do something crazy. I didn't know then, but I quickly learned you could only take so much for so long and then something had to pop! The ones who seemed to take the risks and do the dirty work medicated themselves with alcohol and sometimes over did it. I guess it was maybe like a war and the front line troops were in constant combat and burying their friends while seeing daily what human beings can and did do to each other.

The others did their jobs and saw plenty, but got off of the street as much and as soon as possible. Most of them made it to retirement. A lot of others were killed, disabled, committed suicide, or were fired.

In those days there was no PTSD or breaks from the violence of the street. You were used up and thrown away like a piece of garbage when no longer needed or functional. At first not knowing any better, I found the antics of the senior officers' funny as their way to de-stress. This definitely was not like suburban departments.

One of the strangest stories I heard that later was confirmed by numerous officers, was about a large gruff looking officer who always worked a one-man report car and would give the supervisors fits. He was finally being written up after numerous times for breaking up roll calls by passing some very nasty gas. Another time he was written up was during inspection at a roll call again. The Sergeant was walking the line of officers that were standing at attention and stopped in front of each one checking them up and down. When he came to this particular officer, he yelled, "What the fuck do you think you are doing?" The officer was standing there at attention with his penis hanging out and replied to the Sergeant, "If you're going to work us like horses, we might as well look like fucking horses." When the rest of the officers realized what he did, it totally broke up their roll call. Another suspension for a burnt out cop and a new legend was born. These guys, Vietnam and Detroit combat veterans, were the best in tough situations and I totally trusted them with my life, but still having a little lily white from the suburbs in me, I couldn't figure them out yet. They would willingly risk their lives for this community over and over again while being labeled as white occupation troops by the media.

Daily Runs

When on patrol in the 7th Precinct there weren't very many places we could stop to write reports or to just get out of harm's way temporarily. We were told to stay off Belle Isle as it had its own station. When we needed to get away from the smells of dirty alleys and streets full of garbage, junk, hostile people and a car without air conditioning, we would sometimes sneak onto the Island to write our reports. Being able to enjoy the clean fresh air and not have our heads on a swivel while writing was nice for even a short time. It turned into a cat and mouse game sometimes while trying to get off the Island with the Lieutenants and Sergeants trying to catch you. The Belle Isle patrolling scout cars understood our plight and would keep us abreast of where the supervisors were. I don't think anybody ever got caught or punished. Looking back, I think the supervisors must have loved the excuse to cruise the Island looking for us and the threat of getting caught made our stay brief. We did have tough, but fair supervisors who went through what we were going through and understood.

There also was the Playboy Club on Jefferson and when possible we tried to be around to watch out for the girls at closing. I didn't know if anybody ever got a date, but the girls were knock outs and very friendly. I was learning some girls really did like guys in uniform.

As busy as we usually were, once in a while when writing a report, we would cruise around to the East Town Theatre, bars, or Indian Village. Depending on what end of the Precinct we were working. Indian Village was on our border to the 5th Precinct and once in a while we would get a call of a noisy party or something easy like that. It was an area of mansions and the rich in the middle of a poor ghetto. It technically was in Precinct #5, but when all their cars were busy we got the radio run and loved it. They quieted the band down at our request and usually fed us a plate of food while we talked to and enjoyed the young rich females who seemed to like us inner City cops.

In the Harper and Van Dyke area there was the East Town Theatre an old show that was converted for live entertainment. Most of the time our calls there were to convey an overdosed hippie to the hospital. It wasn't pleasant because we usually had to help the ER staff hold them down, as they shoved a tube down their nose and pumped fluid, mostly bloody from their stomachs. The girls were good looking, skimpily dressed and friendly naïve suburbanites that the locals took advantage of with bad dope, robbery, and assaults.

You never knew what you were going to run into with high hippies, but the locals disappeared when we came around and it usually was not too dangerous for us. We pulled into the alley behind the building one night and right in the middle of it was a spaced out guy with his pants down around his ankles, pumping like heck. We assumed he was having sex with someone right in the middle of a pitch black alley. As we exited our vehicle and shined our flashlights on him, we saw he was alone. My partner that night was used to high people doing crazy things and just said to the guy, "Hey buddy, someone stole your bitch." We took him down to Detroit General Hospital where they had a psych ward, but didn't charge him with anything. I already was getting that strange sense of humor that hardened cops get, as I found the whole situation hilarious especially my partners statement to him. Six months before, I would have found the whole situation shocking.

I was starting to get pretty confident again as I had been through more than most and had gained great training and experience already. I had been shot at a number of times, assaulted, had made numerous varied felony arrests, experienced violence, death and aided seriously injured people all in my short time on the job. Yes, I was feeling cocky, immortal and over confidant in my abilities. I thought I was street smart and not "the lily white from suburbia" any more. I had studied and was taught by the Detroit boys who had combat experience from Vietnam and grew up on the City's tough streets. Then came the wakeup call and I would receive many of them through the years.

We received a radio run to an address on Trombly Street near Chene Street on a disturbance. I pulled up as I was trained to do, one house before the address I was sent to. As I walked up, the narrow steps to the front door, I could see a man standing just inside the door taking aim at me with a rifle. I was trapped as there was nowhere to go, left or right; he had me. At that moment, everything seemed to be in slow motion, as I drew my revolver I expected to hear or feel the shot. Then all of a sudden, he dropped his rifle and put his hands up in the air before I could take aim at him. I then noticed that a backup unit had just arrived and the officers were rapidly approaching with guns drawn and aimed at him.

After handcuffing him I started walking to my scout car when he said to me, "you were a dead man walking until I saw your buddies." Yes, that put me in my place, woke me up and made me realize the danger they put themselves in to help me. That is one very big reason why cops stick together. We don't just think they will risk their lives for each other, we know that they will die for each other and you can't get any closer than that. After that experience and knowing what we go through together daily, it didn't take long to pull away from our old civilian lives. You are changed forever like, Once a Marine Always a Marine; it's the same for cops, Once a Cop Always a Cop. I have been accused, even now, that I would still bleed blue. It's never left me.

Hats Backwards

Some dangerous situations are actually funny, well at least to a cop. We responded to a call of shots being fired from the rear of an upper flat on Townsend Street. Usually the car that gets the run goes in first and draws fire unless the backup beats them there. Nobody wants someone to get killed or hurt on their call so that's an extra reason to hustle. Well another scout car was closer and put out on the radio that there was a sniper and shots had been fired.

So we turned out our lights and swung into the alley very quickly. Then all of a sudden we saw someone on an upper back porch firing shots in our direction. At that time, we were supposed to wear our hats at all times even in the scout car on patrol or we would get written up and lose pay. Well it was very hot in the car without air conditioning and we had our hats on the seat between us. We quickly grabbed our hats as we bailed out of the scout car. My partner got behind a tree and I was behind a telephone pole on the opposite side of the alley; both of us hoping to get a shot at the shooter. When I looked at my partner and he looked at me, while basically pinned down, we both started laughing so hard because we had grabbed the wrong hats. He being a big guy, my hat was just sitting on the top of his head and me, being much smaller, his hat was down to my eyes; we looked like Laurel and Hardy. I don't know if our laughing had anything to do with it, but the shooter then stopped firing. After that situation we both took a lot of teasing for the way we looked in each other's hats, but nobody was surprised by us laughing while in danger. That was the strange sense of humor of an inner City cop.

We were all very into taking the bad guys off of the street. Some of it was pride in what we do and some of it was because we see daily what the predators were doing to the victims. The courts, lawyers, media and general public didn't have a clue to what real victims go through like we did. They saw them well after the victimization was over. The victims know and we know how much they appreciate us and that's what counts. That's why things like this happen. During a shift change one set of officers getting off duty give the set of officers coming on duty there sometimes still running vehicles. I saw the two officers coming on duty jump into the back seat of a scout car because the two officers in the front seat getting off duty wouldn't get out of the vehicle. There was a radio call being dispatched, "Hold up in progress, shots fired, with one down." So all four officers, even the ones no longer on the payroll, responded to protect and serve the victim who needed them. These were the guys who were teaching me by example on how to be the real Police!

I've tried not to use names in this book so the officers who recognize themselves in the stories have a choice if they want to be anonymous. There were two young officers who, not only did their jobs during their working hours, they had a police scanner and responded on their time off to serious radio runs, to back up officers and/or arrest felons.

During that time period, 1970's, we were technically on duty 24/7 and had to live in the City. I think most officers have had to make an off duty arrest or take police action during their careers when off duty. I have and even had people knock on my apartment door needing help. Some of the general public, until they are victims still spat on us, called us pigs and were anti-police. Most people, even I, really didn't know the extent that victims suffered and what cops will do to help them until I was there. I can tell you now that it will change your attitude big time.

I was advised early on not to talk to or trust the press. In the 1970's, the media, like today, was anti-cop and was very good at leaving out or adding to a story with their own spin instead of reporting facts. The media's agenda was anti-military and anti-cop, which in my opinion caused a lot of dangerous problems for first responders and innocent citizens.

Most cops get citizens' complaints or worse written up by a supervisor, but a lot of the time it's an unhappy citizen who either saw only part of the situation or themselves have had numerous run-ins with the authorities. There are some that are totally legitimate and after investigation by supervisors the officers are punished. Supervisors in my time were fair to us, but we were guilty until proven otherwise. Usually the officers that were out there working received more complaints than the ones who weren't. Each complaint had to be investigated on its own merit. I was lucky or just had a way with words with angry citizens, as I only had two unfounded complaints in my career. My first complaint was for laughing. If you knew me you would totally expect that as I was pretty easy going and tried to verbally explain to citizens, when I could, what and why I was doing something. For instance when searching someone, I would tell them, 1) I wasn't going into their pockets, 2) I was patting them down for offensive weapons for their and my safety. I learned quickly that most of the time that communicating with people while doing what you needed to do helped them understand.

When I met resistance with an uncooperative subject I increased my effort and let them know what was going to happen to them and it wouldn't be pleasant. Again, communicating what was going to happen no matter what. Basically I let them know it was their choice. Sometimes they didn't go easy because of anger or emotion and after the fact when calmed down realized they made the choice and it didn't have to be that way. I think that was a big part of why I didn't have very many complaints and the two I did receive had been proven to be unfounded. I made a point to know the law and department rules and tried to make the citizens aware of them while showing respect and humor.

Groceries Went Flying

My first complaint came on a cold windy day while patrolling Lafayette Street near downtown where the wind really whips near the tall buildings. I was driving in the curb lane about 5 mph and checking the front of the businesses when a lady came to the corner of a building that was blocking the wind. She had both arms full of bags that were full of groceries. Just as she left the lee of the building, a strong gust of wind caught her by surprise and her feet went out and up in front of her and her groceries went flying all over the snowy street. I immediately stopped and got out and asked her if she was ok; which she said she was because of her heavy coat.

After I knew she was ok, she said, "That must have looked funny." I said, "Yes, your feet went almost over your head." When she laughed I totally lost it remembering just how funny it did look and couldn't stop laughing. As I helped pickup and repack her groceries, tears were freezing on my face because I laughed so hard. That was my sense of humor let out. Whether I got hurt or someone else, if it wasn't serious, it usually hit me as funny. I still love those blooper type shows and laugh until I can hardly breathe.

A couple of days later I was called into the inspector's office and was quite nervous as to why because that usually meant problems. The last time I was called in I ended up walking a beat on the Belle Isle Bridge in freezing weather for asking about quotas. As normal, I knocked on the door and loudly said, "Request permission to enter sir," and he pointed to the chair in front of his desk and just said "Sit" just exactly like when I was in there before. He told me I had a citizen complaint and proceeded to read it to me. I was shocked as I helped the lady up and she thought it was funny and laughed too. I must have laughed too long and too hard because of my strange sense of humor. As he continued to read the complaint, I started to remember her flip and it just started overcoming me and I went from smiling to actually snickering and the more I could see it in my mind's eye I lost it again and started laughing out loud right there in front of the Inspector. He stopped reading and loudly asked me, "Do you find this funny?" While turning red, with his eyes popping out again, I replied, "But boss, you should have seen it." Same as the other time, he chased me out of his office while yelling, "Get the fuck out of here." The desk officers and Sergeant on duty were cracking up because now I had been run out of his office both times that I had been it. I am normally very respectful to authority except when that sense of humor kicks in. My luck held again as it turned out the lady who filed the citizen's complaint wasn't the lady who had fallen, but someone that saw the incident and misread what was happening. When they talked to the lady who fell, she told them I was nothing but helpful and caring and that we both laughed because it was funny.

Squirrelly Old Lady

We had a call for a possible B&E in progress and to meet a lady that was hearing noises in her basement. She was a little older and seemed a little goofy and we noticed that her windows and doors were barred and locked up tight. Some of our calls were because someone was lonely or needed and wanted some attention or someone to talk to and I thought this was one of those calls. So we searched the house with her to calm her down. As we were walking out another scout car showed up to see if everything was alright and see where we were going to lunch. All of a sudden the lady came out of the house running all upset saying it's a ghost and it's in the basement. All four of us just looked at each other like she was nuts. We all went back into the basement to show her there were no ghost and nothing to worry about. Then we heard it too; a scratchy noise in the drop ceiling. We had her go upstairs and we opened the side door so we could chase whatever it was out of the house. We took out a couple of ceiling tiles and started to tap the other tiles working it toward the opening. All of a sudden a squirrel dropped down and was running all over as we chased it around until we finally chased it up the steps so it could go outside. As fast as it went up those stairs it came right back down making us scatter to get out of its way as it was scared half to death and surprised the heck out of us. The old lady had closed the door after we propped it open and now we were tired, but cracking up. We opened the door again and told her very calmly to get upstairs and not to close the door. Yep, after chasing the squirrel all over again and up the stairs, it came right back down because she had closed the door, again. At that point we were exhausted, but still laughing at ourselves and the old lady. This time one of the guys stayed with her as we repeated our chase until the squirrel went up and out the open door.

Vicious Dog

We responded to a radio run, "A women trapped by a vicious dog." We weren't equipped with dog sticks or nets so I hoped we could help the crew to find the owner or control the dog without the crew that got the call having to shoot it.

Unfortunately, when all our efforts fail and with very few dog catchers available sometimes there was no other way but to shoot the dog, if it attacked.

As a dog lover, I always had a way with dogs, but not this time. It turned into a keystone cop's episode. The four of us went into the back yard and saw that the lady was safe in the rear entrance of the upper flat. A large dog was at her back door at the top of the steps and wouldn't let her out. We whistled, called and tossed stones toward him to get him to leave to no avail. As it turned out, none of us wanted to shoot the dog. So we each tried to climb the steps up and talk it down, but as we were about three quarters of the way to the top, it attacked and chased us down the steps and around the yard until we all had to jump fences to escape. Again, with our goofy sense of humor, we were all cracking up, muddy and exhausted. When it was chasing us the woman would open her door and the dog would go back up the steps. I saw a frozen hose with a metal nozzle on it and poked it straight up to the top of the steps trying to poke the dog away from the door. As I poked the dog, he charged again and the frozen hose bent making the nozzle end come down and hit my partner who was about 10 feet away, on the top of his head. It sounded like a hammer hitting a coconut. We all were laughing so hard we barely made it back over the fence as the dog, apparently having enough of us, took off running into the field across the street. We closed the gate and notified the dog catcher again. We told her to keep calling the dog catcher until he showed up. All we could do was shoot the dog which we really didn't want to do. This little adventure to a lot of people isn't funny, but after all day of danger, sadness and stress, it was to us. When we do get into a lighter situation, or have the temporary opportunity to laugh, we welcome it even if it is at ourselves. They finally had at least one scout car that carried a dog stick in each Precinct because of the shortage of dog catchers.

Dew Drop Inn

One night, while working the midnight shift, we received a radio run to the Dew Drop Inn on Chene Street of a, "B&E in progress, shots fired." We pulled up, as quiet as possible, with our lights out and could see the side door slightly ajar. The door was on the side of the restaurant part of the business. We entered the totally dark building waited for our eyes to adjust while listening for any sounds. I had been to enough B&E's and learned to use the dark and silence to my advantage. I was quite comfortable searching in the dark. I even preferred it; feeling that darkness is to my advantage. My partner quietly went toward the rear of the building and I slid along a wall with my back to it going toward the front of the building with my service revolver drawn. As I got near a door that I later learned was to the bar part of the building, I saw broken glass on the floor. I then heard what sounded like a gun being cocked. I swung around thru the door opening, cocking my gun as I was pulling it up and in front of me. I was suddenly standing face to face with a sweating middle aged black male who had stuck his cocked gun in my face inches from my nose. My weapon was also cocked and inches from his face. I started yelling for him to "Drop it, Freeze, Drop it."

It seemed like we were in slow motion, but it was very clear to me that I had a very dangerous Mexican standoff. With both weapons cocked and fingers on the triggers in a short dark vestibule, no matter who fired first, both of us were going to be shot in the face. Somehow instinctively, by training or a movie I saw, I reached up with my left hand and grabbed his gun with the fat part of my left hand between the cocked hammer and firing pin and pulled it out of his hand. While this was happening, I could hear my partner's footsteps running toward the front of the building. He later said he was waiting to hear shots being fired because of the sound of my voice. It turned out the night porter had just shot at the B&E man who had escaped out the side door seconds before we arrived. He didn't know if we were the burglars coming back to get him and he planned on ambushing them before they got him. He hesitated when he saw my uniform and that gave me enough time to react to what could have been a tragic accident. Luck or someone up there kept me alive again and from killing an innocent victim. During my career, there were many times I could have legally shot someone who was pointing a weapon or taking a shot at me, but like most cops, we don't want to kill anybody even if we are at risk, unless we have to. I can only think this incident added to that frame of mind for me. Other officers experienced it, saw it, or heard about experiences like it and would not shoot until absolutely necessary either. The last thing an officer wants to do is shoot someone and they will do whatever it takes to avoid it whenever possible.

Motor City Madam

Every once in a while my old civilian life called me back. I received offers to return to my old occupation as an Automotive Designer with twice the money that I made as a cop and with the opportunity to make even more. I didn't tell my ex-wife or family because it wasn't even a close choice. I wasn't a civilian anymore and never could be. Sitting at a drafting board in suburbia all day was no longer for me. When I was a draftsman, some of the older guys would go down to a whore house on East Grand Blvd. in Detroit during long lunches. They said it was safe and the Motor City Madam kept everybody safe and the cops didn't bother her or her clients. One day I was turning in a report at the front desk and talking to the desk Sergeant when this sweet white haired little old lady came in. The Sergeant immediately ignored me and asked "How are you today Helen?" She smiled and said, "Fine" and proceeded to put a pile of one hundred dollar bills on the desk that was eye level to her and said, "For the widows and orphans fund." She left and the Sergeant wrote widows and orphans fund on an envelope and put it in a safe behind the desk. I was just amazed at the matter of fact way it happened. I asked him who that was and he said that was rocking chair Helen the Motor City Madam who every so often donated to the fund. Helen wrote a book called Motor City Madam and someday I need to read it.

Trains

Once in a while on the way to a run we would be held up by trains and had to wait until they passed and if another scout car could, they would make our radio run. If it was a serious run and the train had held us up more than 5 minutes, some of the senior officers wrote a report and apparently the rail road was given large fines; the longer the wait, the bigger the fine. Mostly we felt bad for the engineers who were shot at, stoned, and often terrorized as they passed through our Precinct. There were so may B&E's, assaults and property damaged they had their own railroad police in the yards. I didn't know what came first the violent ghetto on both sides of the tracks or the tracks causing the ghetto. I was curious as to whether this was an inner City thing or is crime high all along the railroad tracks. I do know it was quite loud. On Bellevue Street near Jefferson Ave., there was an area with a lot of tracks that they kept quite a few rail road cars parked. They were full of goodies and we had constant radio runs of "B&E Box Car in Progress." Even though Detroit was known as the motor City capital of the world, our scout cars were in pretty bad shape. One of the crews received a brand new car and they were teasing the rest of us about our old beat up vehicles. Well, what goes around comes around; they received a radio run to the dark rail road area of a box car, "B&E in Progress." We responded to assist them and as we pulled up we saw a brand new scout car being pushed down the tracks with the doors open and two uniform police officers chasing it. Apparently when they bailed out to chase a suspect they had stopped on a set of tracks that was about to be used and couldn't get back to their vehicle in time. The B&E man escaped, the vehicle was totaled and the rest of us had a big laugh while they became a legend of a humorous screw up. They were both good cops and it was truly pitch black until the train head light lit up the entire area. It was a hilarious sight.

Officer in Trouble

I learned pretty quickly not to call for a backup or officer in trouble unless really needed because: 1) We were a macho bunch and full of confidence in our ability to handle any situation, 2) When you called for help or support the cars and co-workers came at full speed and a lot of officers could and did get seriously injured, 3) The subject you were trying to arrest could get a hell of an ass kicking when the troops arrived and you didn't want to set that in motion on someone who really didn't need an attitude adjustment.

We were used to having subjects run, wrestle, or resist, so unless we were losing, outnumbered, or weapons were involved, we handled it ourselves. We usually just backed each other up whenever we could. When making an arrest we got our prisoner, the evidence, and got out of there as soon as possible or a crowd would form and then we could really have a problem.

On my first response to an 'Officer in Trouble' call there were two southern brothers working on my shift and both were big, tough guys. So when I heard one of the brother's voice screaming for help with all the background noises of a violent struggle, I was surprised, but knew it was for real. We went at break neck speed with lights and sirens wailing and as we pulled up there was another car that had arrived just before us. Well bad luck for the two guys on top of the officer down because it was his brother responding who proceeded to not only teach them it was unacceptable to gang up on a cop, but totally unhealthy to assault his brother. We ended up having to get the two brothers off of the perpetrators so we could get them all to the hospital.

Over the years, I have responded to a lot of officers calling for help and it gets your adrenaline going hearing someone screaming for help and it always seems like forever for us to get there and for them waiting for help. Unlike now, there were no tasers, mace or bullet proof vest; just black jacks, flashlights and knowing how to fight when needed. As the saying goes, "Today's cops aren't like your grandfather's cops," is very true and this grandfather will testify to that. Testing and standards were a lot higher then and the pay was lower. So you had officers that were doing the job for the love of it instead of for the money and benefits. I truly feel sorry for today's officers who are still doing it for the right reasons "to protect and serve" and have to work with and for people who should never have been accepted in the first place. Police, fire and military should have never been used for "give a kid a job" programs but that is what it became in some cases.

Two Guns

Every day there's a new lesson to be learned that might save your life or someone else's life. To survive you have to learn that quickly and pass it on often to others. One night we received a tip that a guy was in the Jefferson and East Grand Blvd. area and was carrying a gun. As we drove by sure enough there he was fitting the description exactly. We drove past without him knowing he was spotted. We parked the scout car in the alley and approached him from two different directions from between the buildings. He was standing in front of us facing away as I grabbed his left arm and hand that was in his coat pocket, at the same time, my partner grabbed the right arm and hand that was in his other pocket. We both looked at each other and said "Bingo" as we both found a gun. To our total surprise he had a gun in each pocket. There were two very important lessons I learned that night and used throughout my career: 1) Don't stop searching someone or something when you find a weapon, or what you're looking for, keep searching. 2) Obtain and use informants just like 'snitches get stitches' there's also a street creed between cops and street criminals that 'the enemy of my enemy is my friend'.

In other words, we do the dirty work for them and eliminate their enemies or competition. If done right by not telling anybody who they are, and you show them you are honest and trustworthy with them, word gets around that you're a straight shooter. Then you pretty much know what is going on and who is doing it. I've made a lot of good arrest by some of my informant's tips. I truly think my well-being was safer as I was told who was armed or wearing a bullet proof vest. I even had a few informants that I never met, but were told I would act on their information when they called and gave it to me anonymously. I didn't care who they were because they usually were right and I trusted their information. I was working for them too.

Stella-Nurse

One of the characters on the street was Stella. She wore a WWII nurse's uniform with military and police medals all over it. Most people, even suburbanites, knew Stella or knew of her. She hung around Greek Town during the day where they fed her and watched out for her. At night she washed up and slept in the police department headquarters garage usually on boxes. It was common knowledge that you don't mess with Stella or your butt would be in a sling as she was totally protected by the brass and every other officer who worked downtown.

Stella

At times Stella could be very aggressive and would run at you while screaming as loud as she could. We quickly learned to avoid her when downtown going to and from court or having lunch in Greek Town. When we conveyed prisoners' downtown to the 9th floor lockup we would tell them if they made any noise from the scout car to the garage elevator and woke up Stella, we would beat the hell out of them. Strangely they all knew about Stella and didn't want her, or the whole Detroit Police Dept. on their ass. We all stayed out of her way as she was the most protected person in Detroit for years.

I understand Stella passed away in a nursing home at a ripe old age. Her son and police officers tried numerous times over the years to try to set her up with a place to stay, but she always returned to the headquarters garage where she was happy. It was her home before I was a cop and long after I retired.

Real Nurses

Usually when working the day shift, and after a night of partying, a couple of scout cars would make their first stop at either St. Joes or Deaconess Hospitals emergency rooms. Cops always had a good relationship with the ER nurses. We usually could get free beer and would give some to the ER Nurses, who in return, would give some officers a grasshopper (Donatol & Maalox) with some oxygen to get rid of a hangover, when needed. Later, in other Precincts that I worked in, it was pretty much the same. Cops and nurses, especially ER nurses, had a special relationship as we all worked crazy shifts and saw a lot of death, gore and other tortures people would do to each other. Nurses and doctors were never ticketed as we spent a lot of time being put back together by them. The joke was that they would start stitching us up before they numbed us up. At least I thought they were joking.

Badge, Divorce & Lie Detector

Twice during my career, I saw an officer pronounce a couple divorced. The first time I was totally amazed even though I had seen things that a normal person would never believe could happen. In this situation we kept getting called back to an older drunk couple's home who would fight when too drunk. Finally, during one of the weekly calls, one of the senior officers told them they would get along better if they were not married and he proceeded to have them both put their hands on his badge and said, "If you want, like a sea captain can marry you, I can divorce you." They both responded, yes that they wanted him to divorce them. He then pronounced Ester and Thomas divorced. There were no more calls to their house. He said it worked some of the time. Later, while in a different Precinct, I saw basically the same thing done to end another series of calls from an old drunken couple. Yes, I was going into and out of a third world country; or so it seemed.

I saw an officer have a suspect put his arm in the front seat and he looped the radio cord around his wrist telling him it was a lie detector. When he asked a question about whom he was with or if he was arrested before, he would key the mic button which lit up the red light, and then the suspect changed his story as if caught in a lie.

I just couldn't believe how lost some of the people we dealt with were. We had a perpetrator rob a Cunningham's Drug store clerk the same day he had dropped off pictures for development to the same clerk earlier. He had filled out the paperwork for the pictures with his correct name and address. We went to his house and arrested him for armed robbery and recovered all the money.

Street Peds

Another thing that I couldn't figure out was why people insisted on walking in the street or crossing in between traffic lights sometimes when the crosswalk with a light is only 20 to 30 feet away. We had numerous pedestrians killed or seriously injured that way. This did not happen very often in suburbia. If it did you were ticketed or your parents kicked your butt. Working and living in both the suburbs and the City gave me a unique perspective of just how many differences there were. Maybe just maybe they were worried about dogs or a person coming out from between the houses after them, but while walking in the middle of the street and arrogantly refusing to move for cars or crossing streets so close to a crosswalk still baffles me. I can only guess it is an attitude of I can and will do anything I want and nobody can stop me. That's fine until they, or one of their siblings, are hit by a car. That happened a lot more in the inner City and it would usually be a hit and run.

Felony Stops, Inside Roof Light

We were taught, and were in constant awareness, just how dangerous a traffic stop could be because of the possibility of ambushes. I don't think I ever saw the inside roof light in a squad car turned on. When writing or reading at night inside a dark scout car you would use a flash light on your lap that was kept down as low as possible as to not illuminate you. In the 70's, snipers were a very real threat in the City. Just before coming on the job, two officers were ambushed in front of the New Bethel Baptist Church; Aretha Franklin's fathers church that was having the RNA's (Republic of New Africa) first national meeting. One was killed and the other badly shot up but survived. I think most inner City street officers have experienced being shot at one or more times and have heard a lot of gun fire. Not knowing for sure whether or not it is directed at you, can keep you always on high alert.

We were also taught not to stand next to a car door when making a traffic stop. We would usually stand just behind the driver's door with our weapon drawn and hidden behind our leg as the driver would have to turn quite a way around to get a shot at us. The passenger partner would exit the vehicle covering any passenger's movements and sometimes, when necessary, he would have a shotgun aimed at the rear window if a felony stop was made. After my first year when working Precinct Special Operations, most of my stops were felony stops and not traffic enforcement. I liked arresting felons, but not writing traffic tickets and you had to do one or the other and both sometimes.

Upchucking

Some of the calls that no one wants to get are the "one down" or "nobody's seen them for a while" calls. In the winter we have had people frozen to the sidewalk. In the summer we had what was called a stinker and that was one that had been dead in the heat with the rats chewing on their fingers and toes for a long time. The sight and smell could knock you over. As with any dead body, usually with a release by phone from homicide, you still had to stay with the body until the medical examiner released it. That could take many hours and a rookie or junior officer would have to stay with the body the whole time to protect it from foul play. It took a while to get use to them before you could stop gagging. After a while some crews would get so use to it they would actually eat lunch in same the room while waiting. We knew these bodies were people who were loved and going to be missed by families, but we had to limit that emotion to keep doing our job, but still be respectful to their families.

The worst were the burnt bodies as the sight and smell will never leave your memory. One time when I had just over a year on the job and was working with a brand new rookie, we had a call to stand by a fire unit for security, as they were attacked all the time. The house had extensive fire damage and was still smoldering as we searched it with the firemen. My partner who had just days on the street called me to a bedroom pointing out what he thought was a burnt dog. As soon as I saw and smelled it I knew it wasn't a dog. The extremities were mostly burnt off and the body had split open with the intestines still bubbling from the heat. The sweet sickening smell of burnt flesh with the horrific sight was too much for the rookie when he realized it was a human and not an animal. He ran out onto the front lawn and threw up while on all fours for quite a while.

Anyone who has actually smelled a body while it was still burning knows you can never ever forget it. When we were relieved for our lunch, we went to the Clock restaurant for a hamburger which was what I ate most of the time. My partner didn't eat and just had coffee. As I was eating my food I noticed he was staring and didn't look very good. Then the couple seated in the next booth left without finishing their food while looking back at us in a strange way. When we got back to the station for off duty roll call everyone was commenting on how bad we stunk. I didn't realize that the smell had got into our hair and uniforms. I then knew why the couple at the restaurant, which specialized in char-burgers, had walked out. With barely a year on the job at the time, I was already hardened enough to eat lunch no matter what.

Seven Cruiser – (The Big Four)

We responded to a radio run of "shots fired at Mack and Mt. Elliot" to back up a unit that was already there. A crowd was starting to form and we were trying to keep them back for their safety as it was turning into a barricaded gunman situation. I was kneeling behind a two-foot high cinder block wall with my hat on backwards as taught so light wouldn't reflect off of the badge and give my location away to the gunman. I kept yelling at the forming crowd, who kept getting closer and closer, to get back. All of a sudden a volley of shots rang out and the crowd went running in every direction with one guy tripping over a metal garbage can. It stuck between his legs causing him to fall down, crawl, scramble and fall again. It was like a Charlie Chaplin movie scene and I couldn't help myself, as shots were being fired, I was laughing at a bunch of nosey idiots who wouldn't listen and now were running for their lives. I had previously been taught the sound of gunfire and those booms weren't in my direction, but the gawking crowd didn't know that. Once the crowd moved back, I was able to concentrate on the upper apartment of the building where the shots were coming from so no one could escape through my direction.

In the 1970's, we didn't have swat, armored vehicles, bullet proof vest, or any of the equipment they have today. We did have a unit of the best of the best who handled barricaded gunmen, large fights, holdups, shootings in progress, dangerous felony arrest and drug raids. There were four officers, usually large, experienced and tough with the driver in uniform and the other three in sport coats and ties. They drove a big black Chrysler with only a gold decal on each front door that said Detroit Police and had lights in the grill that were hidden until turned on. There was just one car in each Precinct; twelve in the whole City. They came with a reputation of something you didn't want to mess with. The Black community thought they were only hard on them, but the truth was anyone, black, white, even cops who crossed the line would catch their wrath if needed.

They were called the "Big Four" or "The Cruiser." As I saw the Big Four pull up to the building and the four cops get out all at the same time, I was in awe. On the radio they told everyone to hold their fire, plain clothes officers were entering the building. I don't know what happened inside, but a few minutes later they came out with one in custody and carrying a long gun. There were all types of stories about their history going back to the Purple Gang and Mafia days. They had a Thompson sub machine gun sitting on the deck of the rear window in the early days. We respected them and the predators feared them.

1930's Cruiser Crew

Some in the media with their own agenda, even then, believed and repeated like a parrot all kinds of false accusations to the general public that gave the Big Four a reputation of being racist, violent and dangerous. In fact, The Cruiser (Big Four) goes back to 1930, when Detroit was nearly all white, to confront The Purple Gang and organized crime during prohibition. After prohibition, they were used to hunt down violent felons and handle the most dangerous situations in high crime areas.

The crews were integrated in the early sixties under Commissioner Ray Girardin and they didn't ride around harassing law abiding minorities because they didn't have "proper ID" like some claimed, that wasn't their job. They had a real reputation amongst the troops of handling any dangerous situation in a fearless manor and making good arrests almost daily. They didn't waste their time on innocent citizens or misdemeanor violations like the media and some with agendas would like to have people believe.

In 1971 I had the honor to fill in on Seven Cruiser; it had a history going back for years of a unit that could handle anything. I was excited, proud, and not disappointed with the opportunities of working with and learning from these officers that lived up to my high esteem of them.

1990's Cruiser Crew

They were hand chosen by the Inspector who is in charge of the whole Precinct and they worked directly for him. Anything that would have been done improperly would fall directly on his shoulders. Later during some of its history, some politically correct Precinct Inspectors and Administrations disbanded them to the disgust of most of the street officers. Eventually, they were returned to their original duties even in those few Precincts that had tried to change them. The Cruiser Crew at #7 was so close to each other that one of them even turned down a promotion to Sergeant to keep the crew together and it wasn't easy to get promoted. That's loyalty!

The Spinner

The Capuchin Soup Kitchen was located at Mt. Elliott & Lafayette. To the south was an area full of vacant houses with old semi-trailers and junk cars and no visible residents. Usually when we drove down Lafayette there was a large brown dog that would seem to come out of nowhere and chase our blue & white scout car. As he got close enough to the passenger door to see it was a police car, he would pull back and spin around and around, but with regular cars he would keep chasing them. It was crazy to watch and it happened over and over. I asked my senior partner what it was all about and he said he had heard that one time one of the guys opened their door and wacked him in the head to get him out of the street. He didn't stop chasing cars, but he sure remembered the blue & white scout cars and would start spinning. It later became my turn to introduce "the spinner" to new rookies.

Street Parade

I was working my first Thanksgiving holiday & my partner said if we're not busy at 2pm he would show me the real Thanksgiving Day parade. Well we were busy on a report so he drove us over by where the Spinner usually was, but he wasn't anywhere in sight. The reason was that Lafayette Blvd. was lined up with a long line of bums that squatted in the vacant houses and old semi-trailers and were on their way to the Capuchin Soup Kitchen on Mt. Elliott.

The Capuchin put out a big Thanksgiving dinner for them. They waived, smiled, and were a happy, friendly bunch. As I talked to them some would share their stories. To my surprise many of them were neither alcoholics nor drug users. Some were just normal people from all walks of life, lawyer's, executives and professionally educated people who just burned out and couldn't handle the normal everyday stress of life. They had chosen this way of life and didn't want to get rehabbed or bothered. I would occasionally cruise that area and talk to them. Some were a little goofy, but most made sense and were happy to see us looking out for them and never asked for anything. They even enjoyed our curiosity about their life stories. Sometimes when someone asked me what I did for a living, I would tell them I was a street psychologist with a smile on my face. I knew that a lot more was learned from the people on the street than could be learned in any book or a class room. I saw people born, die and survive anyway they could until they couldn't take it anymore. I received an education you couldn't buy or learn any other way but by living it daily and trying to help in any way you could.

Food Competition – Feeding the Cops

Detroit's inner City had its small, but fantastic Bar-B-Q take-out restaurants. One of them was Greens Bar-B-Q on Mack Ave. near Concord St. Greens also happened to be in a Delta One area real close to a Black Panther headquarters. The ribs and food in general was so good to this ex-suburbanite that even with the danger we would go there as you just couldn't get that kind of food outside of the inner City. They had had a couple of shootings there and one person had been shot while in line thru the ceiling! As we stood in line, we could still see the hole above us and would usually have our hands on our guns with the strap unsnapped just in case. Another place was the M&M Shrimp Shack on Conant; just as dangerous and food just as fantastic. The best was when you cruised down an alley on a warm Sunday afternoon and could smell the ribs cooking. Usually somebody, mostly ladies, would flag us over and give us a couple of ribs to try and would tell us it was the best there was and made from their secret sauce. They were very proud and happy to share this experience with us. A lot of times while we were complimenting them while eating their ribs we could see someone down the alley who kept popping out and looking back at us. When we left and got down to the person who was popping out, they too would usually have a couple of ribs for us to try. It was big time competition and we apparently were the judges.

They would tell us how much better their homemade sauce and ribs were and of course we told them all that theirs were the best. To be truthful this lily white from the suburbs had never tasted anything so good before or since, anywhere. I was learning the real diversity that was between the inner City and suburbs that I grew up in. Whether it was the food or different life styles that each didn't really know about the other. I worked and lived in the inner City with my youth being spent in a totally different environment out in the suburbs. I was learning first hand day by day that two different cultures existed just miles apart from each other. I knew it was very important to know and understand the difference to bridge the gap and not be one sided. It wasn't just a white or black thing because some white born Detroiters or a black born suburbanite also had different views of right and wrong behavior. It seemed Detroiters had much more macho attitudes than I grew up with and I was pretty macho myself. Even in the City the outlying Precincts were considered retirement homes for some, as the crime rate was lower than the inner City stations. That was to change in the mid 1970's when the City, except the downtown area, turned into the wild, wild, west.

Racked Shot Guns

I found out really quick that a uniform, or even drawing your revolver didn't automatically get you respect or strike fear in anyone in the inner City like it would in suburbia. Gunfire and exposure to weapons are common place on the City streets. People were used to it as a daily occurrence. I did find out that when you racked a 12 gage riot shot gun loudly, they did pay attention. When outnumbered and dealing with a hostile crowd, it could give you enough time to make your arrest and get the heck out of the area before it could cause a larger disturbance.

One night we responded to a call of another unit requesting back up searching for a man with a gun firing shots. As I was crouched down behind a solid wooden fence in the alley behind the location where he was last seen and slowly quietly moving forward, I heard a shotgun racked right behind me on the other side of the fence. I froze waiting for a blast with the hair on my neck sticking out and could hardly breathe. It seemed like forever before I heard someone loudly say drop it and the area was lit up by flash lights. Afterwards I knew first hand why people paid attention to the sound of a racking shot gun as I was at the business end of one. Later thinking about it, I'm not sure if he even knew I was there, but another lesson was learned.

Celebrate

It didn't take long to figure out there were a lot of people and groups out there that would like to see me and my co-workers dead. So in the summer of 1971 when a Motown Rock and Roll group called Rare Earth came out with a song called, 'I Just Want to Celebrate', I kind of thought of it as my theme song. It had a party beat and caught my attitude of trying to stay alive in my daily hostile environment to party another day like everybody in the ghetto did, but that lifestyle was new to this lily white suburban boy. I spent all of my career and most of my life living to those words and that same beat taking my chances and partying hard. I am sure the song was made for the people and not us cops, but it fit some of us. ♫ I Just Want to Celebrate Another Day of Living ... ♫

School Cars, Scooters & Police Organizations

We also had what were called 'School Cars'. School Cars had one officer inside each school and another patrolling outside in a marked scout car during school hours. There was also a group of Detroit Public School officers that were separate from us who responded to school burglaries and such with us on nights and weekends. We also started what was called the Scooter Patrol that worked the schools and other events like sports, dances, etc. At that time, the City had over 1.5 million residents and 4,500 police officers. We had amateur police sport teams, baseball, football, hockey, and basketball, as well as a department choir and band. They became the City's amateur teams and were followed by the good citizens of the City. The Precincts also had individual teams that played against each other and were followed by the local communities they served.

There were a lot of good citizens, who when the bad apples on the street weren't watching would let us know how they really felt about us and what was happening on the street. We knew and appreciated them too. It seemed then, as now, that only the bad ones got the media favor to the downfall of the good citizens who were being more oppressed by the criminal elements if they spoke out. When asked why cops would want to work in the inner City when it seemed everyone and everything was against them, we would respond, it was because we knew the good people needed us. They couldn't speak up because we couldn't be around at all times to protect them and if they did, they would be in danger in their own neighborhoods when we weren't there.

Moved up - 2nd Man Already

In October of 1971, I was awarded my 2nd Commendation/Citation for "Arrest of two felons for armed robbery." I had forgotten about that arrest as there had been better arrest and situations without a write-up made. I was to learn it was up to the supervisor if he felt like writing up an officer or someone else directed him to do it. We never asked for ourselves, as that was unacceptable and would be kind of like patting yourself on the back. So most of the cops I knew could have been awarded a lot more awards than they received in their careers. We knew who would put it all out for us and the citizens. That is who we respected and wanted them to respect us as peers. Even so, the little ceremony at on-duty roll call with a paid day coming was nice especially for a newly confirmed officer like me who was trying for their respect.

Another surprise was coming my way. I had just over a year on the mean streets of #7 and gained more street experience than most because of the area and group I was being taught by. As mentioned before, it was one of the more dangerous inner City Precincts with mostly young officers because a lot of them transferred out to the other City Precincts and bureaus as soon as they could. I liked the action and the guys I was working with and hadn't even considered leaving. I was second man on my car already with only a year on the street which made me a senior man to our third man and I liked making the calls when I was the senior officer.

Transfer – "Yeah, I can do that!"

One day my junior partner told me he liked the way I worked and that his brother was starting a new unit and he had told his brother about me. He told me his brother wanted me to put in a blue slip transfer request to the Northern District Morality Unit stationed out of the 10th Precinct. He said I would be accepted as his brother was the Commander, but I was to keep it a secret because the unit was not known yet. I asked my partner what a morality unit does and he said you work undercover in plain clothes and go to bars and stuff like our Precinct cleanup crew did, but in a large district. I said to him, "Yeah, I could do that." I was totally shocked that a young low seniority officer could get accepted to a prime assignment like that. I immediately typed up a blue slip requesting a transfer and gave it to the desk Sergeant to be sent up to the Commander. He took it, laughed and said there is no such place and told me that I was not going anywhere with my seniority, but he would forward it.

Normally the transfer procedures were to type up a formal transfer request on a pre-printed form and have it signed by your commanding officer. If he signed it, you were then investigated by the unit you were trying to go to. If all that panned out, then you were put on the bottom of a waiting list and had to reapply every 12 months as the list expired. So with low seniority it was almost impossible to get a transfer to anywhere worthwhile. The back door way was a blue slip memo, but you had to be requested by the Commander of the unit which was always honored. So for young low seniority officers to go anywhere you had to have a good work ethic and know someone in the unit who would vouch for you. That is how I made it without even knowing that was how it was done. I assumed it would be quite a while before I heard anything about any transfer. To my complete surprise, I was called into the inspector's office a couple of days later. Remembering the other times, I had been run out of there with him swearing at me loudly, made me a little nervous.

Just like before, I knocked and requested permission to enter and he pointed to the chair and said "Sit." I sat, held my breath and waited for the swearing to start. I expected it would be for having the nerve to request a transfer before I deserved it. Instead a large smile came across his face as he handed me a copy of a sheet of paper ordering me to be assigned to the Northern District Morality Unit at the 10th Precinct signed by the Commander. I was told to report Monday at 8am in plain clothes for advanced training. It had happened so fast there was no time to think about it. He was totally different even friendly and told me I had done a good job the past year and that I learned fast. He even joked about how I was too short and looked like I was 16 years old and that would help me in my new undercover assignment. He shook my hand and told me the Sergeant would take care of my paperwork. I learned later that he really was a good guy, but liked to scare the hell out of rookies, which he did. The Sergeant told me that since it was Friday and I had Sunday off plus a day off coming for my Commendation, I would have the weekend off and would be done at the 7th. He congratulated me and asked me to come by and visit once and awhile. WOW that was quick, and done with no time to digest just what happened. The guys on my shift that I worked with had all went home while I was in the Inspectors office so I wasn't able to see them before leaving.

Moving On - More to Learn

After I gathered my things, I had a strange feeling that I didn't want to leave these guys and what I was doing here. As I walked out the front door, which we hardly used, and waved goodbye to the desk officers, I looked sadly at the wall of the deceased officers' pictures who had given their all. I stared for a moment at them and thought of my first mentor who was killed protecting one of my classmates the day after we worked together. It all filled my mind as now I really knew what those pictures on the wall meant and to this day, I still tear up thinking about Danny and how he taught us and kept us rookies alive. I have never been much for goodbyes so for me it worked out well and I was heading into a new world on the other side of the City, all by myself.

CHAPTER 3

Northern District Morality Undercover

District Morality - 1st Time Undercover

After my weekend off, which that alone was unusual, I put my uniforms away, stopped shaving and let my hair grow as was the style in 1971 for young men. On Monday morning, I drove to #10 located on Livernois and Elmhurst. It was in a bad part of the City just like #7. I arrived feeling like a rookie again; like my first day on the job and I had no idea what I was getting into. The new unit would be working out of #10 and covering three Precincts, the 10th, 11th and the 12th. The 11th and 12th were outer Precincts in better areas. That was going to be a big change in itself. We would be on a different radio frequency so I wouldn't be hearing any of my old buddies calls that were in the east side Precincts, 5th, 7th & 15th.

I did not meet my benefactor immediately, the Lieutenant in charge who was the older brother of my scout car partner at #7. I did recognize two of the guy's, one was a senior officer from #7 who never let the cat out of the bag about this new unit and the other was the Sergeant at #7 who told me there was no such unit and I wasn't going anywhere when I submitted the transfer slip. They were both totally surprised to see me as they knew people in the right places and had connections to get there. They couldn't figure out how someone who was just past being a rookie and didn't have enough time on the job to have the right connections to get this type of assignment. I thought it best, until I knew different, to keep quiet and let the Lieutenant acknowledge how I got here.

No one knew the Lieutenant, but the rumor was he used to be a priest. My old partner didn't mention that and I couldn't figure out why an ex-priest, with a four-year college degree, would want to be a cop. Especially, one in charge of a unit that was going to be dealing with people who were violating vice laws – pimps, hookers, homosexuals, gamblers, pornographers and liquor laws. It was an undercover unit and his men were all going to be living the lifestyle of it. To my surprise, the Lieutenant did turn out to be an ex-priest. He was a straight laced honest, by the book cop, who liked to work.

We were assigned to four-man crews with each crew led by a Sergeant and at least one officer with vice experience who had come from the Downtown Vice Bureau. We were given a desk drawer at the 10th Precinct to keep our miscellaneous items. We were assigned cars, radios, call numbers, and binders with information on laws, procedures and important numbers. Our unit clerk seemed to have thought of most everything including who was assigned to whom. To my surprise, I was on the crew with the Sergeant from the 7th Precinct that told me there was no such unit. I hoped he wasn't going to be difficult because I got here when a lot of guys with more seniority and experience from the 7th didn't get into the unit. We had one day-shift crew and 2 night-shift crews that were all white, and one night-shift crew that was all black for enforcement of illegal after hour's clubs. That didn't seem strange to me as that was how it was in the Precincts, usually by choice, in the 1970's. Everybody got along and we sometimes worked together when called for but usually weren't assigned together as crews. The theory was it was harder for black officers to pick up prostitutes and white officers to get into illegal after-hours clubs. It didn't take long for us to prove that wrong when we worked on each other's crews.

We had a couple of days to get our office set up and organized. Most of our office equipment was obtained from the World's Medical Relief Association on 12th street. The next step was training. We were sent to the Downtown Vice Bureau for advanced training in Liquor Laws, City Ordinance and Vice Enforcement procedures for two weeks. The first week was mostly in class rooms learning how things were done at the Vice Squad, like the paperwork, laws, procedures and general practices. The second week we actually went out with Vice crews to put into practice what we learned like, undercover buys, liquor violation write ups, license inspections and undercover Accosting and Soliciting (johning) arrest. We learned how to cover our partners who were actually working the case without being to close or too far away and to help if needed. We were taught after obtaining the necessary actions (getting a case) for an Accosting and Soliciting violation, how to stop our vehicle in the right lane so close to a parked vehicle that the defendant only had one way out and that was over you. Well it worked only too well and as Accosting and Soliciting was a morals charge, a lot of arrestees choose to try that way out. Technically it was a misdemeanor, but most people didn't want family, friends or anybody knowing what they were up to and panicked. We understood it was just a misdemeanor violation and didn't want to have to hurt anyone or get injured ourselves.

It was a whole different kind of fear than being shot at or responding to a dangerous violent situation. Being undercover and alone made the hair on the back of the neck stand up and your heart race. Your mind played tricks on you like you were sure someone knew you were a cop or someone looked familiar to you that you might have arrested before.

We weren't supposed to go in unarmed, but because we were searched a lot we took off our weapons and police ID to gain entry or acceptance. We turned into pretty good actors and played our parts as if our lives depended on it and sometimes it did. We were usually alone without close backup and usually the backup consisted of only your partner. There were usually no large crews, wires, or pre-set up conditions like today. We were taught to pass our hand through our hair if on foot or flash our head lights or break lights if in our vehicles when we obtained a legal case and if in trouble, throw a chair or anything though a window. Yes, it was a totally different kind of fear that lasted even when you weren't found out.

I heard some officers, for different reasons, didn't go exactly by the book. Either they didn't want to spend a lot of time getting a complete case or didn't want to take the risks for a misdemeanor arrest. I was known as a straight shooter and didn't accept anything that wasn't a complete legal case no matter the risk or how hard it was to get. If, for instance, I could only get 2 out of 3 parts of a prostitution arrest, it wasn't a legal case and I moved on to try another girl until I got a complete legal arrest of (1) the Accosting, (2) the Price

& (3) the Sex Act. There was talk of some officers just knowing a hooker was a hooker and would just pick her up and make up a case on paper. I was here to enforce laws, not make up laws and if anyone did that when I was working with them, they knew enough to at least talk long enough to the hooker that I could assume they had a case. I think most officers did it the right way. As to the hookers I let out of my car because I didn't have a complete legal case, they thought no cop would do that and I usually got them the second time around.

That brings me to the first few weeks after vice training and working the district with my new unit members. I have never had problems meeting or working with new people. I am a friendly non-threatening person, but for the first time in my life nobody was talking or responding to me and I couldn't figure it out. I thought maybe because I was one of the youngest and least experienced with just over a year on the job. It was like when I was a new rookie at #7, but this time I was being avoided and people stopped talking when I approached and gave me strange looks. One day, after a few weeks of this, my Sergeant and co-workers wanted to meet me in a bar across the street from the station. As soon as I sat down he told me that some of the guys believed I was an undercover officer working for Internal Affairs and watching every little thing they did so they could burn them. I was shocked and told them I wasn't from Internal Affairs and was just a straight by the book cop. When I asked them why they thought that, one of my partners said they wondered how I got in the unit with low seniority and with a last minute blue slip memo transfer rather than a formal transfer like the rest of them. He said rumor was that I was related to a Lieutenant that worked on Commissioner Ray Giradins Commissioner's Squad which was the original Internal Affairs unit. That and being too short to even be a cop lead them to believe I had a special assignment.

Ok, Ok, now I understood the cold shoulder and silent treatment. I explained to them that my uncle helped me to get on the job, but my transfer to the new unit was through the Commander because his younger brother was my scout car partner at #7 and it was a last minute Blue Slip transfer because he requested me. I explained to them that I met the Commander the same time they did and I had no previous contact or discussions with him. We didn't even know each other. I told them I wasn't internal affairs, but I did and always would go by the book. Everyone seemed satisfied and I was totally accepted from then on.

A few days later I heard one of my old partners from #7 had been shot, but would be ok. They said he was lucky as he was hit in a main artery and his partner stayed with him stopping the bleeding until they got him to the hospital. My heart jumped into my throat as I knew if I was still there he probably would have died. He told me when we were working together if he ever got shot to leave him and get the S.O.B. no matter what. As a macho rookie who followed orders given by a macho senior partner, I most likely would have come back to a dead partner. Another lesson and a scary wakeup call for me.

What is "johning?"

We spent a lot of time driving on Woodward Avenue from 6 Mile Road to 8 Mile Road in our private vehicles by ourselves johning for prostitutes. Some corners had groups of them and sometimes they were alone, but usually the pimps were close by and you had to keep an eye out for them or a holdup man trying to take advantage of the situation. The normal procedure was to drive by the prostitutes slowly a couple of times until one of them waves or flags you down. That was the first part of your case called "Accosting," they had to initiate the contact. Then you had to get them to give you a price and a specific sex act they would perform and that was the "Solicitation" part of "Accosting & Soliciting." Usually they would jump into your car and the discussion would begin as you drove on with them. They would touch your waist and basically search you while pretending to feel you up, while they were really looking for a gun. We knew to put our gun under the seat or between the drivers' door and seat so they wouldn't find anything to think "cop." Sometimes we would have an open beer between our legs sipping on it to convince them we weren't cops. They would think that cops couldn't lie to them or drink on duty, but we could and did to act like a real "john". When we had our case we would signal our backup by flashing our lights. That is when it could get dangerous. Being alone and not knowing if your backup could get to you in time to help. He would also be in his private vehicle without lights or sirens.

We took turns johning and covering each other. Sometimes they fight when they think you are alone and will try to escape over the top of you through the driver's door. Since we parked next to a parked car or wall there was no way out on their side. The worst and toughest arrests are the straight males out for a homosexual experience and can't let themselves be charged with a morals charge. They would rather die and take you with them. We don't want to hurt anyone, especially for a misdemeanor violation; much easier said than done. A lot of times the female looking prostitutes were very strong men and that would be a battle. When you pulled out your badge and told them they were under arrest for Accosting & Soliciting, you would kind of tense up, hold your breath and hope for the best.

Woodward Avenue

Woodward Avenue has at least two histories: 1) It is the first paved street in the country and 2) Vice & Crime. Woodward Avenue was one of the busiest streets in Detroit for crime, drugs, sex and just about anything you could think of. Woodward and its cross streets were busy 24/7 with male, female and he-she's for freebies or paid services. There were gay male and gay female bars, private clubs and parks where almost anything goes. X-Rated movies, go-go bars, prostitution bars, blind pigs and gambling houses were either on Woodward or just around the corner. You could, and most likely would, run into almost anything and most of it was illegal and dangerous as everyone wanted to take your money one way or another.

I worked Woodward Avenue most of my career on Vice or Special Operations Felony Units and I saw just about everything people could do to each other. Most people outside of Detroit didn't have a clue that we had our own Amsterdam type area, but it was more violent, dangerous and illegal. The media pretended it didn't exist as it wasn't good for Detroit's image. That was hard to understand when Detroit was the murder capital and already had a tough image.

At first, being young, dumb, and naive to these worldly Vice activities, I was shocked and amazed by what I saw, but went to work trying to make it safer and control the bad elements. I knew it couldn't be stopped and most likely wouldn't be made legal and had to be policed for everyone's safety. So we worked on the complaints and tried to keep it from getting totally out of control.

Street Rules

We had certain street rules: We left the gays alone in gay bars and would only enforce the bars liquor law violations. Since the bars were adult only, anyone going there knew what was happening. They could leave if they didn't like it. On the other hand, in public parks, rest rooms in businesses or on the streets, the laws were enforced to keep the law breakers from totally taking over Woodward Avenue.

Palmer Park

Palmer Park was a large park on the west side of Woodward Avenue, North of 6 Mile Road. It had all the amenities of large parks. It also had nationally well-known areas of homosexual activities which were illegal at the time, but still a very popular pickup place. In the main parking lot, the bridge on the duck pond, the restrooms, statues and fountains were busy pick up places. The Park, along with the 13th floor restroom of the J. L. Hudson's Store, were rated and published in gay magazines as popular and internationally famous pickup locations at the time along with other places in the City, so everyone knew where to find the action. After the pickup, the action took place in cars on the streets of neighborhoods, parking lots and even just off of the trails in the woods where they had made deer type nests. This went on day and night, but most of the complaints were from families trying to enjoy the park during the day. That was when we either did our undercover johning or looked for indecent exposure activities. At night we sometimes totally switched to decoy activities and acted gay to catch what was called "Fairy Hawkers". They were violent predators who acted gay to rob and assault the gay population knowing it most likely wouldn't get reported because of the stigma in the 70's of being gay. It was a strange experience to walk out into the dark woods with someone, hoping that you were about to be assaulted and robbed by a group of fairy hawkers, but that's who we wanted to get off of the street. You never knew when a misdemeanor could turn into a felony, but knowing you were working on a felony arrest somehow made it easier mentally.

Dragon Lady

The Dragon Lady Go-Go Bar was on Woodward Avenue just North of 7 Mile. It was a good size bar with a lot of really good looking dancers. I left my gun and police ID with my Sergeant and was told if I needed help to throw something through the window. I was to spend about an hour or so observing for liquor violations and letting the help get comfortable with me. The way it was done, each of us on the four-man crew had a number of bars we would frequent on a regular basis. Some of the bars or clubs were chosen randomly, but most were based on citizens' complaints that had to be answered. We had small expense accounts that the City would reimburse, but it never covered all our cost. Since we were also reimbursed for our mileage for using our personal vehicles no one complained. Bottom line was if you didn't like it you could go back into uniform instead of being paid to drink in air conditioned bars with hot half naked women. Still unarmed, by yourself and with the hostilities toward cops in the 70's, it was a nerve racking experience until you had a couple of drinks in you.

It didn't take long to get the feel of the level of danger, or to know if you were fitting in. It was a completely different fear to overcome than being shot at and if you looked nervous you could be in a hell of a lot of trouble. So I, like most undercover cops, turned into an actor when needed. The only problem was most of us stayed in character and lived our street persona if we worked it too long. As my hair and beard grew, I entered deeper and deeper into the street culture of the times. I was brought back to reality when making an arrest or mourning another cop killed which continued to happen over and over. We lost another cop on New Year's Eve 1971 to end that year and four more good cops in 1972. There were too many officers shot or seriously injured at that time to remember the actual numbers or situations unless you personally knew them.

High Class Bar Hookers

In 1972, Edjo's was one of the classier Go-Go Bars with expensive, good food that drew a lot of business executive type clientele. At that time, there were smart high class hookers that knew cops couldn't spend a lot of money on them in the bar. If you wanted to talk to them, you had to spend before any price or act of prostitution could be obtained. So what usually would happen is when you exited the bar the not so hot street walkers hanging around the building would hit on you and the competition made getting a case easy. It wasn't unusual to catch a business executive in an expensive suit so drunk that he didn't realize he was having sex in his fancy car with a dirty hooker with open infected scabs all over. Sometimes, I would have loved to take a Polaroid picture and give it to him when he sobered up.

Edjo's was profitable enough with a suburban base it discouraged any inside prostitution. There were plenty enough outside to keep the customers coming and with the threats of the Police Department they could lose a good business. Most of the hooker bars weren't high class and could be dangerous as the pimps or even the hookers robbed their johns quite often. They knew who wasn't a regular and could tell if they didn't know their way around. It also went the other way too where some johns robbed the hookers and usually neither wanted the police involved. This Detail was like being in an X-Rated movie with every kind of sex available and happening all over the place. Unlike the suburbs or inner City Precincts that I came from, it was a totally unbelievable party scene 24/7 of decadent activity and I was right in the middle of it.

It was common knowledge that we couldn't stop it, but we had to control it as best as possible. There had to be a fear to the predators that they might be dealing with undercover cops or they would run amuck. Usually the fines for Accosting and Soliciting were sometimes as low as $25 dollars, but the real cost to them was being locked up and off of the street for a night. The fine usually was considered by them just paying their taxes.

We usually johned for prostitutes and tried not to pick up gay males, but if one put himself between us and the hooker, we let them give us a case and arrested them. Most of them knew we were cruising for the hookers and admitted that they were stupid by trying to pick us up. One night, I had one who kept following me in a red and white Cadillac convertible who actually put two twenty dollar bills between his fingers pointing for me to follow him around a corner while cutting in front of a hooker that was waving at me. So, I did and got a case on him and arrested him. Later I ran into him at a couple of gay bars during routine inspections. He turned out to be a well-known millionaire in that life style who also wrote a book. He told the story of how he got himself arrested by a cop who was trying to avoid him with a laugh and no hard feelings.

Most gays that we dealt with weren't out and were doing their thing in public places like parks, rest rooms and cars. The regular gay culture partied with each other in bars, clubs, and in private. We didn't bother them; only those who accosted us or the public in public places or those that violated indecent exposure laws. In the 70's, Woodward Avenue bars and clubs were one giant party like a Mardi Gras all the time and they really knew how to party. Usually when we checked the bars and clubs for liquor violation, the owners and clientele were friendly knowing we left them alone in their element and only arrested those on the streets. They usually didn't have any problems with that. They understood there was a time and place for most everything. I was even invited to their gay church and events. I think our fairness in enforcing the law was usually appreciated. The gay female bars were pretty much like the male bars but usually not too many males were found in them. They were mostly friendly knowing we weren't there to harass them. There was a rather large, tough looking, female bouncer named Billie at the Amiga's Lounge on Conant and 7 Mile who would tell me which go-go dancers were straight, in case I was interested. They had to act gay for tips while working, but did get very friendly with me at closing time.

I had experienced so many new things in my first year working in an inner City Precinct I thought I had seen it all. Now this outer City area was also, in a different way, something I didn't even know existed. Just when I thought I was on top of things, I was again starting from scratch and realized I had a lot to learn very quickly. I was still a naïve lily white kid from the suburbs working in a totally different world.

Disco

Of the three Precincts in our district two were outside of the inner City and one was in the inner City and mostly black. That made it a little difficult to do undercover work for the white officers. Being too short and looking too young to be a cop helped me get into places other officers couldn't. So off came the gun and police ID and in I would go. I got into Blind Pigs (after hour's clubs), bars and made Sunday liquor buys. One of the bars I was sent into was on Livernois and was one of Detroit's first disco bars. Disco wasn't even known in the white community until around 1972. So this bar was one of the craziest I had ever seen or experienced at the time. It was a black, gay, leather clad, loud dance bar with a wild beat type of music. Everyone was friendly and they didn't seem to hold my whiteness against me. It didn't take long for disco to get popular next in the white gay areas and then to suburban kids.

I was, without knowing it, at the epicenter of the early beginnings of a new culture and life style of the times on Woodward Avenue and the Palmer Park area born from the inner City. Unlike today's Palmer Park, the Woodward Avenue area in the 1970's was a robust wild unofficial red light district of Detroit. There were packed bars, private clubs, restaurants and street action with the crime that goes along with it. I wasn't only getting an education Detroit style, I was getting a worldly education on all types of people good, bad, and just different.

Liquor Buys - Early & Late

Our Sergeant told us on Saturday night to keep drinking and partying all night. Don't shave or clean up as he wanted us to look rough and needy for Sunday morning illegal liquor buys. That sounded fine to me, but I didn't realize just how hard it was without getting too drunk or falling asleep. The next morning the four of us on our crew took turns going into liquor stores and bars attempting to talk the owners into selling us poor slobs liquor for our hangovers with an extra $10 for their trouble. I was pretty surprised just how many risked their liquor license for an extra ten dollars. At first, we felt a little guilty by looking needy and talking our way into Sunday buys from them, but that was the law, no liquor sales allowed before 2pm on Sundays only beer and wine after noon, and they were well aware of it. As to talking them into it, the liquor laws were just the opposite of other laws. You had to prove yourself innocent beyond a doubt when you received a liquor license or you were automatically guilty of the violations. It was kind of like us cops when we were written up on violating department policy. Guilty until proven innocent and we were, like them, giving up some of our rights when receiving our badges and them receiving their liquor license. We both knew the rules and that made it seem fair enough for me. On Sunday mornings we would look like drunken bums, smell like booze, and do liquor law violation write ups. Then back to the office with hangovers to do paperwork all afternoon. That was not fun at all.

Once you write up a store or bar, your cover is blown and they know who you are. Even though we couldn't go to those places under cover anymore, we would periodically give them a routine inspection. Most of the time we would get to know them on a friendly basis and would give them verbal warnings to correct any minor violations. We still sent other undercover officers to check underage sales and violations in case they got greedy again. There were times after an inspection that we would leave another undercover officer there after we left to see what their attitude was after the routine inspection. When I was the one left, I was amazed at some of the joking that would go on with customers at some places about gambling, hookers, watered booze and the comments about how stupid those a-hole cops were.

We would also try and make after hours buys, usually when we had complaints, but sometimes randomly by spending time and getting known in the bar. One way was by buying a round for everyone sitting at the bar just before the 2am cut off time. Then buying the whole bar another round at 2:15am after the cutoff time and that's when greed sometimes showed its ugly head. A lot of vice and liquor laws seemed silly, but if not somewhat enforced some people have the tendency to keep pushing the envelope, until things get totally out of control. I looked at it as to keep the lid on so there wasn't an explosion of illegal activity that the majority didn't want to have in their neighborhoods. Some things we did at first did seem silly, but there was a method to the madness.

We went through the garbage of suspected illegal numbers betting and gambling houses, blind pigs and locations where there were complaints of unusual activity or would quietly listen and peer into bar windows after closing on complaints of after hour activity. Yes, garbage picking, window peeking and hanging around public bathrooms was embarrassing and could be dangerous, but it was also part of the job.

Blending in

When I first went into undercover work I was happy just growing my hair and beard to look like most everyone my age. Clean cut was not a popular look for most young people in the 70's. After a while, I would trim my beard into a goatee and then down to just a mustache, then back to long and wild looking, but did not go back to the clean cut look. Some of the guys dyed their hair and changed their clothing styles dramatically. For me, being short and very young looking got me into places others couldn't get into easily because I didn't look "cop" to anyone. My biggest problem was convincing them I was really a cop or even old enough to be in a bar. More than once I was refused service without ID. The rest of the crew got a big kick out of me getting kicked out of a bar.

The vehicles we used were either our own or borrowed. Sometimes we used demo cars from friendly car dealers. Most plain clothes vehicles were four door Plymouth's that everybody knew were police cars. We couldn't use them for undercover work so we were supplied a goofy looking four door rambler as an undercover vehicle. The first time we were out in the Rambler, four white guys driving in an alley in an all-black area, a 5-year old boy waived at us and said, "Hi Poleez." We weren't fooling anybody and went back to using our personal cars.

Kidnapped

We had numerous complaints about indecent male on male activity in the parking lot of Palmer Park near the Duck Pond. We would get complaints from families that took their kids to the park. Because of these complaints, we would, on a regular basis, sit in our personal vehicles during the day and wait for someone to pull up next to us and hit on us. It was the same as with female prostitutes, we had to let them accost us first and then offer a sex act. The only difference was a price wasn't needed for a legal Accosting and Soliciting case against a male. We had to be careful not to entrap. They had to be the aggressor and we usually acted dumb or naïve until we got them to actually tell us what they wanted. Sometimes they were leery and it took a lot of general conversation before a legal case was obtained. One afternoon, the guy that was hitting on me just wouldn't give me a complete case. At one point he asked me to join him in his car to smoke a joint. I told him I didn't smoke, but would join him. That was a big mistake on my part. As soon as I closed the door he drove off with me. I didn't know it at the time, but my partner/cover man had left his vehicle and was on foot to get closer to us.

He drove me a few blocks away into a private parking lot to a spot that dead ended with over hanging trees. As he pulled in and shut off the car, he told me he wanted to give me oral sex. With that, the case was completed. My cover was nowhere in sight so that left me to make the arrest alone.

I pulled out my badge and police ID holder and told him he was under arrest hoping it would go smoothly. He was about 6'5" tall and around 250 lbs. and I was about half his size. Needless to say, it didn't go well, he panicked and slapped my badge holder out of my hand into the back seat of his car. I had taken off my gun and had it under the seat of my car back at Palmer Park since I wasn't expecting to leave the parking lot. He opened his car door to escape and I instinctively grabbed him as he was slapping the hell out of me. As we were struggling, I saw the butt of a handgun sticking out of his suit coat pocket. So I got a hold of his coat sleeves with a death grip so he could not get the gun. If he did, I didn't have a chance. We were half way in and out of the car door when I saw my partner running toward us all out of breath. I yelled to him, "He's got a gun" and my partner who was a good cop, but a little crazy and had just ran over a mile, pulled his own weapon and yelled, "I got him." I was sure he would start shooting while we were entangled, so I rolled about and kept yelling, "Don't shoot." When my partner got close enough, he put his gun away and together we got handcuffs on him. What a mess. I should not have got into his vehicle while my cover was on foot and my cover shouldn't have got out of his vehicle at all. Lucky for me that big dude was effeminate enough to slap instead of punch and his gun turned out only to be a starter pistol. The fact that I was able to stop my partner from shooting him or me was a good thing too.

It turned out the guy's main concern was that he would be charged with the felonies, smoking dope in front of a cop, having a concealed weapon and assaulting a police officer. Our concern was how stupid and funny we looked. He was extremely happy that we were not going to charge him with the felonies as no one was really hurt and we found the whole situation hilarious, after it was over. We only charged him with the Accosting & Soliciting and he pled guilty. Word got out later about my kidnapping and I caught a lot of teasing about it over the years. It probably wasn't funny to him, but to us cops with our strange sense of humor, we laughed every time the story was told and it became a new legend of strange happenings.

Quotas

I learned not to use the word quotas early in my career. So instead, I asked my Sergeant what was expected, work wise. He told all of us to do as much as we can to answer written complaints from Downtown Vice. He also said there was no such thing as quotas, but (4) Accosting & Soliciting cases male or female, and (4) liquor violation write-ups' minimum per month would be nice. We all understood that was the quota, even though there was no such thing as quotas. The guys on the black crew told us they needed a minimum of (4) Blind Pig Raids a month to justify their existence. We had pretty good bosses who realized this system wouldn't work as well as with traffic tickets because sometimes we worked on and made arrest for, gambling, indecent exposure and we were also used for surveillance and assisting on raids. The best way to justify our existence was to work on and clean up citizens' written complaints. Downtown wanted it their way so we had to spend most of our time johning instead of working cases against the higher ups like pimps and organized crime. So like normal, the quantity and not the quality of the arrest won out.

X-Rated Movies

Our senior partner who came from the Vice section had been seriously injured by a priest when he attempted to arrest him for Accosting and Soliciting. The Stone Burlesque had turned into an X-Rated movie theater and of course he didn't know he was a priest at the time. He knew the City didn't prosecute priests even for resisting arrest on morals charges as they were quietly turned over to the Vatican for punishment as a general rule. We never knew who we were arresting.

We always had open complaints about vice activity in and around the X-Rated shows and we had quite a few of them. The routine was two or three of us would go into one theatre at different times. Then, once our eyes adjusted to the dark and we could see each other, we would take turns going into the bathroom. Our Sergeant told us to stand at the urinal and if the guy on either side smiled at us to smile back and then slowly return to our seat. If he followed and sat next to us, to keep smiling until he hit on us for a Lewd Act or exposed himself. When a case was obtained we were to give the signal of passing our hand through our hair and the Sergeant would come and sit next to him on the other side to make the arrest as quiet as possible. I didn't have a problem with going to watch X-Rated movies while being paid as part of my duty, but going in and out of bath rooms so some guy could pick me up wasn't the best part of the job. Like on the street, these guys really didn't want a morals charge on them and would fight like heck sometimes. Most of them were married and lived a straight life out in suburbia.

Our regular Sergeant didn't try to get cases; he did what he was supposed to do and just backed us up. There were a couple of other Sergeants that wanted their own cases so they could make money from going to court. Those

Sergeants weren't the best at backing us up while chasing after their own cases which put us in danger. We suspected one Sergeant, I'll call Sergeant X, of not getting real cases and was doing the hitting on instead of getting hit on. He would tell us to do like he does and make sure you're not entrapping or illegally arresting anyone like the decoy police women sometimes would. One day in an X-Rated show on John R, North of 6 Mile Road, while he was in the bathroom smiling at one guy, one of our guys who used to work Downtown Vice told us the guy our Sergeant followed into the bathroom was an undercover Vice officer. After they went in and out of the bathroom three times smiling at each other, Sergeant X told us he got a case on him, but he needed us to go into the bathroom for the arrest because he was pretty sure there would be problems with him during the arrest. At the same time the Vice officer told his crew that our Sergeant X was hitting on him, but didn't give him enough for an arrest. When they went into the bathroom for the fourth time we were all cracking up because we knew Sergeant X was about to be outed as a "ray fielder" (that's what the street whores called a cop who doesn't get a complete legal case and lies in their report). When we walked in, Sergeant X advised the undercover Vice Cop he was under arrest for Accosting & Soliciting for an immoral act. Just then the Downtown Vice cops crew came in and the Vice cop identified himself and we all stood there laughing at them and the whole crazy situation. We all left with a very silent Sergeant X who was a good guy, but sure didn't work like us or the way he talked. We were very happy that we had a regular Sergeant on our crew who was a straight shooter and who didn't put up with any B.S. Every once in a while when our Sergeant was off, Sergeant X filled in on our crew and we knew not to trust him completely. We understood why only he could get a case and it most likely wasn't a good one, but we couldn't prove it. Otherwise he was likeable, but now on our radar and we hoped he would learn his lesson.

When first entering the dark show from the brightness outside we couldn't see very well and would run our hand across the seats before we sat down so that we didn't sit in anything icky that may have been deposited by the previous occupant. In all the times I sat down in an X-Rated theater I only saw a problem once and it happened to the right guy. Sergeant X entered the dark show and ran his hand across the seat like always and to our great pleasure he got a hand full of 'something'. He totally lost it and started screaming; causing such a disturbance the management turned the lights up. We were laughing so hard while everybody looked that our undercover operation was over for that day, but it sure was worth it. I don't know what we were thinking with that hand movement before sitting down, but his actions taught us just to look real close after your eyes adjusted to the dark and wear Levis when working the shows.

We wondered why the clientele seemed to know that cops were in the house when we went into some X-Rated shows. We found out eventually that while we paid to enter the show so they didn't know who we were, Sergeant X would show his badge and announce Vice Cop to the ticket taker because he was too cheap to pay. He still claimed the cost on his expense report.

He apparently didn't learn his lesson as a few months later while filling in on another crew he and a female police decoy tried to "ray field" or put a case on each other to the amusement of both crews. It wasn't long before he was back in uniform where he belonged. My year working undercover also taught me a lot, but I don't know where else I could use that education, except maybe as a Hollywood actor. If our acting quality on the street wasn't good enough, you could be in a heck of a dangerous situation and usually alone.

Whore House

We got a call from Downtown Vice that they were going to raid a large whore house on Ralston & State Fair near Rounders Bar that was in our district. There were a couple of reasons why they notified and invited us to the raid. One was to assist with the raid and learn the ropes of handling a large raid. The other reason was a couple of weeks before we were attempting to raid a small gambling house on 7 Mile at the same time as Downtown Vice. As three of us, in plain clothes, crept up with our weapons drawn from the west of the building in the dark alley, we were confronted by four armed males coming from the east of the building also brandishing weapons including shotguns and all in regular clothes. As we aimed at each other, one of our officers recognized one of their officers and we all luckily lowered our weapons and barely avoided a deadly situation. Strange as it sounds we were going to raid the same location at the exact same time. Afterwards we all had a nervous laugh and a drink at a nearby bar as the raid was aborted.

I learned quickly when in plain clothes and undercover with your weapon drawn and being used to being very visible in uniform while armed could be very dangerous. When in uniform we were used to being very visible and would draw our weapons almost daily and thought nothing of it. When in plain clothes or undercover, you had to train your mind, when your adrenaline was pumping, to realize nobody knew you were a cop, especially other cops.

Later in my career, an officer that I once worked undercover with was killed when he and another undercover officer, from a downtown unit, killed each other. We also had five off duty plain clothes Wayne County Sherriff officers shot. One was killed and four wounded when a plain clothes Stress unit attempted to arrest them after seeing them armed. When nobody identified themselves fast enough, they opened fire on each other. So it does happen and I know from my own experience just how quick and easy the unexpected happens. When I or anyone I trained drew our weapons while in plain clothes, we yelled as loud as we could over and over "Police Officer" while holding our badge up for everyone to see especially other cops. Things and situations changed rapidly and at some point in the arrest you had to put your ID and weapon away while attempting to subdue an unwilling suspect and it could and did get dicey.

Salt & Pepper Team

It was generally thought back then that a black cop would have a hard time picking up prostitutes and white cops couldn't get into an all-black blind pig. That is why the crews were separated, but occasionally we did work together. One night I was working with a black officer and we decided to go johning on Woodward for prostitutes. We went one step further and johned together in one car. It didn't take long before two hookers flagged us over and immediately gave us a case. Most likely the hookers believed that myth too and thought no salt & pepper team would be Vice Cops. It was one of the easiest cases I ever got, but the arrest got a little sticky.

The girl my partner got a case on ran between the buildings with my partner in hot pursuit and my girl started running south on Woodward. She stumbled and I caught her about a block away. I was struggling to hang on to her as she was screaming, "Rape, Help, Rape," while I was yelling, "Police Officer" and holding my badge holder up with one hand and hanging on to her with the other hand. A group of hostile looking angry large men were gathering and getting closer and closer to me. The group knew they had a little cop alone without a radio to call for help and an excuse to attack, and they were going for it.

Being hard headed, I had a choice to either let her go or drop my badge holder so I could at least pull my gun. No way was I going to let her go after pulling that trick of yelling rape to get away. I dropped my badge holder, got a death grip on her and started to pull out my gun. They damn well knew I was a cop and they were about to find out the hard way, nobody was going to take my prisoner away. All of a sudden, before I could draw my weapon all the way out, their hands went up and they started backing away. I looked behind me and saw my partner with a big smile dragging his arrest with one hand and pointing his 9mm automatic at them with a look like he would like to light them up and loudly telling them, "Come on, give me a reason or get the fuck out of here, now." After hand cuffing them we headed into the station and were both laughing at what we had gotten into and out of. Strangely, we both enjoyed the craziness of it after it all turned out ok. Usually you didn't get nervous until after the fact and by then you were in the middle of another situation over and over until years later when looking back. One reason the bond between cops is so strong is that we prove to each other, black & white, that we have each other's back no matter the danger or the odds against us. I've always remembered that night and the bond we made. Thanks, Greg.

White Panther Party

John Sinclair, the President of the White Panther Party, was having a meeting at the old Grande Ball Room on Grand River in our district. The Feds were having trouble getting into it and came to our office looking for someone who could get in and let them know what was happening. I was just coming into the office to sign in when one of the Feds asked our Sergeant if I was a cop. At the time my hair and beard were long and scraggly just like the hippies of the day. When they were told that I was a cop they said I would be perfect for what they needed, short, young and baby faced. They were from the FBI's Counter Intelligence Unit and they wanted me to infiltrate a White Panther's Party meeting at the Grande Ballroom. They told me and my Sergeant it could possibly be a long term assignment for me with an option of transferring to the DEA (Drug Enforcement Agency). Apparently they thought they were offering me something I couldn't refuse. I asked my Sergeant if I could have a word with him in private. Once in his office, I explained to him that I had worked with the Feds before and didn't trust all of them. Some weren't street smart and burned their informants by being naïve white suburban types with a degree, usually in accounting. Not my type of cops to take a chance with. I told him I would go in this one time, then they can get one of their own. My Sergeant smiled and said ok and told me I was absolutely right about them and this would be a one-time deal if I wanted it to be.

My Sergeant said he would make sure my crew would be involved as back-up. I, being an ex-lily white from the suburbs, was more worried about the Feds screwing things up than the hippies I was about to infiltrate. I knew a little about John Sinclair and the White Panther Party. Their associates were the dangerous ones, The Black Panther Party, SDS, Weather Under Ground and the Anti-establishment cop haters of what they called "The New Left" with an agenda of protest, resistance and revolution. They had already attacked and wouldn't hesitate to kill or injure cops. They were closely tied to the White Panther Party that was more into drugs, partying and recruiting the suburban youth to their causes with sex, drugs, and Rock & Roll. I wasn't under estimating John Sinclair or his group as he did time for drug sales and being involved in a bombing in the City of Ann Arbor. I knew it could be dangerous as I looked like a revolutionary, but didn't think like one. I decided to act buzzed and dumb. The Feds told us they searched their guy at the door and asked him for a pass the last time they tried to get in. We just smiled at each other wondering how they got into anywhere hoping their other undercover crews were a little more street smart. I asked them what they wanted me to do once in and they said to check for drug use, weapons, and see what generally was going on.

We told the Feds to wait at the 10th Precinct and we would be back in about an hour if everything goes well. If not, they would hear us on the radio or we would be right back. I was a little nervous, but confident in my crew. First we grabbed a hippie looking dude on his way in and took his pass while I took off my gun and police ID. Sure enough they asked for my pass and searched me and the group I walked in with. I quickly spotted a loose chair near the entrance door that I would throw through a window if I needed help, knowing my guys would be watching for that if there was a problem.

I drifted around, checked the john for drug use, and looked to see if any weapons were visible on or around anyone. It basically was a political type rally against authority, and for free living without the hassle of going by "the Mans" laws. They asked everyone to join the cause and come in for the parties. I didn't see anyone of importance like Sinclair or anyone I might recognize from the more violent groups, just a bunch of hippies having a rally.

After a while I left and advised the Feds of what I saw and heard. I told them if they really wanted to know if anything else is going on, they would have to get someone in their trust to go there on a regular basis. They again asked me if I wanted to work with them, and they could arrange it. I politely refused and stayed with my street smart co-workers. They did recruit one of our guys from another crew for the D.E.A. and after about 6-months working Detroit, they transferred him to New York against his wishes; typical Feds. To be fair to the FBI, they didn't have the street experience of inner City cops and were a little naïve to the ways of the mean streets. It is not something you can learn from books or in college.

Babies Abused

We had a file system with Polaroid pictures and information on 3x5 cards of the people we arrested just like Downtown Vice that was separate and private from the main system of records. The Woman's Division had an office right across the hall from our office in the 10th Precinct and they would borrow our Polaroid camera to document the injuries of abused babies or children. Sometimes we would be there and see the scars and damage done to these kids. It was bad enough to see what people did to each other on a daily basis and the general abuse of kids, but torturing them was even more obscene. I knew I could never control myself when investigating or arresting these types of perpetrators.

Heart Surgery

One of the hardest and most rewarding things I have ever done was to go to Children's Hospital. I was working undercover at the time and my young nephew was going through open heart surgery there. I was told by my ex-wife that he wanted his uncle the policeman to come and see him. I hadn't worked uniform for some time so I shaved, got a short haircut, and dug out my uniform figuring he wanted to see a real policeman. I was nervous because I wasn't so tough when seeing sick or injured children and worried about showing my emotions around them. I tentatively entered his room not knowing what to expect and to my utmost pleasure he rushed over to me with a proud smile and grabbed my hand. He had never seen me in my uniform and immediately took me around to show me to his little friends at the hospital who were all excited to see his policeman uncle. The kids were great and I was never so proud of what my uniform did for them for a little while and it reminded me of what I was wearing it for.

Gambling-Mutual Numbers Arrest

One of our functions was enforcement of gambling and most of that was done at night. When on days, we decided to try to work on Mutuals, also called The Numbers Racket. Detroit had a long history going back to the Purple Gang and Italian Mafia, and then it was taken over by Black Organized Crime called the big-four of Detroit which included John Roxborough the boxer Joe Louis's manager (unrelated to the Police Big Four). The Numbers Racket was a multi-million-dollar operation that provided cash for other illegal enterprises like narcotics. It was basically a day-time operation for runners also called bagmen. They walked the alleys and streets picking up cash and bet slips from homes and small businesses, as small as pocket change six days a week. They would drop off bags of money and bet slips to a central office or headquarters that later was moved to a main office and often moved again for security reasons.

The way it worked was you picked 3 numbers between 0 & 999 and bet what amount you wanted to on those numbers. The good part was everybody knew and trusted their runner and you could check on the number coming out because it was configured on a formula from daily horse races, not just made up. The bad part was it was the poorest of the poor's money that was being taken with very slim odds of winning, just false hope. It also produced large sums of cash that was used for illegal purposes and political corruption to advance the agendas of the corrupt, while giving nothing back to the people except more crime. Normally its enforcement fell to a larger unit called the Racket Conspiracy Unit that had more officers trained in surveillance and how to obtain warrants. They had the time and manpower. One of my partners and I decided to see if we could make some arrest and possibly work a case up to the higher ups.

It wasn't easy being two white guys in all black neighborhoods trying not to get noticed. But we looked like hippies trying to score some dope while really watching for older males walking the streets and alleys going to the same houses daily. I remembered from my days working in the factory that the runners would go to the same betters' daily and collected money and bet slips almost always at the same time every day. So we got pretty good at driving by in different vehicles to see the pick up's. With only working a month on days, we didn't have the time needed to work our way up and the runners we arrested wouldn't cooperate with us because they feared their people more than us. Even so, they had to pay a fine and be more careful. We learned how to do surveillance type work and had a change of pace from our normal Vice work. The funny part was when we busted a runner everyone knew and they all claimed their number came in.

Six Month Qualification

There was about a half a dozen of us overdue for our 6-month firearms qualifications and riot training that was supposed to be done by everyone twice a year. I thought I could get away without it by working in an undercover unit, but no luck. Some cops enjoyed going to the Rouge Range firing various weapons and doing riot formations; I wasn't one of them. The range was located on the other side of town, and the weather would be either hot or cold, but we didn't have a choice. At least we didn't have to cut our hair, shave our beards, or wear our uniforms. It went well until they had us firing our guns from longer distances to the targets. Most of us had snub nose revolvers with two inch barrels that weren't very accurate from a distance. Unfortunately, we weren't taking this training as serious as we should have and did a lot of goofing off and laughing as we shot the hell out of the hanging signs that were between us and the targets. Somehow we did well enough to qualify, but the range officers weren't too pleased with our hippie looks and acting like F-troop cops. Near the end of the training day it was time for everybody to put on their gas mask and get gassed while doing riot formation moves. As we marched into the tear gas they were throwing, the uniform officers marched right through it without any problems. When we marched into the tear gas it went right up into our mask, as our beards kept the mask from being sealed. The range officers knew what would happen, but we didn't. So in the end the joke was on us and the range officers seemed to enjoy our distress.

The next time I had to qualify, I shaved, took my department issued gun and took the training more seriously. I think I was starting to live my undercover role a little too much and forgetting I was a police officer and should act like one when necessary and not go completely native unless in character when needed. I was already an experienced street cop having to handle most everything in a very busy inner City Precinct, but apparently I wasn't a cop long enough not to slip a little back into my civilian ways which was good and bad depending on what I was doing.

The Big Kiss

As I said before we had an unwritten, unofficial rule that we only worked gay bars for liquor law violations like any other bar. But, if a gay violated the law in other public places, we would arrest them if they gave us an Accosting & Soliciting case. We had one officer that decided he was going to get a case on a gay bartender, so he could tie the bar into illegal conduct and write the bar up on a liquor violation. We couldn't talk him out of it or stop him, as technically he was attempting to enforce current laws. The Sergeant sent me in first to cover him and I sat at a table near the bar. When he entered he sat at the bar, ordered a drink and he immediately started 'acting' gay and overtly flirting with the bartender. I sat in amazement because he was the one doing the Accosting and that alone would make his arrest illegal and end his attempt at a liquor write-up.

After a while the bartender, who was pretty street smart, started flirting back and then, to the officer's complete surprise, he leaned over the bar, grabbed the officer by the ears and gave him a great big kiss on the mouth. The officer's reaction was priceless. He jumped back wiping his mouth, spitting and swearing at the bartender. The bartender was cracking up. The officer was so furious, I had a hard time grabbing him and getting him out of the bar. I was laughing so hard I could hardly talk. The bartender apparently saw through the phony acting job and turned the tables on him. As we left the bar and walked around the corner to our car where our crew was waiting, he tried very hard to get me to promise that I wouldn't tell anyone what happened. I was still laughing so hard I could hardly walk and said, "Are you nuts? That was the funniest thing I've ever seen, I could never NOT repeat it." Which I did often to his chagrin.

Bitten at the Last Chance

On the south east corner of Woodward and 8 Mile Road at the border between Detroit and the City of Ferndale, there was a bar called the Last Chance and it lived up to its name. It had a rough crowd of the most unlikely people you could ever imagine, bikers, pimps, prostitutes, male & female, with a mixture of hippies thrown in. It was busy day and night with almost every kind of drug and vice activity. I don't have a clue how they did it, but they somehow did their own thing while staying out of each other's way. It was what you could call a tough crowd with one thing in common; they all hated cops with a passion. Needless to say when we went in undercover it usually wasn't a pleasant experience and we had to be careful and hope we weren't recognized. That alone made the hair on the back of your neck stand up as you most likely wouldn't have the time or opportunity to talk your way out of there.

The City and Police Department had been trying to close it down for years, but couldn't seem to tie in any of their employees to any of the illegal activity that was going on in plain view. The back story was an ex-cop who was fired was part owner and schooled everybody that they were welcome, but it would get very dangerous if they even alluded they were allowed to be in there and he claimed he didn't know what anybody was doing was illegal. So the theory was, because of the numerous neighborhood complaints of illegal activity, we were to get as many cases for Accosting and Soliciting inside and outside so they could deem the bar a nuisance, they could then close it down without having to actually tie employees to the activity.

I spent a couple of hours every Friday afternoon for weeks getting known by the employees and clientele hoping someone who worked there would mistakenly tell me how or who could get me drugs or a girl. I could see, like many before me, all I was going to get was a separate arrest. So when one of the hookers again propositioned me saying for $20 she would give me oral sex in my car, I told her ok. Knowing it wasn't safe for me to try and make an arrest in the bar; we walked out together and got into my car. Instead of pulling off and parking next to a wall or another car so she couldn't get out, I identified myself and told her she was under arrest. She immediately opened the passenger door and started running. I quickly caught her and while attempting to put hand cuffs on her she bit me and got away again. Now my cover partner was chasing her with me and as she was running west on east bound 8 Mile, there was a bridge on Woodward Avenue going over 8 Mile with a sidewalk going under it. Just as she was starting to go under it she looked back at us, misjudged the opening, hitting the wall at full speed and knocked herself out temporarily. Then my crazy sense of humor got to me and I was laughing so hard I could hardly get the hand cuffs on her. It was like watching TV bloopers, but this was real. I went from being nervous to cracking up in minutes and then I realized that I was bleeding and was just bit by a hooker. We didn't have an AIDS epidemic in 1972, but I thought I better get it cleaned and maybe a shot so I didn't get infected. We drove over to the ER at Holy Cross Hospital on East Outer Drive. We knew the nurses there and sometimes would bring them beer like we used to do when I was in the 7th at St. Joes and Deaconess Hospitals. It was always good to take care of people that would be taking care of you.

One of the nurses brought me into the treatment area and handed me a flimsy opened back hospital gown and told me to put it on behind the curtain. I took a few steps toward the curtain and suddenly realized that I didn't need to get naked for a small bite on my baby finger. As I turned around to question her about the gown, a group of nurses were standing there smiling at me. We all had a good laugh at the joke they were trying to play on me.

It was my first time of many to be treated there and the doctor asked me if I wanted the rest of the day off to which I replied, sure. By the time I went back to the station the rumor mill had said I had a big fight with a prostitute and my finger was almost bitten off. The Sergeant told me to take the rest of the day off and report to the medical section the next day to see if I could return to work. Now I realized why the doctor wrapped up half my hand instead of just my little finger. It was ok with me so I left and went to the local bar where we sometimes stopped after work. When some of the guys came in later my hand was sweating so I started to remove the bandages. Before I knew it, I had a bunch of cops around me trying to get a look at my damaged hand. So, I slowly unwrapped the Ace bandage, pulled the tape off of the gauze wrapping, then finally pulled off the little band aid that was covering the small ½" cut. I received loud booing and cat calls from the guys who were hoping to see a mangled hand all the while laughing and calling me names as I laughed at their sick curiosity.

Mixed Crew

One night when I came into work my partner had called in sick and the rest of my crew were off that night. As I was thinking of whether or not to stay, the Sergeant on the black crew said they had a spot for me to fill in if I wanted to. Usually they worked their areas and we worked ours overlapping sometimes. I liked the idea of being the minority on the crew and learning from those that lived and worked in the area. Our first stop was Club 23 on Livernois, which was Detroit Tiger, Willie Horton's bar named after his baseball jersey number. It was one of their pit stops and everybody there was nice and friendly; it was a good start. Then they took me to a drive-thru funeral parlor on 14th street where the casket was on an angle facing a window and as you drove through you stopped at the window and paid your respects. I had never heard of or seen anything like it and if somebody would have told me without me actually seeing it, I wouldn't have believed them. Naturally for me I found it hilarious and they found my naivety about it hilarious. We then got our private vehicles and I johned on 14th street where they showed me some hookers. But the hookers didn't want any part of a white boy cruising so far in the inner City and when I slowed down they went the other way. Then we took turns stopping in small corner bars, having a drink and looking around for liquor violations.

One of the bars I went into had an all-black clientele and even though I had done that before, this one was in a rougher area and I wasn't too welcomed. As I walked in and sat at the bar the open hostility was very apparent with first stares then dirty looks to finally loud comments. I was nervous, but wasn't going to leave until I finished my beer and checked for violations. The more I ignored the rowdy group at the end of the bar the louder and angrier they got and I was sure there was going to be a problem when I had to walk by them to leave. It suddenly dawned on me that since I never worked with this crew before, I didn't know if they had the same signal as my crew did of throwing something through the door or window, if we were in trouble. As I was finishing my beer, the little barmaid who had witnessed the harassment and apparently had enough of their attitude, came over and told me, "don't worry honey, I'm half white." She then proceeded over to the group of harassers and read them the riot act to which they all quieted down. I was quite impressed on how the little lady ran her bar and her attitude on race. It wasn't long ago that I didn't fully understand either side of race relations and now I was learning by experience the good and bad of both sides first hand by experiencing it in real life situations.

Company Party

Our commanding officer invited us over to his place for a little get together with some of his friends for food and drinks. We were carried as working and appreciated what he was doing for us, so most everyone showed up. When I arrived, I was struck by the difference between the way we looked and his friends who were in suits and ties and clean shaven. Our group looked like a bunch of derelicts unshaven, long hair, wearing blue jeans and looking totally out of place. As we socialized, his friends were serving us drinks, snacks and treating us like celebrities. They were totally enjoying our war stories and the situations we got ourselves into, and out of. The more we drank, the more they served and the more graphic our stories got. We all had a pretty good time even if it was a bit high class for us street boys. At the end of the party when everyone was leaving I was having a conversation with my Commanding officer about working with his younger brother and telling him he was a good street cop. He told me that's what his brother said about me too and that I hadn't let him down. I then mentioned to him that his civilian friends really got a graphic earful about the goings on of Detroit's vice undercover world as we all loosened up and told some of our experiences. He laughed and said they were all priests from suburbia but don't worry about it they loved the stories and had a great time. The next day most of us were a little embarrassed as we thought back to our vivid descriptions of situations that would have even shocked us a few months ago before we were wallowing in it. Now it was just part of our daily lives, except telling it to priests who now had some stories of their own to tell. Once again, I experienced the meeting of two different worlds.

Off Duty Harassment

Once in a while I would hook up with my civilian friends that I had grown up with, but found we didn't have much in common anymore. One Friday night I stopped in a bar called Gabriel's to have a pop with them as I was not drinking at the time to clean up my system. I had the long hair, beard and was dressed like a hippie. I parked my car on Gratiot in front of the bar, where there was a fire hydrant and the curb was painted yellow for 15 feet from the hydrant showing where not to park. I was in the bar for 3 hours socializing with my old friends, having a good time. When I left at closing I found a ticket on my windshield for parking within 15 feet of a fire hydrant. I thought I was far enough away from it, but my front bumper was six inches into the zone. By looking at the ticket I saw that it was written within minutes of me parking there. Ok, I did park there even if maybe it was a bit cheesy, it was the law and I broke it. Maybe because I had a Corvette or they had problems with that bar clientele and enforced everything, either way I knew better and didn't have a problem with it. As soon as I pulled off from the curb, I was hit with lights and sirens and a spot light in my eyes as I was pulled over. A young Roseville officer walked up to my door and said, "Get out of the car asshole; you don't learn do you?" I was shocked and said, "Excuse me sir" and he replied, "You heard me asshole." So I replied, "Yes sir" and got out of my car. He then told me to go to the scout car and asked me how long I had been in the bar? I told him a couple of hours and he said more like three. I was shocked as I was wearing a pop up holster with a large .357 Magnum with big rubber grips completely visible that he hadn't even noticed. As we were walking to his car he asked me if I knew what a breathalyzer was and when I said, "Yes sir, I do" he just said "It figures." I was perplexed as to why I was even stopped without any traffic violation; maybe my car or my hippie look. If so, they must have seen me enter the bar at 11pm and assumed I must be drunk by now, or maybe they just didn't like hippies who drove Corvettes, or thought it would be just an easy drunk driving arrest. Either way, they were about to get a surprise and taught a lesson.

I was born and raised in Roseville and use to work out at a gym with the Chief of Police and also went through school with a couple of good Roseville cops.

He opened the rear door of the squad car and told me to get in right behind his partner who was behind the wheel and had never even exited his vehicle. He got in the right front seat and said to his partner, "He's been busted for drunk driving before," and the driver asked me how many times I had been arrested. When I replied that I had never been arrested for drunk driving, he asked me how I knew about a breathalyzer. I told him that I had been present for a lot of them when they were administered. At that, he asked me in a tentative voice, are you a police officer? When I replied, yes sir, he asked if I was armed and I replied I most certainly am. He turned around and looked at my fully exposed .357 which could have been seen from a block away. I showed him my police ID while they were both rapidly apologizing. I truly cared for my fellow officers and these guys needed an attitude adjustment so I verbally gave them one. I explained that real cops don't cherry pick bars for drunk drivers or treat people without respect and you just don't know who you're dealing with and sometimes it turns out to be an armed undercover cop who doesn't even drink. I was hoping they would get the message. I wasn't mad, just disappointed in them and would do the same if one of my partners acted like that. The next day at work I explained what happened to my boss and he called the Roseville Chief of Police and asked him what kind of officers worked for him while mostly embarrassing the Chief. They asked me what I wanted done with them and I said if they got the message, a good ass chewing, but nothing in their files would be fair enough unless this was normal for them. Working plain clothes and undercover gives you an insight on how some officers treat civilians and why sometimes there is a lack of respect. Respect is earned and it goes both ways.

It was only a few months later another officer was killed. I remembered him as Officer Stocker who had received the Medal of Valor at my Academy graduation just two years before being killed on July 31st. He was shot in the head through the front door of a residence and his partner was critically wounded while investigating a stolen rifle complaint.

Flasher

We got a call that there was a flasher in front of Cunningham's Drug store at 8 Mile and Dequindre flashing on weekends and by the time a scout car got there he was always gone. Two of us took our private cars and sat in the parking lot for only about 10 minutes and sure enough this goof ball stands right in front of the store opening and closing his trench coat with nothing on under it except for his shoes, socks and the bottom part of his pants legs held up by elastic bands. It was crazy just like you saw in a cartoon, but this was real. I now had about 2 years on the job one in uniform in a busy Precinct and another undercover with Detroit's wild sub-culture and I thought I had seen and experienced most everything. Unbeknownst to me this was just the beginning of a life very few people would experience or even believe existed.

The End of Northern District

We had been together about a year now and were trained and experienced in all types of vice and undercover work. So it came as a complete surprise to us when we were told the unit would be eliminated. We were shocked because our arrest, write ups and enforcement numbers were good. No one had been disciplined nor had there been any accusations of bad behavior made. We had a week's notices and were told that they would try to honor our transfer request. We were told that although we did a good job, they wanted to do the enforcement at the Precinct level instead of the district level. After thinking about it, I didn't care if I went back to #7 with the guys who broke me in as it was a sad experience leaving them after what we had went through together. Now I was a little more rounded out than I was when I left #7. Heck, I now had two-years good street experience and might even get my own car as senior man in an inner City Precinct, which was most young cop's goal. The 7th Precinct was on the Eastside and a lot closer to home. I knew most of the guys, supervisors and my way around the area. With only a little more than two-years seniority, I couldn't get transferred anywhere good anyway. So a low seniority Precinct was my best bet. The downside was, but couldn't be avoided, I'd have to shave, cut my hair and go back in uniform. In the 1970's radical culture, being young, clean shaven and with short hair anyone looking at me would think I had to be a cop, ex-con or military which could get you harassed or even spat on. At that time, cops and the military were hated by some groups.

So, I decided that I would request to go back where I came from, if possible. Just like #7, I got to know and like these guys and we would all be going in different directions to start a new phase of our careers. I would definitely miss all the guys on my crew that had been together for the whole time. So to my surprise when I told my crew chief, Sergeant B who I had worked with at #7 before, that I would like to go back to #7, with a big smile on his face he told me our crew, the four of us, would all be going to the 11th Precinct Special Operations Section as the Precinct's new Morality Crew. Wow, what a pleasant surprise, no haircut, shave or uniform and a North Eastside Precinct with the whole crew still together to boot. Apparently he didn't just have pull to get here he had enough pull to go where he wanted. The 11th was the busiest for vice activity because it was mixed and on the border of suburbia from where most of the johns came from and Woodward (our red light area) would still be ours to work. We also had the option, to work for the Federal Government because we had a year of undercover work so the Feds would waive their four-year college degree requirement for us and hire us direct, but I wasn't interested; I was staying in Detroit. It had everything a young cop could want in my book. We were already used to working the 11th, but didn't know the personnel who worked there. The next night Sergeant B took us to see our new office and meet some of the Special Ops crews we would be working with. He seemed to know most of the supervisors and a lot of the officers. We were welcomed by everyone and introduced around to the night shift.

When we returned to our offices at the 10th Precinct a City employee was screwing metal property tags with serial numbers that said property of City of Detroit 10th Precinct on our furniture. We were given the weekend off and told to report to #11 on Monday morning at 11am which was the time that our day shift of 11am - 7pm would start so we could get our office together and get organized.

11th Precinct – Davison & Conant (1970)

We were allowed to keep one of our four door Plymouth vehicles, but the office equipment was to stay at #10 because that's where it was registered. Sergeant B. was having none of that, he told us to meet him in the 10th Precinct parking lot at 1am and not to let anybody know. When I pulled in he and the rest of the crew were starting to take the office windows out. We then took out our desks and office equipment that we had scrounged from the World Medical Relief Center and he said the 10th Precinct had no claim on it. Nothing on the property tags said anything about our almost defunct Northern District Morality Unit and it was going with us. We were laughing our asses off as uniform officers were coming and going and the front desk personnel had no idea we were robbing them.

When we got all the equipment to the 11th, we removed all the tags and set up our office in the middle of the night with the 11th Precinct personnel giving us hippie looking dude's strange looks. As we first pulled up to the 11th on Davison and Conant, I was pleased to see the lights were still on in the outer offices. That didn't happen in the inner City's 7th and 10th Precincts that I had worked in because the Precincts would sometime get shot at after dark. This is going to be different and I like the way it was starting.

CHAPTER 4

The 11th Precinct Special Operations

Precinct Morality 2nd Time - Undercover

November 1972 was a new start once again; the third time in a little more than two years on the job. I was in a new Precinct, with new bosses, and new co-workers, but doing the same type of work with the same partners and Sergeant (crew chief). I was pleasantly surprised that I already knew some of the guys from the Academy and the 7th Precinct. My old partner from my first days at #7 who taught me the sounds of gun fire and calmed me down when we were under fire, was there working the accident car. It turned out they also dispersed the central accident prevention section where he had transferred to earlier. They still had the main downtown units, but they were also operating Precinct Special Operation units of Narcotics, Morality, Cruisers (Big Four) and B&E Cars under one Lieutenant, with a Sergeant as a crew chief on each crew. The idea was, and it was a good one, that we would be more involved and

familiar at the Precinct level, opposed to everything coming from downtown. The neighborhoods would have more control and involvement through their Precinct Inspectors who had to answer to the local citizens. It also worked out that as a specialty unit working mostly nights together from 7pm - 3am or 8pm - 4am without attending regular roll calls, we all immediately became close and took pride in our unique unit. Unlike Northern District Morality where we had misdemeanor type quotas and we were not supposed to get involved in other types of enforcement, here we all worked together.

Our first priority was Vice enforcement, and we also backed up the shift cars on felony runs, went on raids with Narcotics and the Cruiser with a lot of latitude to get involved wherever we were needed. I liked it immediately, no shift supervisors or radio runs directing us. Our Sergeant treated us like an equal with street experience and let us work alone most of the time. Sounds nuts, but now I can scare myself both ways with the hair on my neck standing up while working undercover and with the heart pounding fear of making felony arrest of hostile violent felons too. It was two different types of adrenaline rushes and very addictive. I didn't know then, but I had already slipped into a mental state that I had to prove myself to myself almost daily and that I not only belonged there working with the best trained and most experienced police officers in the country, but now even more being assigned with the cream of the crop in Precinct Special Operations. Almost all of the officers here and especially in Precinct Special Operations were very motivated and seemed to be a happy bunch working in this diverse ethnic area.

December 1972

It didn't take long to go from the frying pan into the fire now that we would also be working felony type crimes instead of mostly misdemeanors like we had for the past year. December had always been a dangerous month for cops and businesses because the have-not's take advantage of the haves in a very violent way not caring who got hurt or killed. Our four-man crew met a four-man Stress crew at a local restaurant bar called Club Polski on Conant for lunch. It was my first time meeting the other crew, but some of the guys knew each other. They warned us of a trio who was holding up dope houses and we all agreed to work together if and when needed. They were a good bunch of guys and became instant new friends. We left and went our way and they went their way. Later that night all four were shot up while sitting on a dope house watching for the trio that we had talked about that were holding up dope houses. The trio turned out to be Brown, Boyd and Bethune. Luckily they survived, but when you have met or personally know the officers killed or wounded it seems to hit harder, even though they all hurt you a lot.

On December 8th Officer Gerald James Riley was killed while trying to stop a hold up at Michigan National Bank while off duty. He had the drop on what he thought was the only hold up man and handed off his young son to a nearby woman. The second hold up man shot him and then assassinated him in front of his son while he was lying on the floor by shooting him in the face.

On December 18th three of us were working in plain clothes and driving a department unmarked Plymouth when a scout car received a radio run to the Bali Hai Motel on a "hold up in progress on 8 Mile Road." We parked on 7 Mile Road hoping for a quick description in case they might head our way. While we were waiting, a white Rambler with one white male driver and two passengers sitting in the back seat passed by us coming from the direction of the hold up. We started following it as it weaved from one side street to another in no apparent pattern or direction. It seemed like forever and we didn't want them to run as we had no lights or sirens for pursuit. We continued to follow them into Highland Park. Finally, after about 15 minutes of following from a distance the description of the 3 suspects with the license plate number and vehicle description came over the radio. It matched perfect and our gut feelings were correct. With our adrenaline pumping we cut them off at Woodward and Church Street in Highland Park. We all knew this month had already been dangerous and the fact that I was newly back in the game of making felony stops I was a little uptight to say the least. As soon as our vehicle came to a stop, I bailed out of the rear seat with my gun drawn and laid across the trunk of our car while looking at all three suspects so they couldn't get a first shot at us. Almost immediately, our car started going again and I was standing just a few feet away from them in the middle of the street. My partners had jumped out and in the excitement left the car in gear, so it kept going. I was standing there alone while my partners were chasing our car. Luckily our driver reached in and put it in park after only a few feet.

I had lost my cover, but still had the drop on them and they had decided not to shoot it out knowing they couldn't get away. Afterward, we all had a little laugh about our not so perfect felony stop with a sigh of relief and renewed knowledge that we were back in the big game and better kick it up a notch or two. I was later awarded my <u>3rd Citation/Commendation</u> for "Arresting three felons for armed robbery." It later turned out Mr. Troha was on parole and was a semi-famous criminal from Chicago. That is probably why they didn't shoot it out as he was older and experienced.

Just a little over a week from our arrest and a couple of weeks from the four Stress officers being ambushed, two more Stress officers were ambushed. On December 27, 1972 the same trio, Brown, Boyd & Bethune, were in the middle of robbing dope houses again which was their normal M.O. Officer Robert Bradford Jr. was shot and assassinated while lying on the ground wounded and Officer Robert Dooley was seriously wounded and died of his wounds years later. Boyd & Bethune were later killed in shoot outs with police in other states as there were massive manhunts for them throughout the country. Brown was later arrested and was brought back to Detroit for trial, but was found not guilty by a jury who later said they didn't like that he was hunted like a dog. Brown was made out by radical left wing organizations as a Robin Hood type who was closing dope houses with the help of the media who were anti-Stress Unit and didn't care to look at the facts. Losing these brave young officers hurt like hell, but the media making Brown, Boyd & Bethune out to be heroes by the works of radical revolutionaries, was putting salt in our wounds. Brown was shot years later in 1984 and killed by an unknown assailant. All three had violent histories and ties to radical groups like the Black Panthers. As some say, the year of 1972 was ending with a bang and we were on the wrong end of it with too many funerals and black bands on our badges. I mourned 14 Police Officers killed in the line of duty and I don't even know how many where shot in just my first 2-1/2 years on the job. The fact is, it was going to get a lot worse for us cops on the streets that we were trying to protect and serve in our community.

Characters

The 11th Precinct was a lot larger than the 7th or 10th Precinct's that I had worked at and more diverse in 1973. It still had good areas and decent businesses, but wasn't like a suburb anymore. There also were projects and high crime areas like my old Precincts. It had its characters, but nobody seemed as burned out as the guys that I had previously worked with who were working daily in combat type situations. It wouldn't be too long before #11 caught up with the inner City Precincts in crime and violence. The citizens that could leave left in droves in the mid to late 1970's to the northern suburbs. The ones that couldn't were victimized by the violent predators. The cops in #11, myself included, were right in the middle of a new war zone. It was going to turn into another Fort Apache, but bigger. At the time though, most crimes were being solved, up to 90% of homicides and violent crimes. The standards were still high for new recruits and the officers and supervisors were top notch.

New Year's 1973 – Life Changes

1972 ended with a number of cops being shot which continued into 1973. On January 27, 1973, Officer Harold Carlson was killed in the line of duty. I was into my 3rd year on the street and didn't have any naïve suburban traits left in me anymore. I had become hardened and streetwise by what I saw and experienced daily.

I no longer had much in common with my old suburban civilian friends and saw very little of them including relatives. There wasn't anything left in my marriage after separating 5 or 6 times and going back together; I couldn't do it anymore and it wasn't fair to our kids. When we were together we fought all the time and I couldn't take putting the kids through it over and over again. So early in 1973, after the beginning of another separation, I went to a lawyer, paid him in cash and told him to represent my wife. I then went to her and told her to go to the lawyer and file for a divorce. The divorce was final in May of 1973. I had been married with children since I was 18 years old and when taking the kids home on Sunday nights it broke my heart that we just couldn't be a normal family. I told myself it was better for them than living in an unstable situation being in the middle of a broken marriage full of hostility, anger and separations. They were able to move back to the suburbs for better schools, less crime and the possibility of a family life with parents who weren't going in different directions. I got the children on the weekends that I wasn't working and they were able to grow up in a normal world.

Not having a family to come home to nightly and working the hard streets of Detroit is what led me to start really living one day at a time. I might not be here tomorrow like a lot of my friends and coworkers. It was the beginning of a mindset that made me a little reckless and I was never afraid of anything or anybody anyway. I thought that I had done the right thing for my kids and tried to stay out of the way so I wouldn't be interfering into their new and better suburban family life. Looking back, I wish I would have been more involved, but that would have been almost impossible at the time with the situation as it was. But I still wish I had.

Van Dyke Avenue

Woodward Avenue was our main red light area, but Van Dyke Avenue also had numerous go-go bars, blind pigs and regular bars. Van Dyke & 7 Mile had Vandy's, Rumpus, Duchess and Fancy Pants all competing with each other for local and suburban customers. Woodward and Van Dyke both ran north and south and were the busiest vice areas. The 11th Precinct was busy businesswise, even though in 1973 cops weren't generally liked by the anti-war crowd and revolutionaries. Our business people and citizens in #11 seemed to like us around, most likely because they needed us. They were cooperative and that was a pleasant change from what I was used to. We still had those that resisted when arrested, but now we had some witnesses that actually told the truth and didn't go by 'snitches get stitches' or stick to a made up story.

Go-Go Joe

Working the topless go-go bars, I kept running into one man who most of the dancers violated the ordinance of mingling with. That was the touching or being touched while performing in a Group D license establishment. I eventually ran into him in numerous regular dance bars too, but at those bars his dancing was legal. I am glad I didn't try to enforce the minor violations as he was pretty famous around town. I don't know how old he was but he was bald and looked about 80 or 90. When the dancers saw him sitting at the stage, they would immediately go over to him and with the crowd roaring, they would rub their breast on top of his bald head until he got up and did a wild dance, which was quite professional. The whole crowd would be cheering and enjoying the show. It never got out of control and he never touched the girls so we just let everybody have fun. I was used to seeing him all over town for years, but pretty surprised to see how famous he was in the regular dance bars too. I never heard him speak; he just had a giant smile on his face and danced and danced. That was why he was known in the 70's as Detroit's Go-Go Joe.

Monkey Woman

We had some extremely talented topless Go-Go dancers in the numerous bars. Not just good looking, but good dancers who put on a good show that you could tell they worked at and took pride in. One of them was called 'Monkey Woman' and the club owners actually had a metal bar attached to the ceiling so she could swing, flip and do all kinds of aerobics on it. When she was working at certain clubs they actually advertised her in the weekly bar papers. Unfortunately, when she wasn't performing some of the other girls, after a few drinks, would try her routines and took some nasty falls or looked extremely foolish to the delight of the crowd.

After a bar was written up, or given a warning for a violation, you were then known and no longer undercover in that particular establishment with the people that were there at the time. Eventually you ended up being known by most of the employees and dancers at the bar and it would turn into a semi-friendly game of cat and mouse. When we wrote them a violation ticket, we usually did it in the privacy of their office while a waitress brought us a drink. Some owners were outright hostile and would try to get the bar crowd worked up against us. But they learned that wasn't a good idea when they had to appear at the Liquor Control Commission that could shut them down and put them out of business. Mostly a violation was handled very professionally by both parties without any future animosities.

They all tried to push the law to the limits and we tried to keep them from running amuck. When they thought we weren't there, they would have one of the girls do a set bottomless, so word got around and drew in customers from their competitors. Those girls also made better tips. When we were in undercover mode we were pretty good actors, but not as good as most dancers. I got to know a lot of dancers quite well and they showed us their real self when around just us. They knew how to make a customer think he was special to her, squeezing tips out of them then going on to the next one. It was a job to most of them and the customers had their egos built by half naked beautiful friendly young girls. I guess it was a win-win for both parties, if they understood the game. Some of the girls were going to college or happily married and had their heads together. There were others that were being played by players who gave them drugs and took most of their earnings almost like pimps. Most all of them were attracted to bad boys, which included the undercover cops. We were street bad (hard asses), but protective of the girls and they liked that.

Talford

We had some complaints from the local liquor stores in the area of Conant & Nevada that people were selling booze from a hallway of a vacant building during the day. I was used to after-hour's clubs, but this was my first experience of illegal alcohol sales (bottle joints) during the day. We watched it for a couple of days and sure enough some bum looking types would enter a doorway and then come out with a can of beer or pint of booze. They were selling apparent stolen alcohol cheaper than the stores could and on Sundays when the licensed establishment couldn't. While watching it we noticed a large 6'4" or 6'5" dark skinned black male whose face was all scared up and real scary looking. He was always around and walking in and out of traffic harassing anybody he could, apparently trying to get someone to buy him some booze. So on a Sunday morning I pulled up to him in my private vehicle and asked him where I could get some booze and if he knew, I would buy him some too.

He got all excited almost pulling me from my car while repeating, "Come on, hurry up." He took me into the vacant building and grabbed two pints of whiskey and a 6 pack of beer from a cooler and put them on a make shift counter. The man behind the counter said twenty bucks and while I was paying him the other guy behind the counter was playing with a large buck knife. He walked over to the door looking at me the whole time while blocking the doorway. I got a bad feeling that I was about to be robbed and or assaulted. As I walked to the door he smiled and moved aside most likely just having some fun intimidating whitey – a game that was played often in Detroit. As we left, I gave Talford the beer and one pint of whiskey, keeping one pint for evidence and hoping to make a good informant out of Talford later.

As I met up with my Sergeant we called for a couple of marked scout cars to assist on the raid. It wasn't the biggest raid for sure and we ended up with only one arrest and a trunk load of booze, but we closed a complaint and met a real character named Talford who I would run into numerous times in the future. As we were collecting the evidence and taking away the prisoner a crowd started to form and they all wanted to kill Talford who just eliminated their cheap booze supply. He had climbed into the front seat of one of the marked scout cars and was howling like a police siren while pretending to drive it and enjoying a cold beer. At this point, I realized he wasn't going to be much of an informant since he was truly nuts. I asked the scout car crew to take Talford anywhere he wanted to go so the crowd could calm down and not attack him. He didn't seem to have enough sense to be worried.

A few days later while driving in the same area, I saw Talford in the middle of the intersection directing traffic. He was walking up to car windows causing people to roll them up as he was yelling into them loudly, "I'll kill you." He was big and ugly and nobody wanted to mess with him. I was glad the crowd didn't get him after the raid. I asked around my new Precinct about him and was told he had been around that corner forever. He acted violent, but never really hurt anyone and nobody complained about him. So everyone left him alone unless he got naked when directing traffic, which I heard he did now and then; even in the winter. Years later when I was stopped at that light and Talford would walk up to my window, I would roll it down and yell at him before he could yell at me, "I'll kill you." He would take off running, it seemed like he just liked to scare you, but not be scared by you. Much later when I was working the (Big Four) Cruiser, we would drive by and he would get all excited and run around slapping the other guys in the back of the head yelling, "I'm the Big Four" over and over.

Another time we were responding to a radio run of "Hold up in progress of a beer truck driver at Conant and Nevada." With a call like this we would respond without the siren, but as fast as we can with only the blue lights on until we were almost in sight. Then turn them off so not to spook the perpetrators. That was called running silent and as we were doing that we both kind of looked at each other at the same time with the same thought, beer, Conant & Nevada, Talford. Sure enough as we pulled up there was a new white suburbanite beer truck driver all upset and telling us the perp said, "Give me a beer," and then said real loud, "I'll kill you." When we described Talford to him he said that's the one. After we explained that Talford was harmless and all talk, he agreed it probably wasn't a hold up as he just walked away. We warned the driver that not all of them were as harmless as Talford and to be careful. That was the first and last time we ever saw that driver.

Years later while working a gun car in uniform, all the shift cars were busy and dispatch was asking for a volunteer to meet the City physician on a violent commitment. That type of call wasn't our normal, but I had done a few when I was a rookie working regular shifts at #7 and hot as it was without air conditioning in our cars, a hospital with air conditioning sounded like a nice change of pace.

The way it worked was a scout car crew would meet the doctor and stand by for his safety. He then interviewed the patient because someone, usually a relative, requested for them to be committed for observation because of dangerous and or violent behavior. This wasn't the first or last time I volunteered for something I didn't have to do for a dumb reason. The doctor read his file and talked to him for a while. Then he suddenly, without giving us a heads up to get in position if he resisted, said loudly, "Take him." As soon as he did that, the patient threw a water glass full of vodka into my face, bouncing the glass off my forehead and then stomped on my big toe with his heal bruising the heck out of it. After a brief struggle we got the cuffs on him.

All the way down to the Psych ward of Detroit General Hospital my partner was laughing at me saying yeah great idea volunteering for a Psycho run. Well as my partner was filling out a conveyance report, I was looking through the large plate glass windows at all the patients walking around to see what goofy things they might be doing. When all of a sudden I saw my old friend Talford who I hadn't seen in years walking around yelling at whoever was nearest to him. I excitedly yelled over to my partner, "Hey they got Talford in here." One of the City physicians standing near me came over, introduced himself in broken English and asked me if I knew Talford. After I replied that I knew him for years, he started reading a report to me that stated that he directs traffic in the street. Before he finished, I interrupted him and finished his sentence saying, "At Conant & Nevada." I then told him to get him back out there because traffic was all fucked up. The look on his face was priceless as my partner and I walked away without smiling and looking serious.

With a bump on my forehead and a big toe throbbing, I wasn't in any mood to be talking to a goofy psychiatrist after the one that we had just dealt with. I was by then getting a little goofy myself and would rather be dealing with someone I understood like Talford or the people of the street. I never saw Talford again, but I always remembered him with a smile to this day – what a character!

The Real Mayor

Like Talford with his group, the "Mayor of Six Mile" had a group of drinking buddies who hung out just a half mile away at Conant & 6 Mile behind a liquor store. Normally we didn't have any serious problems with them, but every so often we had a complaint that they were hanging around the front door harassing customers for money. The "Mayor" was in charge and they all did what he told them to do. So when we had a complaint we took it to the "Mayor." He was supplied with brooms, rakes and garbage bags by the owner and took his crew in the back to clean up their normal drinking area. They usually were out there all summer long. I was curious where they all went in the winter. When I asked them I was told they got welfare and went to Florida. Stupid, they weren't.

Yard Sale

There was a house with a double wide lot on Joseph Campau near the Hamtramck border with what looked like the biggest yard sale I had ever seen. The owner had a large hand painted sign that said, "Things for Sale". My partner spotted a set of golf clubs with bag & cart that looked pretty good. The yard equipment, lamps, tables and everything else looked in pretty good shape too. He was friendly and described everything in detail. When asked how much for the golf clubs he said a million and a half dollars. After asking him about some other items they were the same price. When my partner told him that the prices were ridiculous, he got mad and basically ordered us to leave. We left laughing and saying if he sold only one item he would be rich. A neighbor lady flagged us over and told us he was nuts and prone to violence. She said everyday he hauled all the stuff out and then back in every night. Unfortunately, he got worse and started catching squirrels, skinning and boiling them alive in a large tub on the sidewalk and then tried to sell them. That was when the neighbors called the police. When the police arrived, he grabbed a rake and went after an officer who ended up shooting and killing him. That night the neighbors stole all his stuff and ransacked his house. The 11th Precinct, even though it was near the border of the suburbs, was turning into an inner City Precinct like #7 and sadly I was there to see it happen.

Hit & Run Injury Accident

I was newly single and living with two other cops, sleeping on the couch of a two bedroom apartment on East Outer Dr. & Van Dyke. The couch was fine for me, I couldn't afford anything else and we all worked different shifts, so it worked out.

So far I was pretty lucky and only had to get involved a couple of time's making off duty arrests as technically we were never off duty. We had to live in the City which kept more cops in the City and on the street when off duty without extra pay. One day I was just pulling out of my new apartment complex when a car side swiped another car that had a family with two children in it. He then took off failing to stop to see if anyone was injured, as there was extensive damage. I attempted to follow him as he sped up and changed direction from one street to another attempting to lose me. I kept blowing my horn as I followed him hoping for him to stop or gain the notice of a scout car. Neither happened, but as he was approaching 8 Mile Road while heading North on Mt. Elliott, I was able to cut him off because of traffic congestion. I didn't have a radio or back up, so not knowing why he was running or if he was armed or wanted, I decided to move fast. As I got up to his driver's window, he had it almost rolled all the way up and I just got the barrel of my gun into the last two inches while showing him my badge and holder and yelling over and over police officer. He then pushed open his door, knocking me back and started to get out. About that same time as he was struggling to get away, two rather large guys helped me hold him until a scout car arrived.

I learned a few things that day: 1) There were still some citizens that would help a cop in need. 2) Doing the right thing doesn't always matter. When you risk your life, vehicle, and job making an off duty arrest and some would refuse to prosecute if paid off, you might think twice. 3) It also meant paperwork, on my time, so someone didn't have to pay their insurance deductible. The hit & run driver gets away with it and I learn why some cops didn't get involved off duty unless it was a last resort.

The Apartment

Our apartment complex was in #11 and close to Holy Cross Hospital. Outer Drive East Apartments were full of cops, nurses and social workers mostly single, professional working class. It was right around the corner from Gino's Falcon Show Bar and Bowling Alley on Van Dyke & E. Outer Drive – a very popular dance bar. On Sunday afternoons a large group of the single residents hung out at the pool and in the early evening the girls would cook up a large dinner with whatever the group brought to them. It was great and there would be the most unusual variety of food that you could imagine.

My roommates and I didn't cook much so most of our food was delivered daily from the local pizza joints or picked up fast food. We worked and ate at different times so sometimes pizza was actually delivered to our apartment 3 times a day. They knew us well and made good tips so if we needed cigarettes, milk or something they didn't have they made special stops for us. We didn't have food for the Sunday parties so we supplied the beer because we knew a beer truck driver who would actually deliver 10 or more cases for us right at our apartment door at cost.

I enjoyed the girls company, they were young, good looking, nice, educated and professional, but seemed to be looking for a relationship. Being freshly divorced, broke, and with an attitude of life is short, the last thing I wanted was to date a nice, marriageable girl. No way, I was going to live to the limits of my life and stay single. I was married at 18 years old. No more marriage for me. The ladies I dated were going to be like me and not looking for long term relationships. To my total surprise, there were a whole lot of hot, nice females who were thinking the same thing and liked crazy cops who lived on the edge. I also learned to approach the best looking girl in the room; as most nice guys didn't because they were afraid of them, and most of the guys that did acted like jerks trying to be cool. I had learned that being upfront with women, or even someone you were about to arrest made things a lot easier. Even the ladies at the Sunday apartment dinners appreciated my honesty with them, but still teased me about the action at my apartment.

After a while one of my roommates got married and then I not only had my own bedroom, but a designated parking spot too. As time went on the clientele of the complex was changing just like the rest of the 11th Precinct and the professional types started moving out as the low life's started moving in.

One day when I came home the same car had parked in my designated parking spot again so I parked in the visitors' lot and went to the pool. When I came back from the pool she had left and came back and was again parking in my spot. So from my balcony I asked her nicely to please park in her own spot or the visitors lot as she was parking in my spot. With an attitude, she told me to fuck off and said she would park wherever she wanted. Instead of arguing or fighting with her, I just called for a tow truck, got my ticket book and proceeded to write her a $100.00 towing ticket for parking in another's designated spot, while still wearing my bathing suit and covered in suntan oil. All the while she screamed and threw a fit as the tow truck hauled her car to the yard where she would also be charged for storage. It was bad enough to have to put up with the ignorant attitude while working, but I wasn't going to when at home. That was just the start of a nice area going bad.

As time went on Detroit's good citizens who could leave the City did and my nice apartment complex changed rapidly. We had idiots breaking the washers and dryers for the complex and even taking a dump in one. There were constant neighbor troubles and I had people pounding on my door in the middle of the night looking for help from their husbands on family troubles. Burglary, purse snatching and stolen cars also started happening. Unfortunately, it was getting just like a project with gunfire heard and druggies hanging about.

One afternoon we responded to a call of shots fired and I ended up in a foot chase with a suspect who was shooting into a suspected dope house apartment. As I was chasing him armed with an M1 carbine we ran right past my Sunday dinner group who was at the pool. They waved and said "Hi" and I waved back as I was going by in full pursuit. When they realized what was happening they all had a strange look on their faces and stopped waving in mid wave. I lost sight of my suspect and decided then and there, like most of the other tenants, it was time to leave. Our little Shangri-La was no more. The apartment was the first time that I moved because of the City going downhill and driving out the law abiding tax paying good citizens. It would repeat itself over and over as neighborhoods changed, but cops still had to live in Detroit. I eventually moved into and out of 4 different neighborhoods that were nice, good areas and then became crime ridden as they changed. Gun fire was the normal sound of the night even when at home tying to sleep. Unfortunately, if you had to live in the City, like we did, you got somewhat use to it.

Gino's Falcon Show Bar

Right around the corner from our apartment complex was Gino's Falcon Show Bar where I spent many evenings. In the early 1970's they had Monday night show time with live entertainment and the place would be packed to see, Joey Van, Gene Taylor, Willie Tyler and Lester, Mickey Denton to name a few. They also had great house and visiting bands, and even had some talented amateur acts like Jerry (Kazoo) who played a little kazoo to top tunes of the day. The place was always packed with good looking girls and that alone made it a hang-out for us cops. I ended up being friends for years with the owner and most of the employees. Two of the toughest guys that I went through school with in the suburbs, turned out to be bouncers at the bar. We were all surprised to see each other and they were shocked that I had become a cop because I was just as wild as they were during our school days, only smaller. The cops in the bar would help them and they would help us when needed as there were some pretty good battles at the bar. As a cop in the 70's without mace, tasers or vests, we had to do a lot of fighting with our fist and hands on and off duty.

In those days you had to earn your respect without special equipment designed to make it easier. We really didn't like to fight, but had to quite often. In my case, it made me angry. If forced into a fight, I would make sure they realized they made a big mistake. Probably not politically correct for today's attitudes, but usually most people learned there was a price to pay for bad behavior, especially when they got violent.

Most of the time the bouncers, with our help, were able to physically remove the rowdy's in the bar. It was a large bar and one night we had a nut that wanted to fight everybody. We subdued him and bum rushed him out the back door as that was where the fight started. A couple of minutes later he was back and we had to battle with him again and throw him out the back door again. Finally, after the third time we had to throw him out, the bouncers at the front door were told not to let him in any more. We were exhausted and he just wouldn't quit and kept coming back in. One door didn't know what was going on at the other door and the place was packed so they had trouble keeping up with him.

I was now living full time in the fast lane on and off duty. I didn't have to wait in the long line or pay cover or for drinks. Instead of valet parking, I would park my car in the gas station across the street and the kids working there would pull it inside and clean the heck out of it while I was at the bar. When I entered the bar the bouncers shook my hand and girls gave me a hug. I liked it and my ego soared, so I spent more and more time at the bar getting the VIP treatment.

They had a goofy looking valet parking the cars that wore a leather world war one flyers hat and acted as strange as he looked. I asked the owner one night if he was alright mentally and he had quite a laugh. He explained the valet was actually a math teacher who was extremely smart and just making extra tips entertaining the clientele. He later bought his own sports bar on Van Dyke. I got to know him and his neighborhood friends through the owner as they were all a bunch of fun characters. One became a judge and others successful business owners later in life. All good polish kids from the neighborhood. Quite often when I left the bar with a young lady my car would be parked in front of the gas station clean and shiny and my apartment was just around the corner. Sometimes when I was working, I tried to make last call at Gino's and if I ran into one of those young ladies that I had previously met, I would drop them off at my apartment in my unmarked or private vehicle and then go to the station, finish my paperwork and meet them at my place. As a young newly single man this cop business really could have some perks you couldn't get anywhere else. Gino's was like my Cheers Bar from the TV show, but with a lot more action.

Duchess Lounge

The Duchess Lounge was on Van Dyke North of 7 Mile Road and just down the street from Gino's and around the corner from my apartment. The difference was it was a topless club and at the time (early 70's) it was one of the better ones with good looking girls and wait staff. If I was off-duty on the weekend you could usually find me at Gino's or The Duchess where I knew most everyone from the owners to the bar-backs. Monday nights were busy at the Duchess because they were the only bar to have Monday night Go-Go Guys for the ladies, well before the Foxy Frenchman type groups that became the craze later. Men weren't allowed in except for a few cops and the male employees. I got teased about going up there on Male Go-Go night, but it was a blast watching the ladies and then having a bunch of females after you. One of my goofy partners would actually dance a couple of sets then waited tables while getting mugged by the ladies and making a lot of tips. We had a ball with them. It wasn't all fun and games though because we had some pretty good battles helping the bouncers when they needed it on the regular nights. It was the same in most of the bars where we were known and not undercover anymore. We cut the bouncers some slack as they mostly didn't want to fight and would rather remove someone who was acting up peacefully but ended up fighting way more than they wanted to. Being friendly with bouncers could and did get me into a lot of brawls, because I just couldn't leave them outnumbered and do nothing. We were supposed to arrest and make a report every time we got into something, but it was so often and if nobody was seriously injured we just sent them on their way. A few times they sued the bar, but when their attorneys read our deposition and saw that we were police officers, they dropped their lawsuit as we were pretty good witnesses.

Still Johning

We still went johning on Woodward Avenue almost nightly arresting hookers, he-shes and male prostitutes. There were always new ones and the old ones knew better than to out us, or they would be arrested daily for loitering by us and the scout cars that patrolled Woodward. A lot of them were arrested so many times they didn't remember us and we didn't remember them, but just in case though, we changed our appearance every once in a while. I would let my hair grow long then cut it short, grow a beard then cut it down to a goatee, then go clean shaven with just a mustache. The minor changes worked enough that sometimes I got a case on a girl for a second, or sometimes a third time. The harder part was using your same personal vehicle because they would remember your car and would just leave the area while you were johning. Our answer to that was to beg or borrow another vehicle to use. We weren't supposed to take our gun and badge off, but we wouldn't be able to get into, or make undercover buys or arrests if caught with them. The supervisors knew we had to stretch department rules, but never the laws. It was our supervisors that we handed our guns and ID to when we went into situations where we would be searched. To get the job done we had to take a chance sometimes.

I personally had a rule of 'Just do it' and somehow I survived with that attitude. One night I was johning up and down Woodward getting no action and thought maybe somebody put the word out that my car was a vice unit which sometimes happens. So I went back to the station and talked my roommate into letting me use his brand new Corvette as he was working nights that month. Sure enough at my first pass by a group of ladies that were standing together, one flagged me over and jumped in as soon as I stopped. She told me to go down the street to the DeLido Motel where she had a room. After some small talk she said, "You're a cop, I've seen you before." I pulled over to the curb and told her to get out and that I was no cop and don't want nothing to do with any cops if they were around. She then told me to go on to the motel and she was just testing me because real cops wouldn't tell a whore to get out once they got in their car. I used that trick many times on prostitutes and it always worked as they really thought we couldn't lie to them or it was an illegal arrest. Unfortunately, I heard some cops would make up a case if a hooker got as far as getting in to their car and they didn't get the complete case. I found it was a little more time and effort to do it completely legal, and if you didn't get the legal case, you would always get it the next time because they thought for sure you wouldn't let them get out if you were a cop.

Even the judges knew who was really playing the game 100% honestly because a hooker in court would plead not guilty to some of the cases then when my case came up they would plead guilty. After that happened on different girls and cases the judges knew I was getting good cases. If a case was close or you had to fight to arrest them, the judge would really stick it to them instead of the usual $25 fine.

As I drove toward the DeLido Motel parking lot she told me I had to pay for the room and she would give me oral sex for $20 and anything else would cost more. I then parked facing where my cover car should be and flicked my head lights on and off to signal them that I had a case. I reached for my badge holder telling her I'd pay her now and as I pulled my ID out she pulled a knife and we struggled and fell out of the passenger door onto the parking lot. After wrestling and yelling police officer numerous times a small crowd started to form and that got the attention of my cover officers who pulled up and helped me handcuff her. They had missed my signal, but saw the disturbance. By the time I got into the station with my arrest, word had spread about my fight with a hooker armed with a knife. When my roommate heard he wasn't very happy about the situation in his brand new Corvette and let me know about it.

Two things came to my mind, one was that I could have been stabbed like my Uncle was years before when he worked the Vice Squad and the other was never to borrow a roommates new Corvette because he was pissed.

1973 Ends

As 1973 came to an end, we had two more officers shot and killed, Officer Robert T. Moore on 11/8/73 and Sgt. Alvis P. Morris Jr. on 11/12/73, just days apart. During the last few months of 1973 Coleman A. Young was running for Mayor as an anti-cop candidate against John Nichols the law & order Police Commissioner. Young won after stirring up the populace to a dangerous level toward the police with his political rhetoric. It was dangerous enough before Coleman Young, but his election win and a radical Black Power agenda put us right in the middle of a target.

The day after Christmas 1973, I lost my most-staunch supporter and mentor when my Grandfather, who had lived with me all my youth, passed away. I realized that divorce, death, violence and working in Detroit's gutters daily were already taking its toll on me. I was still young, but not naïve anymore and saw more death than most people would experience in a lifetime. For some strange reason, I wasn't afraid of dying, but had a hard time with the death of others and tried not to face it and I just kept moving on. As the New Year was starting we had four more officers shot and two died of their wounds. I didn't know it then, but 1974 wasn't only going to be deadly, it would really affect me for the rest of my life.

Precinct Morality 3rd Time - Conspiracy Cases

The new Mayor took office in January 1974. He let everybody know, he won and they lost. The law & order crowd was done and he believed law & order was, "just to keep the Nig'… in line," which he told the press often. His Police Chief, Philip G. Tannian, who we called Elmer Fudd from the Bugs Bunny cartoon, was a yes man who took his orders from Frank Blount the #2 in charge. Tannian was only a token and Blount, with Coleman's direction, tried to, and somewhat succeeded in, enforcing more traffic violations, arrest and general laws in white areas. It was well known that the higher ups didn't want gambling, liquor, traffic or even narcotics enforced in black areas as much as before. To do that, they had to change the complexion of the street cops. We were enforcing the laws wherever and to whoever broke them. They immediately started to divide the police department on race. Promotions, transfers, assignments, etc. were no longer being strictly done by seniority and merit, but by race and their unique affirmative action rules. Only blacks and females were considered in their rules to be a minority, not Indians, Hispanics or any other race or ethnicity. For every white male promoted, there was 1 black male, or 1 black female or 1 white female promoted. Meaning a white male was only promoted, even with higher scores, for every other opening. Even if a white male scored 90% on the exam he sometimes could not get promoted. A minority, on the other hand, with this system, could get promoted from their list scoring 70%. There were also numerous non-test Mayoral promotions that used to be only for the Mayors bodyguards periodically. These promotions were also used to gain control of street enforcement and divide the police department on racial lines. Standards were lowered and minority hiring radically expanded and rushed to a dangerous level of incompetence. The Police Academy rules were eased and went from 13 weeks plus 2 weeks extra street training to 8 weeks total. While this was happening, crime skyrocketed and the attitude on the street became more and more violent and anti-cop, mirroring the Mayor and his cohort's attitude toward the cops. That was my opinion of how and when the big change started in 1974. As the story goes, illegal gambling profits helped to swing the election and from then on enforcement of gambling conspiracy cases were frowned on; especially mutual bets (numbers), which were done mostly in the inner City communities. The Racket Conspiracy Unit downtown had been basically neutered by downtown politics. Then my Lieutenant, who was in charge of our Precinct Special Operations Units, asked us if anybody in our unit had ever made any arrests or worked surveillance on gambling or conspiracies. There were only two in our unit, one of my partner's and me.

We were the only two who had made illegal numbers arrest while working Northern District Morality. Our Lieutenant set us up with the Organized Crime Prosecutor downtown that would be coordinating our cases with the

Organized Crime sections and the Racket Conspiracy Unit so no one would be working on the same cases. Our meeting with the Prosecutor went well, but he was skeptical that we would get anywhere as the other units had completely stopped any type of Gambling Conspiracy Enforcement. He also advised us to be very careful of leaks as that could end our investigations. The Lieutenant told us we were on our own with only the help of the Organized Crime Prosecutor. No one, including our Commanding officers, were even to ask us what we were doing. We were to advise them to contact the Prosecutor if they needed information. Unknown to us at that time, the Administration had already planned to eliminate all the Gambling Conspiracy Units with their new reorganization which would in my opinion (Surprise, Surprise) give the black organized crime group their reward for backing this new Administration. Looking back, our Lieutenant was pretty smart and knew it would take some time before anyone knew what we were doing out in the Precinct as this type of work just wasn't done at the Precinct level.

My partner, though his downtown connections, obtained old military type radios that used about 8-10 C-cell batteries and were on a frequency that hadn't been used in ages and were very secure. Without being on the police radio frequency, no one was able to monitor our communications. We used the radios when my partner was in a police helicopter by air and I was in a private vehicle on the ground to communicate the direction of the numbers runners so we could find the main office of the runner to get to the higher ups. It worked great on each and every case with the pilots keeping our presence and helicopter use a complete secret. They wouldn't ask what the end game was because we told them that a breach would end our investigation.

With this assignment, to avoid questions and curiosity of what we were doing, we did not set foot anywhere near or around the station. We would call the desk and tell the Sergeant to put us on duty in the morning, and then call in the afternoon and tell him to put us off duty. It was kind of like out of sight out of mind. We were on our own to do whatever it took to do the job. With my partner's connections, we got an old surveillance van that had not been used in years by Downtown Vice. He was able to get it without any paperwork or explanation. The old van had one way windows in the back and a disguised entry door from the cab to the back of the van. It hadn't been used for so long, it was never missed. We also would borrow for short term some of their new surveillance equipment like campers, again through his connections without paperwork. Step vans, trucks, demos and used cars from local car dealers were also available just for the asking.

I was amazed at the silence we got from everyone, civilians to supervisors, when we told them that if anyone leaked information about our investigations to the City, it would be shut down. It was very apparent that this Administration was immediately shutting down units and putting their insiders in positions that they could control like, executive officers, Internal Affairs, Precinct Inspectors, Personnel section (recruiting) and the newly formed Board of Civilian Police Commissioners to name a few. The others in charge quickly got the message to go along or else. That was just the Police Department, the rest of the City was also being rapidly changed by Affirmative Action and with rewards, to their loyal followers whether they were qualified or not. Overnight our fair & equal world turned one sided and it wasn't even being hidden. It was becoming very clear to us that what we were doing, if found out, could have repercussions on us instead of rewards. Just months before this kind of work would be encouraged and good results were acknowledged and rewarded. That was before the mass changes in the City. There seemed to be many reasons for the change in enforcement.

The Mayor himself was accused of being a bagman for the numbers racket years before and was under investigation by a young vice officer who had a file named File-88 that documented his actions and ties to the Black Organized Crime Group that took over gambling from the Italian Mafia. That young vice officer that had File-88 was rapidly moved up the ranks to Chief of Police until he was sent to prison years later. Unknown to us at the time, we were about to be sticking it to the Mayor's apparent benefactors who helped put him in office.

They thought that they had eliminated and controlled all the enforcement against the Black Organized Crime Groups on the illegal numbers rackets. It made millions of dollars off the backs of the poor and contributed to government corruption and narcotics operations. Later another top executive deputy chief, Frank Blount, had to retire early while under investigation and his protégé Deputy Chief Harvel supposedly committed suicide by shooting himself 'twice' in the chest.

It was found out later that the Italian Mafia was still getting paid by the Black Organized Crime group when an FBI probe was leaked that taped Giacalone and Eddie Wingate, the Mayor's old friend and head of the numbers organization, about an illegal numbers investigation by the FBI effectively ending it.

I didn't know then, but I suspect now, the reason we were successful in every one of our Conspiracy to Violate State Gambling cases was because no one except us two and the Organized Crime Prosecutor, who was rich and untouchable, knew what we were working on. Even the FBI's case was leaked and I don't think there was another case after ours, ever.

Our Lieutenant sure stirred the pot by cutting us loose and hooking us up with an honest prosecutor who seemed to really enjoy what we were doing. We followed our bag man runner to their drop off house and then set up surveillance for 4-6 weeks using the vehicles and techniques mentioned before.

We had an informant that we sent to the house who made direct bets to confirm the illegal betting activity going on at the location and confirm who was running it. We spent weeks in our surveillance vehicles freezing or sweating depending on the weather. One of us watched the activity of the subjects and what they were bringing into the location through binoculars and the other recorded what was observed in a journal. We would describe the subjects using an ID like John Doe #1, #2, #3, etc. with a description of each subject. We rotated between watching and recording the acts, so we both knew who our John Does were. They were so confident that they openly carried cash and bet slips in their hands sometimes or brown paper lunch bags.

For a conspiracy warrant we had to have 7-day surveillance so that meant no days off sitting quietly in the back of a stuffy cold or hot van. Not exciting or fun like I was used to, but knowing this was off limits under this new Administration made it easier. It was still boring which was new to me; I hadn't experienced being bored in the last 3 plus years.

My partner would take care of our informant by taking him to the methadone clinic, etc. and told me the informant said the houses he was going to give us were part of a dangerous organization that was politically connected. He mentioned the name Wingate and was scared if anyone found out he would be done for and maybe we would be too. We decided to keep that information to ourselves, but to be very careful from then on, even off duty by changing our travel routes and habits. I was happy that my kids and ex-wife were now in suburbia, out of harm's way. If they were going to follow me or get information from the Police Department, I was listed as single and living in the City. I figured they would try and eventually stop us before anything violent would happen to us, but our informant would be in immense danger. From then on and throughout my career I made it a habit to pay attention to my surroundings and not be naively trusting. Paranoia will keep you alive in this business as I later found out in run-ins with those that are connected to organized crime.

The First Conspiracy Raid

Once we had enough evidence, we typed up our warrant request, had it signed by the Organized Crime Prosecutor, and then raided our first upper level gambling organization location. It couldn't have gone any better; they were caught totally off guard thinking they were protected and untouchable. We confiscated money, bet slips and most important, their books containing house locations, runner's names and their routes. The damage we caused was that all their main houses and collections points had to be shut down and relocated at great expense and trouble to the whole organization. Most of their customers would claim they had bet the winning numbers for the day of the raid because the winning number was determined by the daily horse races and customers knew it. We had just kicked open a big hornet's nest and we knew it. They would now know who went rogue and would be under pressure to stop us. This was going to get harder for us and more dangerous from then on. A few days later we were summoned to meet with the Organized Crime Prosecutor at his office.

As we entered, he had a big smile on his face and kept shaking our hands and patting us on the back saying great job over and over. He proceeded to tell us we had a perfect case for the felony of Conspiracy to Violate State Gambling laws and the defendant's lawyers knew it. They wanted to make a plea deal. He made it clear it was 100% our choice and he could win at trial. We knew a trial would take time and with only two of us we couldn't start another case until the trial was over. So we decided to let them plead guilty to Engaging in an Illegal Occupation. Then we could go after more of their location's and disrupt their activities, and give everybody involved a great big headache. We were hoping to cause discord among the organized crime groups and politicians who were supposed to be protecting them. The prosecutor was extremely happy with our choice to stir things up and go after them, but warned us it would be harder now and to be very careful as we were the only ones working these cases and would be hanging out there all alone. The surveillance part was boring, but I sure liked this part of poking the bear in the eye when we weren't supposed to. Our Lieutenant, who most likely knew a lot more about the damage we did, was ecstatic with us. He reiterated to us to keep going, but be careful on and off duty and he would cover for us as long as he could. We took a few days off and partied like hell.

Conspiracy Case #2

We went through basically the same procedure as our first case using the helicopter and equipment that we borrowed before. The difference was that the pilots now knew what we were doing when we borrowed the equipment. They were still more than willing to help and keep quiet. We drove around and around following each other sometimes to protect our target location so we couldn't be followed. My partner checked with his connections downtown and helicopter crews periodically to make sure no one was on to us without us knowing. I learned how to follow and surveil subjects from my training at Downtown Vice years before and watched for signs of that happening. I'll never know for sure, but I did eventually spot what could have been surveillance on me a few times. One time, two white males, in a mostly black area, seemed to be behind me after a couple of turns. To be sure, I made a quick right turn off of Van Dyke onto a side street and then another quick right turn on the first side street and turned around in the first driveway so that I was going directly back at them if they were following me, and they were.

I pulled up to their driver's window, with my driver's window, side by side, and matter-of-factly told them they were pretty sloppy. They both had very surprised expressions and drove off without responding. Maybe paranoia, but we were still doing what wasn't supposed to be done and got another conviction with more books, evidence and more headaches for the illegal operators like the first raid.

Conspiracy Raids #3, #4, #5

After a couple of days off we set up a file cabinet with a padlock in our Morality/Narcotics office because the books and paperwork were loaded with information and connections to the illegal numbers racket with names, locations and information that we hadn't even digested yet. We were trying to keep hitting them every six weeks or so because you had to have that much surveillance to obtain warrants. With just two of us, we didn't have enough time to go higher yet. We decided to keep disrupting their operations while collecting information for later use. Still no one openly questioned us on what we were doing, but we were told everyone, including us and our Precinct Narcotics Unit, had to have our informants finger printed and photographed. Then they would be given ID numbers to be kept downtown. Stupid we weren't. We were not about to get our informant killed or outed by sloppy file keeping or even worse, corrupt cops or politicians who might want our rogue operation stopped. So we did what any street smart cops would do, we just ignored the request. We stayed out of sight as we raided and got convictions, books & evidence on third and fourth conspiracy cases to the delight of the Organized Crime Prosecutor and our Lieutenant who were now feeling the heat. We, two determined cops, had done our job and got 100% convictions on more cases than all of Organized Crime and the Racket Conspiracy Squad had gotten in years and did it in only a matter of months. It was all done by just the two of us, with no help or support. In my recollections, normally there would be a big deal made and others would be trying to take credit for big arrests, but not for our cases. There was just dead silence from the higher ups.

WILLIAM L. CAHALAN
PROSECUTING ATTORNEY

PETER KARAPETIAN
CHIEF ASSISTANT

COUNTY OF WAYNE
OFFICE OF THE PROSECUTING ATTORNEY
DETROIT, MICHIGAN

FRANK MURPHY HALL OF JUSTICE
1441 ST. ANTOINE STREET
DETROIT, MICHIGAN 48226
TEL. 224-5777

May 15, 1974

Inspector Revel Brawner
Detroit Police Department
11th Precinct Station
3812 E. Davison
Detroit, Michigan 48234

Re: People v. Smith;
People v. Ashton;
People v. Jenkins;
People v. Middlebrook

Dear Inspector Brawner:

This will advise you that two of your officers assigned to the Vice Bureau have been in contact with this office on numerous occasions in the past few months, successfully preparing and completing four gambling cases. These officers are Officers David Kap and Albert Boudreau, both of whom individually and jointly have done excellent work in preparing and processing these cases. They have performed their duties with diligence, ingenuity and considerable skill.

It is unusual to have such ability and skill arising out of a precinct unit because ordinarily we see this type of building only in the specialized units such as the Rackets Conspiracy Section.

I wish to bring this matter to your attention as I believe a commendation of their work and ability is in order. I further appreciate the fact that other officers, including one of your Lieutenants cooperated greatly when it became necessary to execute search warrants in these cases.

Very truly yours,

ROBERT STEVENS
ASSISTANT PROSECUTING ATTORNEY

cc - Officer D. Kap
Officer A. Boudreau

While we were finishing up our 5th and final conspiracy case, also with guilty pleas just like the other four, we received a copy of a letter sent to our Precinct Inspector from Robert Stevens the Organized Crime Prosecuting Attorney advising our Inspector that a commendation was in order on our work and ability in gambling cases with our diligence, ingenuity and considerable skill that was unusual at the Precinct level and only built in specialized Units like the Rackets Conspiracy Section. We received no Commendation or even a Letter of Appreciation from our Inspector. He didn't even give us a copy of the Prosecutors letter that was sent to him and copied to us, just dead silence. Our Inspector was not aware of our activities until he received the letter. The Prosecutor was trying to give us acknowledgement for our work which resulted in him accidentally outing us.

In my opinion our Inspector had only one way out if he wanted to get along with the political higher-ups. Instead of rewards, that we really didn't expect, we were immediately disbanded and placed back in uniform in one of the most dangerous assignments. A Special Ops Unit called The 80-Series Felony Car that was usually voluntary. This unit handled only priority 1 and 2 calls in progress and actively hunted violent felons.

I was fine with the change as I was bored to death with surveillance type work and welcomed going back into the action that I originally signed up for, and was good at. My poor partner hadn't worked uniform in years and never worked in high crime areas; he was totally lost and upset with the change. He immediately started working on a transfer through his Downtown connections. In the meantime, he took our file cabinet with all the books of the gambling organizations information home and hid it.

Sure enough they still wanted to register our informant. Since our detail was so abruptly ended, as if it never existed, we no longer used an informant. We gave them nothing. They were very insistent and wanted to know who he was very badly. We said we would take his identity to our grave as we promised him. I was also asked a few times by supervisors about what happened to our gambling case files. I found that strange because they had nothing to do with gambling cases and shouldn't even have known about them. When asked, I responded that I didn't know where they were and that they were in the Morality office locked in a file cabinet the last time I saw them. I never heard or asked what happened to the files which contained a lot of information on Black Organized Gambling houses that in my opinion this new Administration didn't want to be used.

My partner was transferred to the Organized Crime Surveillance Section Downtown and not to long later, at 29 years old, had a brain aneurysm that crippled him and caused a loss of memory. I don't know to this day what happened to the files and they were never mentioned to me again. I was always a little curious as to what happened and why all the silence as we opened one hornets nest after another until they just abruptly stopped us while we were having more success than all Downtown units combined. Case after case without the slightest acknowledgement and then rewarded with a transfer to one of the most dangerous assignments in the City. Both the helicopter pilot and his observer were later killed in a crash over the Detroit River.

1974, in my opinion, was the real beginning of Detroit's downfall, but I was going to do my part to help the good people no matter what and enjoy the journey. While we were working Conspiracies, four more officers were shot by a barricaded gunman on January 16, 1974 with two dying from their wounds, Sgt. Leonard M. Todd & Officer Edward Pakula Jr.

Then it hit home again as one of our Precinct Special Operations partners and friend Officer Gerald A. Morrison was ambushed, beaten, shot and killed on March 11, 1974 while investigating a local bar in plain clothes by the owner who he returned fire on and killed. Gerry was a good cop and we used to like to tease and joke with each other. It was another reminder that working the bars was still dangerous.

On May 25, 1974, we lost another officer, Brendt L. Stephens, who was shot and killed while chasing an armed suspect.

Police Week goofing around for a young citizen with Officer Gerald A. Morrison

CHAPTER 5

The 80 Series - Felony Cars

11-81

AT OUR FIRST ROLL CALL in years, before my partner's transfer came through, the Lieutenant was amazed because my partner had all his equipment on in the wrong locations - gun, ammo and handcuff case. The Lieutenant actually asked him, "Where in the hell is your weapon, officer?" It was in an old style flap holster in the middle of his back out of sight. The Lieutenant adjusted his equipment and introduced us to everybody who mostly knew each other from their regular shift work. There were six of us working the 80-Series, three assigned to each car designated 11-80 and 11-81. All of the officers were hand-picked and would be working with limited supervision on the new 80-Series Units as Felony Gun Cars and would only receive priority 1 and 2 runs and back up shift cars to serious runs. This was to be our first and last roll call and we wouldn't have a direct supervisor as everyone was experienced.

We were to check the teletypes for crimes, the desk for special attentions, the Detective Bureau, and also make ourselves available to assist in raids, barricaded gunmen, etc. We were part of the Precinct Special Operations Unit and would work two shifts,

7pm - 3am and 11am - 7pm. Tickets and misdemeanor arrest were good, but felony arrests were the priority of these new units. We were supplied with new scout cars without shields so we could work as three man units, when necessary. We carried the extra-large bullet proof vest (there weren't smaller vest at that time), shotgun, M1 Carbine and tear gas gun with masks in each unit for raids and barricaded gunmen runs as there were no such thing as SWAT units in the 1970's.

The Precinct Cruiser or Big Four had been eliminated as was S.T.R.E.S.S. and was missed. Apparently our units were to try and fill that gap as violent crimes were increasing throughout the City, but especially in the 11th Precinct as the law abiding whites and blacks fled and the neighborhoods changed. The guys in this unit were experienced and go getters. They knew we were Vice undercover cops who were put into a tough situation and they tried to lookout for us by backing us up on our runs. We knew where the bars were, but not how the addresses in the Precinct were configured. When we had a hot call they would key their radio mic's and blurt out the bar that was the closest. We would then start going in the right direction to respond quickly as we figured out the addresses.

The dispatchers, who usually wouldn't tolerate any unprofessional chatter, must have been clued in because they never questioned it. It didn't take long for me to get into the groove with these guys and my new assignment. It was exactly what I liked. I had a really good base and more street experience than anyone thought because of my inner City training from working at the 7th. The 11th precinct was just starting to get as rough. I wasn't just one of those plain clothes partying Vice guys; I had handled homicides, shootings and knew how to handle myself in tough situations. My new partners and co-workers were pleasantly pleased that they not only didn't have to babysit me, but could totally trust and depend on me.

Yes, this was even better than old #7. All of the guys in Special Operations were gung ho and anxious to put the bad guys away. The parts I didn't like about being in uniform, we usually didn't have to do like, accident reports, traffic enforcement, dead bodies, and special details, or take reports on crimes that were long over. Depending on how you look at it, I was allowed to be in the middle of what was happening now over and over all night long 24/7 and that was what I was here for and worked with guys that felt the same. I took my job seriously and my off duty partying just as seriously, especially on our boats.

Before my partner transferred, he introduced me to two officers from aviation, the crew that took him up when we were working on Organized Crime Gambling Surveillance. One of them re-did the canvas on my boat and I was just getting to know him when their police helicopter crashed in the Detroit River after a collision with a small plane. On June 28, 1974 we lost two more fine officers, Byron B. Soule Jr. and Jon Ryckman from the aviation section.

Too many funerals, too many widows and orphans of good young men who died violently because they chose to protect and serve in a dangerous community where some really needed them and others hated them. Some ignored their sacrifice and some, us that knew them, and buried them, hurt for them and their families for the rest of our lives.

When our Lieutenant of Precinct Special Operations, who we would do anything for, asked a special favor of us when we were working the day shift from 11am - 7pm which was slow for us. He asked something I really didn't want to do and he made it clear we didn't have to. He asked if we would be pallbearers for a deceased 90 year-old Detroit Cop, requested by his widow who was in her 90's. Six of us went out to suburbia with our white gloves on and took turns standing by his casket in two's and then carrying his casket to his grave. We weren't an honor guard and kind of made it up as we went along. Of all the sad funerals that I attended, this one made me feel proud and good that we could give this family something to remember and that his Blue family still cared. I didn't know who he was or whether the department supplied pall bearing for non-duty deaths or if the Lieutenant just wanted to give him a special send off. I did know his widow hugged us with tears in her eyes and was proud too of his send off by his Boys in Blue, as she called us.

I spent my on-duty time getting to know my new partners and the regular shift crews by going to shootings, hold-ups, and showing up to back them up or even beating them to very serious radio runs when I could. I was proving to them, and to myself, that although small, I wasn't afraid of anything or anybody. I was working with a new bunch of guys and like #7, Northern District

Morality, and #11 Special Ops, I was still the smallest cop in the crew and in Detroit at the time. The new Chief had just eliminated the height requirement completely and it would be a while before it would be noticed with the other changes the new Administration was making to change this department that the new Mayor made clear that he hated.

With the new lowered standards, they were mass hiring females and recruiting in inner City high crime areas. An Officer Candidate School was created to prep the minorities for the promotional exams. Civilians replaced light duty officers who knew street situations and how to relay information on 911 calls with people who didn't have any street experience making it more dangerous for us and the public. For instance, the operators would ask the caller a bunch of questions that were formatted that didn't exactly pertain to their call and never pass on the pertinent information to the cops on the street. On a shooting call, sometimes all we would get was a disturbance or a family trouble which did not prepare us properly for what we were going into.

Before the change, light duty officers were there to heal from their various injuries and they would know what to ask and would pass on pertinent information like, description of the perp, weapons, directions, condition of the injured, etc., etc. They knew by their own street experience, what information was needed and whether or not it was a phony or real call. There were never enough scout cars to waste their time on false runs. Experienced cops could determine that, opposed to civilians sending a car to every call while those in real need had to wait for help.

After the change we could really tell the difference as we were getting calls like a Burglary in Progress that was 12 hours old or a phony shooting because they didn't want to wait or go to the Police station to make a minor report. Cops who couldn't work the street because of an injury would screen calls much better than unqualified civilians.

In 1974, I didn't know just how bad it would get. At that time, before all the changes took effect, I worked with a good bunch of cops who I trusted with my life and well-being. We really would die for each other and didn't hesitate to risk our lives for the citizens we were there to protect.

11-81 Choir Practice

When I worked Morality we didn't have Choir Practice because our job was, on most nights, to drink all night to blend in. The new 80-Series Gun cars did though. Joseph Wambaugh's book, "The Choir Boys" came out in 1975 after our end of shift drinking parties had already started, but we quickly picked up the name as most of us read his books. His books were an accurate depiction of what we were actually living on a daily basis. It was funny how real his books were. The movies, as usual, were not as good as the books because of the re-writes that were done. Even Mr. Wambaugh wouldn't promote some of the movies because the story line was changed to push an anti-cop agenda, instead of the truth and were inaccurate to the books story line. Still, any big city cop, at that time, saw themselves or somebody they worked with in the stories he wrote.

We worked 7pm - 3am and usually one of our units would pick up a couple of cases of beer at a local party store located near the station just before the 2am closing. After we got off duty at 3am, we would all meet in the furthest corner of the parking lot. One of my partners would park his big old gray nine-passenger station wagon that we called "The Gray Ghost" there. We would meet in rain, snow or even tornado warnings, nothing would stop us. It was our unwinding session and got really crazy at times; we had a lot of steam to blow off, and it was better than therapy. If you were early enough to get a seat in the Gray Ghost, it would be a little more comfortable even with all the windows open. At that time, everybody smoked which made it hard to breathe in the car or even move; in 1974 Special Operations Cops were pretty big guys. When the Gray Ghost was full with all the seats taken, some of us would be standing outside the car drinking beer telling stories of the night's experiences with an inch or so of snow on our heads while dancing around to keep warm. Women officers, regular shift guys, and supervisors weren't accepted at our "Choir Practice" unless they were proven go-getters and, if they brought more beer. Special Ops and Choir Practice was something that had to be earned. The Precinct Cruiser (Big Four), Eighty-Series, B&E Car, Precinct Narcotics, Morality Crews and officers who were accepted as fill-ins were the main group.

Some of the regular shift supervisors, who liked to work, would stop by for a quick beer and a laugh then move on. The Police Chaplin who we called "The Rev", liked to ride with us because we didn't have shields in our cars and only handled serious in-progress calls, would have a beer with us and then leave before it got wild.

There was a public library next to the police station that backed up to a large park with baseball fields called, Jane field. Both were closed and off limits to the public at night. The library parking lot wasn't visible or near anything so it was perfect for our new Choir Practice location for years. During these times, someone would always end up doing something goofy, crazy, or sometimes dangerous after a few beers. One night one of our Sergeants bet my old morality partner, once a Marine and quite a character, that he couldn't climb the prep radio tower. The radio tower was over 100 feet high and was fenced in. After a few more beers and with a bunch of guys egging him on, he agreed to do it for $50. Up he went without looking down and he touched the giant light bulb on the top. He then turned around and looked down at us in his victory pose and then totally freaked out, clinging to the ladder and yelling for us to call the fire department to get him down.

We were all drunk and in uniform telling him we can't call the fire department. He had to climb down himself. That went on for quite a while, yelling at him to come down and him clinging on to the ladder and yelling back to us in panic because of the height. It was getting close to day light and we had to leave so one of the guys said I'll get him down and started slowly shooting at the big bulb just above him. It worked! He came down so fast it looked like he was repelling out of a helicopter. It was like a comedy stunt in a movie and we were all laughing so hard we could hardly stop him from attacking the cop who was doing the shooting. After he calmed down, the Sergeant gave him the $50 and we all left still laughing our butts off. He had just become one more of the legends of the Detroit Police Department. It was frowned on for women or civilians to attend our choir practice because of trust and the guys couldn't open up as they could and would amongst each other. There was one woman who loved cops and was totally trusted by this wild bunch. We didn't hit on her as we accepted her as a true supporter who knew our inner feelings and we all liked and respected her. She could take it and dish it out just like the rest of us. She eventually bought the bar next door to the station and renamed it The Precinct Pub and immediately turned it into a cop bar. Every so often, after closing her bar, she would still stop by our Choir Practice with a big bag of beer at 3am. She could write a book of her own from what she had seen and heard. Hopefully, if she does the X-Rated parts will get left out or at least cleaned up.

Bobby

I spent the end of 1974 working 11-81 with great partners in a great unit with supervisors who supported us. We were making a lot of felony arrests and taking guns off the streets on pat down searches by our units. On the two 80-Series cars we quite often worked on each other's units so we all became close and knew how each other worked under pressure. There was never, no matter how bad the call, a time that I remember any of us having to call for a backup. We knew as soon as one of our units could get to us, they would. Sometimes both of our cars would respond to the same call or at least be heading in that direction. There just were no dead beats on our units. We faced danger daily together and partied nightly at our Choir Practices with everyone very close to each other.

It was just before Christmas, I was single and wanted the night off to go partying at my favorite bar, Gino's Falcon Show Bar on Van Dyke. The problem was one of our two units was already shut down and just two of us were working leaving only one unit running. I complained that I was senior and the Sergeants gave the night off to officers that had less seniority. Then one of the younger officers from 11-80 volunteered to work with my regular partner so I could have the night off. I gladly accepted his offer and thanked him for working for me. I had worked with him numerous times. He was a quiet, nice guy and a good street cop who liked working with us.

Thinking no more about it, I went to the bar. A short time later one of the other cops who was at the bar asked if I heard that a cop had just been shot and killed from #11. I don't know why, but I somehow knew it was Bobby. Everything seemed to go silent and I felt an emptiness in the pit of my stomach and felt dizzy. I told myself to calm down as one of the guys went to the station to get the details. When he came back he told us it was 11-80 conveying a prisoner and Officer Hogue was shot in the back of the head and killed instantly. My regular partner had to rollout of the still moving scout car while shooting it out with the suspect who was finally shot and killed by a responding Tactical Mobile Unit officer. The suspect had emptied his hidden gun at my regular partner after shooting Bobby and then removed Bobby's gun from his holster and continued firing at my regular partner.

December 21, 1974, Robert John Hogue, my friend and Eighty-Series Partner, was killed while taking my place and working for me. It was a nightmare come true and I blamed myself for not being there and letting them both down. I don't think either of them had worked much together before and weren't used to how each other worked. When I saw my partner again, he was totally changed, we looked at each other with tears in our eyes and he said, "Why weren't you there?" I knew what he meant and he didn't say it to blame me, but he knew if I was there, it wouldn't have happened. Even though he didn't say those words to be mean, I have never forgotten them. There is nothing anybody could have said to me because I have never forgiven myself and have been unable to talk, write or face it until now while writing this book. My partner and I were never the same. We never talked about it after, but sometimes there would be moments when a thought of Bobby would come over me and I think at the same time him too, and we both would have to shake off the tears forming in our eyes.

The funeral was on Christmas Eve, and a lot like the other Police funerals I've attended – flags folded, taps, 21-gun salute and big tough macho cops with tears running down their cheeks with widows and orphans in shock. TMU covered our Precinct and we were up front again just like my first funeral at #7 when my first mentor was killed on my day off four years before. There had been 23 officers killed in my short four-year career so far, but this one completely tore my heart out. It wasn't supposed to be this way and it happened because I wasn't there. I was still living in the apartment with my old partner from #7 who worked the Accident Car and we usually didn't talk work as we were doing opposite types of duties. The next day was my second Christmas since being divorced and I didn't feel very Christmassy. I had bought toys and spent the day at my ex-wife's house with the kids playing and I couldn't help but think about Bobby's family, his widow and little boy at Christmas. I was quiet and not very festive and my ex-wife got mad because of my mood. I was glad the kids were happy and playing with their new toys. I tried to tell her about what happened and why I was a little down, but like before, she didn't want to hear about it. So with no one to talk to about the guilt and pain I felt, I just stopped trying to talk about it to anybody.

It was a slow depressing ride home missing my family and knowing Bobby's family was missing him. I thought about him often as they put us right back in the same scout car without a shield every day that reminded us over and over what happened. We worked even harder taking more chances almost suicidal and pushing the limits on and off duty. Everything changed in my senior partner after the shooting. He was a church going good husband and father and then hit the bottle, got divorced and went wild just like me. We were still hard working honest cops, but emotionally I totally withdrew and held everything I saw and felt inside to survive and carry on like a lot of us did. Unlike today, there wasn't any help for us except the so called Police Psychiatrist who was a suburban social worker who specialized in sexual disorders. He didn't even have a degree in psychology let alone psychiatry. The department didn't require or offer any serious type of help, but would put you on what we called 'The rubber gun squad' which nobody wanted. The City didn't recognize P.T.S.D., Post-Traumatic Stress Disorder; they didn't want to be responsible to treat us or retire us. So we tightened our belts and carried on without treatment. I had enough seniority to get an inside job or go to a bureau, but I couldn't leave the street and not be out there. I had to prove to myself that I still had it and wasn't afraid daily.

Somebody had to do the dirty dangerous work and that was right up our alley as some of us didn't know anything else. The funny thing is, we needed to work to survive, but we were pushing the limits on the street like it could be the last day and lived the same way off duty. Loosing Bobby changed me and my partner's life forever.

In just under 5 years on the job there were twenty-three officers killed and 10 more that committed suicide. Three of the suicides were co-workers and numerous others were shot and wounded. When we first received our badges as rookies, our blood type was taped to the back. As innocent rookies we didn't think about it. My rookie innocents were long gone now.

11-81 / Under Fire

March 15, 1975, Officer James Watts died a year after being wounded during a Narco raid. Highland Park Detective, John Paul Tsolis, was also killed during that Narco raid on April 16, 1974.

On April 14, 1975 I received my 4th Citation/Commendation for "Arresting two felons for assault with intent to commit murder while placing my life in great danger." While working 11-81 we received a radio call on a disturbance by two men with a rifle at the Blue Moon Lounge on 8 Mile, firing shots inside the bar. As we pulled up the patrons of the bar pointed out a vehicle that was just pulling away from the curb and told us they just shot at them, trying to kill them. We pursued the vehicle through side streets with lights and sirens at a high rate of speed turning left and right. They tried to lose us and after a while with us still on their tail, the passenger hung out the window and started firing shots directly at us until we curbed their vehicle at Amrad & Caldwell. After a brief struggle both subjects were placed under arrest. This was the 5th time that I had knowingly been shot at and I couldn't count how many times I heard gunfire in our general area or had looked down the barrel of a gun before a subject dropped it. After losing so many co-workers and seeing so many victims of violence day after day I was so angry that it scared me. I just wanted to kill them and almost did before he tossed his now empty rifle.

There came a point that I didn't know what to do; I didn't want to get off the streets, that was my life now and I know I was good at it. Strangely, I still wasn't scared of dying; just being disabled and unable to do my job. At that point I was feeling very angry at the predators and disgusted by what was starting to happen to the City and the Police Department that I loved. I was frustrated because I didn't know what to do about it, so I did what I always did, put one foot in front of the other. Each and every day was a new and different challenge. One minute to the next you would go from calm to chaos and then back again leaving no time to dwell on the past. I tried not to think about what I saw people do to each other and even how supposedly normal people ignore the plight of real victims. They just didn't know and didn't want to know about their suffering unless they were personally affected.

On duty I was always busy, but off duty sometimes when things slowed the old mind would slip back to the past. My solution for that was to be around the people who had the same problem. There came a point that I was very seldom around civilians any more as they didn't understand. I had totally and completely turned into one of those guys I saw who had that far away stare. I would wonder what those eyes had seen; now I knew. The only relief was women, booze or the next battle which I always found. Surprisingly, my system worked and a lot of women respected my being upfront with them instead of playing head games with their emotions. I was not husband material anymore with my job and life style and it worked for me.

The House – Moving Back

Finally, after sitting vacant for months my ex-wife decided it would be easier for her to sell my house back to me for cash opposed to paying a realtor. In the 1970's whites were dumping their houses at a loss because of the changing City. The Administration was actively enforcing residency requirements for cops and fire fighters so, being alone, broke, and with our apartment building becoming a haven for crime, it was time to move. My roommate had all the furniture from the apartment and my ex left the kitchen appliances with the washer and dryer for a fee, of course. With child support for four children, school clothes, and miscellaneous expenses, I didn't have much to live on with a cops pay. I didn't need or want a lot but to help with expenses, I had two roommates move in paying rent and part of the utilities, and we split the food three ways. I basically lived on the cheap which worked out well on my budget. It did feel a little strange and sad moving back in the same house that used to be my family's home, with my kids running around and with the same neighbors with their kids. I was glad that my kids were safe and happy in suburbia where they could grow up and not see the changes in me or the City. Whether it was the right decision or not, I didn't want my kids to grow up hardened. I remembered when I was a naïve lily white kid from suburbia growing up and it was better out there than in the changing City where you had to be hard to survive.

Luke & Bolton's Bar Riot

My partner and I were animal lovers and a lot of the citizens weren't and others just turned their heads to animal cruelty to avoid trouble. There was an anti-cruelty organization on Conant that was in our Precinct. When we saw an abused animal we would just go in the yard and take it and we didn't care if the owners came out to try to stop us. Most of the dogs were in pretty bad shape, but the girls at Anti-Cruelty were volunteers who really cared and appreciated us rescuing the dogs because they couldn't. Now, looking back, we probably shouldn't have done it the way we did, but nobody else cared so we just got the job done like always, our way. After losing Bobby I think we both became more hardened and definitely different than before and maybe with a mindset that might have been a little suicidal or at least more than willing to push the limits.

We would stop and check on the injured and sick dogs that we brought in to see how they were doing, when we could. On one visit, since I had just moved back into my house I thought I would ask if they had a dog for me. We were working days so just before the end of our shift we went over to Anti-Cruelty to find me a dog. The girls were all excited about it and they said they had the perfect dog for me that had been hard for them to place. When they went into the back to get him I said to my partner, "Did they say, hard to place?" He said don't worry about it you're doing a good thing. Yeah, that was easy for him to say. When they came out with Luke, I stepped back and put my hand on my gun. I had never seen a dog that big – he was huge. They told me he was a 10 month old Harlequin Great Dane and was gentle, but frisky because he was still a pup. He had his shots and was ready to go. He was a smart dog too; he walked past everyone, right to me and leaned on me as if he knew he was going home with me. She handed me his leash and we just walked out to the scout car. He climbed in the back seat and off we went. We must have looked pretty strange driving into the station by some of the looks we got. We had the cars without the shield and Luke just sat like a person as calm as could be, looking out the side window at the people that were staring back. His head nearly touched the roof of the car. We had to laugh as we must have looked like a new type of dog car with a black and white Marmaduke type dog. I was amazed at how calm he was and easy going being a pup in new surroundings.

When we pulled into the station to check off duty the Sergeant advised us we were not going anywhere. We were told to get our riot gear, helmet with shield, gas mask and riot stick and meet up in the garage area immediately. I told the Sergeant that I had just picked up a dog from Anti Cruelty and had no one to pick him up. I asked if he could be put in the fenced-in auto pound behind the station. He said ok and I locked Luke in the pound with a big bowl of food and water and an old blanket from a rear car seat that was there.

I told the front desk personnel that he was there and left a note with the big bag of dog food behind the desk so that they would take care of him. I also told them to notify the next shift that he was friendly because I didn't know when I would be back at the station.

We were formed into 8-man riot squads with a Sergeant in charge and loaded into two cars and headed out to Livernois and Fenkell where a riot was beginning. It started when a white bar owner shot and killed a black man who was breaking into a car in the parking lot of Bob Bolton's Bar. When confronted, the suspect went toward the owner armed with a screw driver and was shot by the bar owner. A crowd formed and an older white passerby was beaten to death with a chunk of concrete. Of course the rumors said it was a black kid that was just innocently walking by and was shot in the back by the white bar owner. When we pulled up into the staging area we were directed to park our vehicles right behind a double line of vehicles parked in the middle turn lanes of Livernois. All the police cars were parked front to back and side to side with no way of moving after the vehicle behind pulled up to your rear. We were told to leave the keys in the ignition, what for we didn't know as there was no way to move the cars.

Our Sergeant was an old salt who had been through the 67 & 68 riots and asked the Lieutenant why the cars weren't being parked at an angle so they could be pulled out if necessary. The Lieutenant sarcastically told him the new command didn't have a clue and weren't listening to anybody. That sure didn't make us feel very confident of surviving this riot in one piece. We began marching toward the roar of the crowd to the police line, the closer we got the louder it was. We could see the police line had been pushed back and some of the scout cars in the middle of the street were burning and rocks, concrete and other objects were being thrown at the police line. Suddenly our Sergeant said, "Halt, fuck this cluster fuck, we'll hold this corner," and he deployed us on the four corners of the street. The squads behind us marched forward into the smoke and ear splitting roar of the crowd and burning scout cars. Nobody said anything but we all kind of smiled at each other pleased with our experienced Sergeant's decision to claim the corner. Still with the heat in the 90's, smoke, noise and being right behind the line wasn't a very pleasant duty either. After a while, our old World War II steel pot helmets, that were war surplus and painted blue with a giant shield bolted to them, were so uncomfortable we used them to sit on instead of wearing them. People watching riots on TV, including me at one time, didn't have a clue what it was like for the cops during a riot situation. It is miserable, dangerous and very nerve racking to say the least. The only good thing is we have each other and trust each other and that got us through the long hours.

As the sun was setting, I saw a phone booth about a half block away and got permission from my Sergeant to call the station and see how my new puppy was doing. When the Sergeant on the desk answered the phone he was shocked that I was calling from the riot area to check on my dog. He told me the dog wouldn't let anybody into the auto pound and they couldn't release any cars, but that was ok and they would take care of the dog until I was relieved. He then asked me where I was and how I was calling. I told him I was in a phone booth on Livernois near Fenkell. There was a brief silence then he asked me if the light in the phone booth was on? When I told him it was, he said, "Are you nuts, didn't you ever hear of snipers?" With that, I answered, yes, hung up and looked around sheepishly as it was dark already. I had to laugh knowing the desk Sergeant was probably telling everyone what a nut I was calling from the middle of a riot in a lighted phone booth, in full riot gear, to check on a dog. Oh well, it wasn't the first time or last time I would be known for doing something crazy.

We were hot, tired, hungry and thirsty without anything to drink or eat for hours when all of a sudden an old car pulled up with a couple of old white guys inside. They were totally out of place in this war zone. They opened up their trunk and passed out sandwiches and pop for all of us. When we asked who they were and who sent them they told us they were from the Salvation Army and they just came on their own. We shook hands and thanked them and they headed off to another squad with the more than welcome and needed goodies.

I had been on duty 13 hours already with more to go before we were relieved. When we were back in the staging area the Red Cross had set up a trailer with coffee, pop and various snacks for the rear guard people and were actually selling it. Ever since that day, I gladly donate to the Salvation Army who actually came into harm's way with food and drink for us, without charging, and kept doing it until the disturbance was over days later. What they did meant a lot to us guys and I, for one, have always remembered it.

We were put on 12 hour shifts until further notice so I called my ex-wife who agreed to keep my puppy for the next few days. I got Luke out of the auto pound and he jumped into the back seat of my car and we headed to suburbia. When my ex got a look at Luke she was scared of him because of his size. His head was as big as a female lion, but the kids were all over him and he loved it. With Luke safe and sound, I headed back to Detroit for a few hours sleep then back to my corner on Livernois for riot duty. This time I picked up some Arby's Roast Beef sandwiches and stuck them inside my shirt with the rest of the squad laughing thinking I was nuts. They thought they would feed us. Five to six hours later when no one came with food or drink and we were joking about catching a rat to eat, I pulled the Arby's from my shirt and we all had a bite each. Old stinky Arby's tasted great as we thought that was going to be all we would eat. A couple of hours later, here comes some Salvation Army guys with sandwiches and pop again, which was very much appreciated. Now we knew our commanding officers weren't going to take care of us anymore than they did the burnt up scout cars. They were in the back area, far from harm's way having coffee and donuts with the Red Cross. Our new Police Chief and his hand-picked Deputy Chiefs from the Mayor's office were of the same mind set as the Mayor; they didn't like or care much about us street cops, or so it seemed. The next day we were relieved to go back to our Precinct duties but still on 12 hour shifts. I was amazed to see a lot of our businesses had been looted in small sections all over the Precinct.

The media played up the Livernois riot, but ignored the numerous little riots in the Precincts. When I went back on eight hours again and was able to pick up Luke, I was happy to see my ex wasn't scared of him anymore. He was roaming around upstairs with the kids and they loved his visit. As Luke and I were leaving and saying our goodbye's a large Doberman from the neighborhood came running toward us barking and growling. Not knowing the dog, I was just about to draw my gun when easy going Luke let out the loudest bark I had ever heard. The Doberman stopped in his tracks and he took off at full speed leaving us all laughing. Luke jumped in the back seat just like before and we headed to his new home.

I didn't know it at the time, but found out later, why we were ordered not to shoot and why there was such a large show of force during the riot. The Mayor and his family owned Young's Bar-B-Q Lounge Restaurant right next to Bob Bolton's Bar and the rioters were friends and customers of the owners of the Bar-B-Q Lounge. It got worse for the Young family later as the DEA was investigating the lounge for the sale of narcotics and involvement in the numbers operation. The Mayor's brother-in-law, Willie Volson, and dope king pin Kenny Garrett with some of his deputy Police Chiefs started falling one by one. One Deputy Chief killed himself by shooting himself 'twice' in the chest, another Deputy Chief retired early while under investigation, and another Deputy Chief was accused of supplying Federal subpoena information to the Mayor's Administration.

Looking back, I realized how lucky I was by just getting put back in uniform after busting a lot of their numbers houses. No wonder our informant was so scared back then, he knew who was now in charge of everything and their criminal connections. It also made me think maybe that was why our gambling conspiracy files were so important to some.

Getting back into working the 80-Series car kept me busy and my mind off of the past until we had two more officers shot in our Precinct. One was shot in the arm by a B&E man at Cunningham's Drug Store at 7 Mile and Van Dyke. When we went to visit one of them at the hospital, there was a metal bowl full of ice with bottles of beer in it. Somehow he got the doctor to write him a prescription for beer instead of drugs for pain and muscle shock. I wondered how in the hell he got the doctor to do that. My partner had the fortunate assignment of standing guard outside the door for security and he was half in the bag. Seems the prescription was being shared. As I left his room, I thought, as goofy as I was, this was even strange to me.

The other officer was shot while being held at gun point as two B&E men got the drop on him in an alley behind a commercial building. They had the gun up next to his head as responding units were pulling up and they thought the officers wouldn't shoot because they had the cop as a hostage. Wrong. The Officer knew the boys would be coming in shooting and as they approached he turned his head so he would get an angle wound instead of a straight on shot right through the head. The Officer was hit in the side of the mouth, knocking out some teeth and ending up near his ear. Both suspects were shot and arrested. I was told as a rookie if taken as a hostage the responding officers would shoot, so take whatever action you could. I don't remember if this was an official rule or a street thing, but these guys were a total different bunch than the ones who taught me that, years ago.

Suicidal Police Wife

Dispatch put out information that a female driving a white Ford with its license plate number was wanted for investigation. It was also put out over the radio that she was armed with her police officer husband's gun and was suicidal and to use extreme caution. My partner was driving and as I was writing the information down he suddenly said, there she is. I looked up and she was right in front of us and I thought "Oh shit" and turned on our overhead lights and siren. It happened so fast I didn't have time to think, but I knew I would rather be chasing a felon with a gun opposed to stopping a cop's suicidal wife with one. As we pulled her over, I thought about suicides by cop and I didn't want to kill anybody especially a troubled cop's wife who was armed. When she stopped she immediately got out of her vehicle with the gun in her right hand waving it all around and in our direction. She was crying and visibly very upset. I had at the same time exited my passenger door, drew my weapon, cocked it and had her in my sights with my finger on the trigger while yelling for her to drop it. She then slapped the gun on the roof of her car and stepped back to my great relief. My partner and I then hurried to her and placed handcuffs on her while securing the weapon. She then turned to me and said, "Were you really going to shoot me?" I replied, "If I had to." I hadn't time to digest what just happened yet and what or who really controlled my trigger pull. Was it experience, luck, good police work, or somebody else? All I know is I, most likely, would have gave her first shot if it was at me, but if she would have pointed her gun directly at my partner, I would have fired. It's hard to explain, but I think most cops knew they were out there to take the risk of harm to themselves, but not to risk others. Any way you look at it when you come that close to taking a human life it's scary especially when it's someone who needs help.

Narco Raids

One of the 80-Series functions was to be the uniform assist on Narco Raids because of our ability to work as a team and we all were highly experienced. I volunteered to be the shotgun man who was to go in first right after the ram men knocked the door open. Our bulletproof vests in the 70's were big and heavy and when I put it on it went all the way down to my knees. Being the smallest cop in the unit I usually got teased that if I ever fell over with the big vest on I would be like a turtle on its back and couldn't get up. Being the smallest did have a big advantage though, as soon as the usually two biggest cops hit the door with the ram, I would then quickly enter squatted down to about two feet high while screaming and racking the shot gun. I pointed it all around, like a crazy man with the other officers rushing in right behind me. With all the noise, sudden excitement, people and animals would usually freeze and some even including pit bulls would lose control of their bowels. At the same time, if through advance buys we knew that they had weapons, sometimes we would have officers throw old flashlight batteries through the windows. A shotgun man with an old beat up 12-gage would break out the bath room window to stop anyone from flushing the dope down the toilet. It was all pre-planned and choreographed to each location before the raid to make it safer for everybody, including the defendants. We didn't have flash bombs in the 70's so we were the flash bomb.

I don't remember how many raids I went on, but it was a hell of a lot of them and unbelievable adrenaline rushes each and every time entering the unknown. Sometimes we had to get creative so not to get shot. One dope house was an upper flat with a rear entrance and a long set of enclosed steps in a hallway that gave us no cover or escape from the bottom to the top with a steel door at the end. So the raiding party hid in the back of the building, while we pulled up in front next to their car with our roof light flashing. One of the Narco crew had parked a car at an angle almost touching their car to make it look like an accident. After noticing someone looking out the upper window in front, we walked around to the back and casually walked up the back steps from bottom to top. The adrenaline was pumping as there was no escape if they were on to us. When we got to the top I knocked and asked if they had a brown Ford in front and that it was just hit by a drunk driver. He said yes and as soon as he cracked the door we bum rushed ourselves in yelling, "Police, search warrant," and our downstairs crew rushed up. It was a perfect raid and no injuries. Not all raids go smoothly, but all the ones I was on were planned and executed well. We had a good Narcotics crew at #11 Special Ops. They had their hands full as the gangs were fighting it out to control the heroin trade.

The City was wide open and called the murder & arson capital as rival gangs murdered each other and burned each other's dope pads. For us street cops we didn't mind that so much, but as to why the higher-ups seemed to ignore it bothered us. We had a good idea years later when some of the top brass were being investigated by Federal Narcotics agents.

The brother-in-law of a former partner of mine and friend had worked in Organized Narcotics Surveillance; he told my former partner that he had turned in an audio tape that his surveillance team had made of some top brass of the police department meeting with top narcotic crime people. When he asked about the tape later he was told, "What tape?" We all were trying to figure it out, what happened to his investigation and ours suddenly ending. We guessed it most likely came all the way from the top and there was nothing we could do about it. He and his partner were moved to organized crime surveillance away from Narcotics to following the Italian Mafia around. He also told him he thought there was something fishy about Jimmy Hoffa's disappearance. Hoffa was on 7-day, 24-hour surveillance. He said when the Feds dropped surveillance, either the Wayne County Organized Crime Task Force, or his unit picked up the surveillance. Hoffa was always being watched except for the few minutes he disappeared. It seemed suspicious to us at the time. In my opinion, his disappearance was either a planned surveillance screw-up or a real mistake that was taken advantage of. There was no explanation of how it could have happened, to my knowledge.

Gangs / Motorcycle Clubs

The main East Side black gangs were the BK's (Black Killers) and Errol Flynn's strangely named after the white movie star. The Errol Flynn's were pretty smart knowing we would shake them down every chance we could. Unless we got the gun car that carried all their weapons we would come up empty. They passed out their guns just before shooting somebody or something up, and then would put the guns back in one vehicle; leaving them clean when we stopped them. They dressed well and were pretty clean cut looking unlike the street pushers we were used to and highly successful. This group fooled a lot of people for a while including the Mayor who announced they would be patrolling some east side area's like a neighborhood watch group. They were watching the Van Dyke and Harper area which was our area and burglaries and street crime went nuts. The Mayor's, 'Give a gang member a job watching neighborhoods' plan, was quietly ended with the increase in crime from the group that was doing the patrolling. The other gangs looked and acted like thugs and that made it easier for us to catch them dirty, which we did. Our motorcycle gangs, like the Renegades on 8 Mile, and the Outlaws at Mt. Elliott and 7 Mile, were smart enough to do their dirt in other areas and not in our Precinct where their club houses were located. When we did arrest them for something they were usually cooperative as they knew we could screw with them over and over. Some cops got macho on them, but as long as they cooperated we treated them fairly, like men. I have, on numerous occasions, run into some of them that I had arrested before while being off duty and by myself in a bar with no problems. It was explained to me that there was mutual respect because I didn't beat on them while they were handcuffed, or lie in court. Apparently, word got around and I never had a problem on or off duty, as I often partied in the same bars they did and with some of the same females.

CHAPTER 6

Morality Undercover Again

Precinct Morality 4th Time

There came a time after five years on the job, on the front line, where I knew I was getting burnt out. So, I thought about transferring downtown to the graphic arts section. With my design engineering background, I thought it might be possible. Then again, I thought with Automotive Design booming, I could triple my pay by going back into that field. I made a quick call to Modern Engineering and they were interested in talking money with me. When it came right down to it, I just couldn't do it. Too much of my life was here with these guys and I couldn't leave. I decided to go back to Morality which would give me a little break and a different type of excitement. There was an opening that would keep me in the Special Ops group in the same Precinct with the same guys, but back undercover.

Not much had changed; every night we went johning for prostitutes. The turnover rate of hookers made it easier to pick them up. The newer ones didn't know who I was and the older ones knew I would leave them mostly alone if they didn't out me or cause problems. Most of the street female hookers were junkies and a lot of them had pimps. The better looking cleaner girls usually worked the bars and looked down on the street girls. Being experienced morality officers our inexperienced fill-in Sergeants let us go out alone to lock up hookers and write up bars, and they would just sign the paperwork at the end of the night. The only problem was our old Sergeant X from Northern District and the early days in Precinct Morality was the regular Sergeant on the crew. He mostly let us senior guys work alone, but sometimes went with us. He tried to fit in and reward us with what he thought was a reward for good work by spending an evening at the drive-in or at his house playing Euchre. We would rather be left alone to work the streets or just have a couple of hours off early, but we played along like we liked playing cards or watching movies.

It was early December and bar closing time at 2:30am I was heading toward the station with the Sergeant and another officer in the back seat. Scout Car 11-6 put out information on the radio of 2 white males with a white female in the back seat, driving a black Pontiac and was armed. They were heading to Bisco's Bar on East 7 Mile and Shield Street, to kill the owner. The driver was armed with a sawed off shotgun and passenger had a pistol. We were plain clothes undercover with long hair and beards driving in an unmarked car and headed in their direction. I knew Bisco's had a reputation for assaulting customers and even had an injunction against the police not to enter their premises. With the detailed radio information and knowing the owner had a lot of enemy's, it sounded like we were in the right place at the right time. An undercover morality crew didn't have to respond to these types of calls, but we usually did. The Sergeant and my partner in the back seat were of the mindset not to respond. Even though we were right on it, my Sergeant told me to head into the station. Since I was driving and knowing my uniformed friends would be responding, I turned into the parking lot of Bisco's taking a quick look for the wanted vehicle then headed west in the alley with my lights out. All the while, my Sergeant and partner were grumbling that it was almost time to get off duty. As I got to the street at the mouth of the alley, I saw a black Pontiac with 2 white males and 1 white female sitting in it. The motor was running; they were on Shield Street facing 7 Mile watching the corner of the bar for the owner to come out side to his car. I quickly backed up a couple of feet so they couldn't see our vehicle and not to spook them. We put out the location of the vehicle and confirmation that they were waiting out on the radio and we exited our vehicle. My partners were back far enough that they didn't have them in sight and were discussing what to do next and wanting to wait for uniform cars. I told them we might not have time as the owner could come around the corner any second and that we had the advantage being behind and to the side of them. A few seconds later an 80-Series unit with my friend Reverend Lund in it came around the corner heading head-on to the armed suspect's and directly in the line of fire. I immediately charged the vehicle seeing the driver raising the sawed off shot gun and put my .357 next to his head and said loudly, "Drop it Mother Fucker, Freeze."

As this was happening, my two partners had frozen and were still back at the mouth of the alley where they couldn't see the scout car coming into the line of fire. My old partners from the 80-Series and Reverend Lund quickly exited their vehicle thinking I was alone and ordered the passengers out of the vehicle at gun point. Then after the fact, the Sergeant and my partner came around the corner to assist the 80-Series officers handle the evidence and prisoners. We went into the station to type up the report and as I was typing it Rev. Lund and the officers thanked me for charging the vehicle and possibly keeping anyone from getting hurt. Rev. Lund, knowing that I had not been baptized and knew it was a close call and that I had a lot of close calls in my career, told me he would baptize me in my own blood if needed, if I was a true believer and wanted him to. I replied that I was, and to go ahead, when needed.

The Rev and a few others were saying a Departmental Citation could be in order. After hearing that, my Sergeant said he would type the report which he never did and was now, after hearing awards being mentioned. Of course in his report he did it all while we just assisted. Anyway, I got my 5th Commendation/Citation instead of a Departmental Citation and they got the same. Anyone who is either in the Military or Cop business has had this happen to them at one time or another. As it is said, "What goes around comes around." When Reverend Lund and the 80-Series crew heard about his taking credit and getting the same award as I did, they told the real story to his embarrassment. I didn't really care, but it was nice to have the police Chaplin talking good about you. Also most of the days I was working, the Sergeant didn't go out with us, but met us later to sign all the reports. My other partner that night who went along without saying anything and accepting his award quit the job and took over his dad's Bar and eventually ended up in Federal Prison. Like I said, "What goes around ..." Most all of my partners were good hardworking honest cops. Another irony was that the bar owner who hated cops and obtained an injunction against cops in or around his establishment, was the very one whose life I probably saved by risking mine by violating his injunction. We never got a thank you from him and didn't expect one, but I hope he still didn't hate cops for doing their jobs.

Luke – Christmas 1975

1975 was ending and there was good and bad news for me. The bad news was I had to give my buddy Luke away or my roommates were going to move out and I couldn't afford that. I had a friend who was a bouncer at Gino's and the Duchess who had his own house and was a dog nut. He was 6'6" tall and when he met Luke they hit it off immediately. Two big dudes – I was happy and sad, but knew I couldn't keep him. A couple of years later he bought a beer and wine store on Van Dyke. I enjoyed visiting him and Luke quite often at the store, as he waited on his customers Luke would sit behind the counter quietly as if he was watching his back in case of trouble. Sure enough, two hold up men came in and had him at gun point when Luke attacked and was shot and killed by the gunman. That gave my friend enough time to grab his own gun and shoot the shooter with the other hold up man running out of the store. I felt terrible that Luke had been killed, but proud that the abandoned Harlequin Great Dane that I rescued years before was a real police dog and died a hero in my eyes. Usually after a store owner shoots or kills a hold up man the neighborhood thugs get the message not to screw with that store. From then on he never had a problem with the locals.

The good news was I had my house back and a stable place where I could spend all day Christmas day with my kids. I went to Toys-R-Us and tried to buy all four of them an equal amount of presents with spending an equal amount of money and that was totally impossible. Their piles just kept getting bigger and bigger and they loved it. Nothing like a guilt ridden Dad who didn't get to see them enough and wanted to spoil them when he could. We had a fantastic Christmas Day in 1975 and many more in every place that I lived. Christmas day was my special day with my kids.

Party House

With three single cops living in my house, it quickly turned into a party house. We had some rules: 1) When someone brought home a female, the others after a little while, would excuse themselves to their rooms so that he could be alone with the girl. That usually worked out pretty well. 2) The girls could spend the night, not the weekend, as some of them didn't want to leave the next day.

The difference between working undercover and partying off duty became blurred as I was almost doing the same thing in the same places. I used to joke that the only difference between us and a biker was our badges. We even partied with a lot of their girls who thought we were bad boys like the bikers. I guess I was, except I didn't do drugs. I had been undercover off and on for a lot of years and was more used to that wild life than how normal people lived and the way normal people thought. I had been in bed with the same girls who would tell me about their boyfriend's business activities and their connections to organized crime. With the violence and death that I had seen, I really did live one day at a time.

I tried to put everything I could in a 24-hour period. I "dated" dancers, waitresses, bar maids, nurses, and even groupies. Mostly night or shift workers like us who liked to live a little on the wild side at times. The places I went to were on the edge of society, the lower edge. I was still a hard working honest cop, but I was more at home with these people than the people of my old civilian life in the suburbs. Detroit was my City now and I was living it to the fullest – the good and the bad. Not all cops were like us, most cops went home to their families, but some cops lived the street life on and off duty unless when with family or civilian friends for short periods of time.

1976 A New Year

With the 1976 New Year, I was nearing 6 years on the job and on my fourth tour on Morality working undercover. Because of the lifestyle and drinking that was a part of being on a Morality unit, two years was usually the limit for this assignment. There were a few of us, in spite of the rule, that just kept getting back into it over and over. When starting to get burned out on Morality Undercover work, I would go to the 80-Series Felony cars until I would start burning out there. I would be jumping back and forth between two stressful jobs. Most guys would get off the street for a while, get into a bureau, or go back on a shift, instead of chasing one felony arrest after another. I didn't know why, but I had to constantly prove myself to myself everyday which would later catch up to me.

During this time as standards were dropped, we started to really notice the change in the quality of the officers and the new supervisors being hired or promoted. Another bad sign was the Federal investigations of our newly appointed deputy chiefs.

The Administration thought it was a good idea to save money by laying off cops because of budget shortfalls. Their plan was to lay off 1,000 cops by affirmative action, not by seniority. This would leave the less qualified and inexperienced officers working and the more qualified and experienced white officers laid-off. The plan was stopped due to a lawsuit and they ended up laying off the last hired.

Between the layoffs and officers manning the Mini Stations, the Precincts had limited coverage. We had four Mini-Stations in our Precinct that were funded by the Federal government. They took away shift officers so the shifts were lucky if they could put 2 or 3 scout cars on the street to cover 12 scout car areas. That was extremely dangerous for the citizens and the cops because there was no back up when needed. Even so, a lot of the street officers would rather work shorthanded than with unqualified officers who should not have been hired in the first place. The trained experienced officers trusted each other, black and white, but had a problem with those that were being hired and promoted in too much of a rush in order to change the racial aspect of the Department. It was too much, too fast and many should not have been hired.

In August of 1976 Cobo Hall, Downtown Detroit's Entertainment Center, was having a rock concert when the BK's (Black Killers) and the Errol Flynn Gangs forced their way into the concert which was being attended by mostly white suburbanite kids. The gangs robbed, assaulted and raped numerous kids. One girl was gang raped right outside on the sidewalk by numerous gang members. All the while the new command officers refused to let the officers at the scene take action. The commanding officers claimed they were outnumbered so they didn't let the officers take action until the local stores started to get looted and burned. The gangs had been coddled by this Administration and officer's layoffs were at a dangerous level. Even so, we, as Detroit Police Officers were embarrassed and livid by cops being held back when people were in desperate need. We, all of us, outnumbered or not, would always go toward danger to help, not away from it. With all the bad press, the Administration tried to deny that they held us back, but they didn't get away with it. They immediately called back the laid off officers (proving the layoffs weren't really needed) and stepped up enforcement against the gangs that they had been trying to placate. At that point, it was too late; the white flight sped up and downtown businesses were empty. The press at the time reported that you could shoot a cannon downtown after 6pm and not hit anyone.

Chief Tannian was fired and replaced by Chief Hart because Tannian didn't tell the Mayor that they were being investigated by the Feds. Deputy Chief Harvell, also under investigation, was buried without the Mayor or any of his reps attending the funeral. My opinion was that somebody thought Harvell was cooperating with the Feds and as was the case even then, "snitches get stitches." The circumstance of his death was curious. It seems to me to be highly unusually that somebody commits suicide by shooting themselves 'twice' in the chest, minutes apart.

The Academy changed and lost certification from when I was there. During this time, mid-seventies, the "MLEOTC" refused to certify the Police Academy for lack of training and with 60% of rejections for drug use. Watching and living through the changing department, our morale was shot. We kept working because of pride in ourselves and our friends that we had buried and we all cared about the good people that needed us.

Hookers Compete

I was johning Woodward Ave. one night and had a hooker give me only half a case. I parked my car took a drink of the beer I had with me and then threw the empty bottle in the alley, breaking the bottle. I staggered into the State Fair Bar and sat down next to a different hooker who asked me to buy her a beer; which I did. The other hooker, who was now sure I wasn't a cop, sat down on the other side of me and gave me a complete case with the offer of $20 for a blow job in my car. Before I could tell her she was under arrest, the other hooker said she would give me a blow job for $15 and the bidding was on. They were both arguing back and forth saying they saw me first until finally one went down to $5. The other one wouldn't go that low, but kept insisting she saw me first and saying that the other one was a pig and no good. I finally gave my partner the signal (hand through hair) that I had a case. He asked me which one was going and when I told him both, he gave me a look like I was bull shitting him until they begged me to say they were charging twenty bucks instead of five. They said they would plead guilty because the bidding was embarrassing. My partner and I were cracking up because that had never happened before, that we knew of.

There were many reasons why hookers hooked and I never was interested in finding out. I had gotten to know a lot of the long term regulars over the years and would actually help us sometimes by giving us information and we could joke back and forth with some of them. There was one hooker that had been arrested numerous times over the years working the street, her name was Carmen. She confused me because she was extremely clean, intelligent and knock-out hot. She didn't have a pimp, no drug habit and she came from a rich, good suburban family from West Bloomfield, an upper class suburb.

Carmen only worked a few days a month and I assumed it was for the money. I had to ask her and told her she didn't have to answer, but I was curious why she walked the streets and didn't just work the bars or be a call girl. She said she didn't have a pimp, and didn't do drugs, but had to really be careful because pimps kept after her. She said even though working the bars or being a call girl would be safer than the streets, she liked the danger and excitement on the street; it turned her on. She could have been a high class hooker any time, but she chose to work Woodward Avenue. I was surprised by her answer, but understood. I worked the streets, in a different way, because I enjoyed the danger and excitement.

We had a few others that would only be out on the street working at the end of the month to pay their rent. Most of the street girls though were pretty rough addicts that had pimps and could be dangerous. There was another hooker named April who was quite the character and would keep getting pregnant. One time we were looking for a murder suspect who had hung out on Woodward by the name of John Wayne something, supposedly armed and had stated he wouldn't be taken alive. One night April flagged us over and told us he was in the parking lot of the Last Chance Bar at Woodward and 8 Mile. She didn't have to, but she told us to be careful because he had his gun on the seat next to him and he was wearing a bullet proof vest. In those day's cops didn't even have bullet proof vests. This guy must have been a real pro as the Feds were all over Woodward for a week looking for him. Sure enough he was sitting in his car and April most likely saved our lives. As we approached, he reached for the gun on his car seat. We pointed our guns directly at his head, not his body, and he dropped the gun and raised his hands in surrender. A good bust of a violent wanted man and we beat the Feds again all because of April. We told the Precinct Commander and he put out the word to everybody, including Downtown Vice, that April was not to be bothered ever again as she saved two officers lives. Ours!

We later talked to April and told her no one was going to bother her and if she ever needed help we would help her as long as she didn't commit any other crimes. She must have told the other hookers because from then on some of the ones that we knew waived us down to offer their help with street information. April loved the attention and sometimes when new officers were riding with a senior officer who knew April, the senior officer would pull up next to April to explain to the new officer that April was protected by the Commander and never to mess with her. She was usually pregnant or just had a baby, and when meeting a new officer, April would pull out her breast and squirt him with breast milk. The senior officer would then speed off laughing. At first the officers would be mad until it was their turn to pull the joke on someone else.

Woodward Avenue was the border line between the 11th and 12th Precinct, but it was the 11th's responsibility. Once in a while, for what reason I don't know, the guys from the 12th would lock up one of our hookers. One night one of their scout cars wanted to know if a particular hooker who was pregnant and said she was in labor was really in labor or just trying not to get locked up. We told them that the hooker had pulled that trick before and went right back to Woodward working. It turned out she wasn't lying this time. She had her baby at the 12th Precinct. The whole Precinct was mad at us and we loved it. Couldn't help but laugh at them every time we crossed paths.

We also had fortune tellers that ripped people off telling them they had to buy candles or such, or bad things would happen to them. I did enjoy going in to see them while undercover. When they hit me up for more money, I would tell them no, the bad things are happening to you now as you are under arrest. So much for physic ability; they should have saw us coming. Some consider it a harmless crime, but these people were preying on poor gullible victims who didn't have anything but troubles.

Hummers Lounge

I reported to the station for work and was told we had a complaint of bottomless dancing and mingling with customers at Hummers Lounge on Davison near Van Dyke. It was an industrial out of the way area that didn't get a lot of attention or traffic at night. Vice had tried to get in, but they said it seemed as if most of the large crowd knew each other and nothing happened when they did get in. The bar was usually never very busy, but when I got there it had a line out the door to get in. While I was in line I heard some guys talking about where they worked and I was familiar with the places. As I got near the door the two bouncers were asking everybody where they worked or who they knew as this was a private party. It was very apparent they were screening their customers. This was perfect for me because I knew most of the engineering companies and worked for some of them in the past. When I got to the door I just said Modern Engineering and I was passed right in. I stood by the bar until a seat at the bar opened up where I could face the bartender and see the dancers from the mirror behind him. After a while I saw the dancers look at the bartender who nodded to them and then they dropped their bottoms. This happened three times by three different girls, but I also wanted to make sure I had tied the bar into it or only the girls would be ticketed.

I ordered another beer and asked the bartender how often they dropped or flashed? He surprised me and said, "When we are sure no cops are in here; just you guys and your friends" (meaning, engineers & draftsmen - my old occupation). Bingo, I had a perfect case. I finished my beer and left. We had a large crowd and called for a couple of scout cars and went back in. With cases like this we could either write tickets at the scene or arrest everyone and make them post bond. It depended on cooperation and attitude. In this case, they cooperated and didn't incite the large crowd as that happened often in other raids. We wrote tickets to the 3 girls and bartender for allowing improper conduct at the scene and released them to appear. We also wrote the bar up on a liquor violation for allowing improper conduct and to appear at the Liquor Commission.

Everyone pled guilty at traffic court and paid their fines. When I went to appear at the liquor commission I was in for a surprise. I walked in and ran into an old friend that I worked with in 1968 at Highland Park Engineering. I had changed since then, now a cop with long hair, a full beard and a hippie look. I asked him what he was doing there and he said some jerk cop wrote up his bar. I then asked him what bar was his and he said "Hummers." I told him I was the jerk cop who wrote his bar up and we both laughed. He told me he was going to plead guilty as he didn't condone what had happened. I told him I would talk to the liquor commission about their full cooperation at the time of the raid. Which I did and also told them I was sure this would be a one-time thing as I knew the owner from way back. They gave him a fine and a strong warning. After the hearing he apologized and asked me to stop by the bar so we could talk about old times. He was a pretty good guy and it appeared his partner was the one who was involved in the violations.

Florida Vacation

I was burning the candle at both ends still working Morality and hitting the bars on my days off. I had a furlough (vacation) coming up, but no money to go anywhere. A girl I was seeing at the time, on and off, suggested that we drive to Ft. Lauderdale and she would pay since she knew I didn't have any money. I agreed, even though I didn't want a serious relationship and didn't want to give her mixed signals. I told her I would pay her back when I could. She wanted to go and may have thought the trip would bring us closer, but after a week, she flew back and I stayed. She expected us to be a couple and do things couples do on vacation, which was not me. It was a mistake letting my defenses down and going with her. After that trip I realized, she was more serious than I was. Even though I thought she knew I didn't want a serious relationship, she would spoil me, buy me things, mother me and try to tame me. She was a good person, but I knew this was not for me and I was not the guy she wanted me to be, so I moved on.

While in Florida I looked up an old friend and stayed with him for a couple of weeks. It did turn out to be just what I needed, to be away from my street life and be around regular civilians. The only reminder of Detroit was when I was going into a bar on the Ft. Lauderdale strip a couple of bouncers were fighting with a guy in the front doorway. They had knocked him out and he was laying there when I stepped over him and said excuse me to the bouncers. This and more was normal to my life so I didn't think anything about it and went up to the bar and ordered a beer. The employees stared at me in astonishment and the barmaid actually asked me, "Didn't that brother you?" I replied, "No, I'm a Vice cop from Detroit." She laughed and told me the beer was on her. After a while the two bouncers came over and wanted to know if I had been shot or had ever killed anyone. Detroit's reputation got around and I would always get those questions when out of the City. I spent the rest of the day there eating and drinking for free. They took care of cops like the local businesses did back in Detroit. I usually didn't advertise it, but if asked, I would say I was a Detroit cop and I would usually get free drinks and the same round of questions, no matter where I was, "How bad is it in Detroit?", "Have you ever been shot?", "Have you shot anyone?"

In the 70's a lot of people were anti-cop and anti-military, but the business owners usually love having cops around and took care of us even when in another City, which always surprised me. Mostly though I was relaxing and enjoying the first vacation out of town since becoming a cop 6 years prior. My childhood friend introduced me to his friend who was Chief of Police in Lauderhill, Fl. The Chief told me he had trouble getting his officers to patrol a certain high crime area. When I told him that would be the only kind of area that I would work, and currently did work in Detroit, he immediately offered me a job at full pay with promised promotions as soon as eligible. It was tempting, but it paid less and I wasn't too keen on working with guys who didn't want to work where they were needed. If I wanted to ride around writing tickets and doing reports, which I didn't, I could do that in Detroit. Still my chances of getting promoted as a white male in Detroit was slim to none and that was why we were losing good officers and gaining less qualified ones. I decided I would rather stay with the guys I knew who have my back in hell or high water no matter what.

New Girl

Almost immediately upon returning home from Florida with a renewed attitude to not think about the past and move on, I met a beautiful young girl. She was a suburban girl working as the new barmaid at Nikki's Lounge at 6 Mile and Davison. She was quiet and unassuming and didn't either know, or care, that she was knockout beautiful. She had a nice, sweet smile, good attitude and was not hardened by the City. I wasn't looking to settle down and commit to anyone, but there was something about her that was different from anybody I had met before.

Everyone wanted to go out with her, especially me, but she wasn't interested in dating anyone at the bar. She didn't care either way that I was a cop and was the only person that charged me for drinks and treated me like any other customer. I was intrigued; most girls either loved or hated cops, but were never just ho-hum. I asked her out, and after asking the other waitresses about me and hearing I was a nice guy, she agreed. She then turned the tables on me and let me know she wasn't interested in a serious relationship or commitment. That should have been perfect for me, but for some reason, it only made me more interested. She was young, innocent and not remotely my type, but we starting seeing each other at a slow steady pace, without any exclusive commitment.

CHAPTER 7

The 80 Series Again

11-82

AGAIN I WAS GETTING WORN out working undercover for the fourth time and needed to get back in uniform. I didn't want to work shifts, write tickets or do reports of old crimes with supervisors all over me. Lucky for me, an opening came up on the 80-Series and I was able to stay in Special Ops with the go-getters and guys I liked working with.

I was put on Scout Car 11-82 with two officers that I hadn't worked with, but heard good things about that turned out to be true. It was also around the time they were putting women in regular scout cars on the rotating shifts. The women from the Woman's Division didn't want any part of it and some of the new hires didn't want to work; they were in it for a paycheck and never planned on working the street. Either way they were all new and inexperienced and I was still planning on going from hold up to shootings and back again over and over like I always did. We started on our day shift from 11am - 7pm and as senior officer, I was driving and getting to know my new partner. I saw an oil and water slick on Dequindre going south toward 6 Mile and a bunch of parked cars that had just been hit. I told my new partner I was going to follow it and we can get a cup of coffee while doing the accident report. Big, Big mistake. As a felony gun car we didn't need to do accident investigations and my partner was giving me a strange look like he didn't know what to make of me. This was not a good way to start with a new Special Ops 80-Series partner and it only got worse. After about a half mile of damaged parked vehicles we came up on our culprit with the front end of his car smoking and leaking fluid. Good I thought a simple arrest to break the ice and a cup of coffee to boot. We could get to know each other before getting into anything serious. Wrong again and my time out of uniform was showing. I was about to be put right back into the reality of the street.

We approached the driver who was out of his car now and happened to be a very large guy. He immediately knocked down my partner who chipped a bone in his elbow. It was now apparent he was high and knew karate since he just took down my partner who was also a pretty tough guy. I had been in a lot of battles and knew I had to move fast and get close so he didn't have the room to get a good whack on me. I grabbed him so close it was as if I was tightly hugging him and he still brought his knee up over and over striking me in the ribs so hard that he bruised my ribs and tore the muscles between them. That gave my partner time to get up and we wrestled him to the ground as a police women reached in to help, broke her nail, and then immediately backed off. After continuing to struggle, we finally got him handcuffed. We turned him over to the responding scout car and headed to Holy Cross Hospital as we knew we were injured, but didn't know how bad. My first encounter back on the street wasn't a good one. My first experience with a police woman, who happened to be 3 inches taller than me, wasn't very positive either. My new partner did well and I felt good about working with him after doing battle, and even getting injured, but we got our man.

I learned later that my new partner was a good cop and a hard worker and one of the biggest characters I have ever met. At the hospital, they x-rayed my partner's arm then were x-raying me when a nurse came in scolding me about smoking in the hospital. I was in such pain that I couldn't hardly breathe or talk and hadn't smoked in years. She was so mad at me she wouldn't listen and kept yelling as she walked away. When they were done x-raying me, I gingerly got up and walked out into the hallway were my partner was sitting in a chair outside the x-ray room door. He had a big smile on his face as he was holding a half put out cigarette butt and said while laughing, the nurse caught him holding the lit cigarette and he told her it wasn't his it was the little cops who was getting x-rayed. I tried not to laugh as it hurt too bad. Later, when I got back to the gurney to get wrapped up, he was on his knees talking to my uniform that he had laid out. He had put my boots on the floor and draped my pants and shirt across the gurney with my hat lying on top. It looked like someone, a cop, had just vaporized and the uniform fell straight on to the gurney. He was saying over and over, "My God, what did they do to you, where's my partner?" Pain or not, I had to crack up but it hurt. All I could do is wave to the nurses trying to tell them to get him out of there, which they did. He was a character and a little nutty at times, but one hell of a good cop who liked to work like me, and was scared of nothing. What a memorable first experience with a new partner. We would work together for years after that with a lot of mutual trust and definitely a lot of laughter. Over the years we got into and out of a lot of situations with only a few injuries, but usually laughed about it after. We were both put on disability to heal up for a few weeks and my girlfriend didn't want me to be all alone all day so she brought her dog, Henna, over to keep me company for a day. Henna was a very friendly 3 year old Irish Setter. It was a nice thought, but I was on the couch, flat on my back, unable to move without pain and my friend Henna decided to climb on my chest, licking my face and wouldn't get off of me. I didn't have the strength to get her off for quite a while, but I couldn't help but laugh later. She was a good dog and was just being friendly. After a few weeks off work, I came back and reminded myself I was on a felony car again and should be looking for felons; which was what I was good at.

Police Chaplin

I was back working in a scout car without a shield again and liked that except it reminded me of Bobby and that still hurt a lot. I tried not to think about it and keep my mind busy. Reverend Lund the police Chaplin asked if he could ride with us and I immediately said ok. He liked dealing with felonies and riding without a shield. He never preached to us or interfered in any way. He was just there if we or a citizen needed him. There were no swat teams in those days and we handled the barricaded gunman and hostage type situations. He always offered to go in and talk to anybody who was in that situation and I always refused to let him go into any dangerous situations alone.

I understood his reasons, but it was our job. I had been in that position with a gunman before and learned how dangerous and unpredictable it could be.

Years before when I lived in the apartment we had a group who hung out at the pool and we had a smorgasbord type dinner together in the evening. One man who we ate with a few Sundays who lived in the apartment complex had barricaded himself after firing a bunch of shots. I was off duty and seeing a group of cops taking cover at his apartment I volunteered to the Sergeant in charge to talk to him. Big mistake, he wasn't the guy that I knew by the pool, he was rattling on incoherently and threatened to kill me, and himself. I backed off, but learned first-hand not to get to close when someone is violently out of their mind and irrational. I wasn't going to be responsible for getting the police Chaplin hurt or killed so I refused Reverend Lund's request to try to talk to anyone in a violent situation.

On 3/3/76, Police Chaplin William Paris was shot in the head and killed by a disturbed barricaded gunman who had also shot a hotel manager. He also shot and wounded a TAC officer who was trying to rescue the Chaplin before the Police sniper shot him.

One Police Chaplin, one Police Matron and twenty-six Detroit Police Officers had been killed in my short 6 years on the job. I didn't know any difference as this was just the way it was in the 70's – constant violence and death

On 10/16/76, Lt. Johnnie Shoates was shot in the head while off duty and trying to stop an armed robbery. He laid in a coma for ten years until passing. Unlike other departments, we were always on duty and required to live in the City and take action whether we had back up, radios or were alone. The only problem was that we knew the City and the courts wouldn't back us up if we did have to get involved in something off duty. Working officers were very grateful to know that there was an anonymous group of business people called the 100 Club of Detroit. The 100 Club consisted of 100 business people who helped the family of a Detroit Police Officer killed in the line of duty. They would pay off the widow's mortgage and all existing bills and guarantee the orphan children free college educations. That was a giant relief to us knowing that if anything happened to us as we risked our lives daily, our families would be taken care of by some amazing caring people and our Blue family.

Internal Affairs

While on patrol on East 8 Mile Road near Woodward we observed a black female lying on the side of the road bleeding from the face with scrapes on her knees and elbows. She told us a john punched her in the face, took her money and threw her out of his moving car. We had EMS check her out and clean her up while we made a report and put out his description. She did not want to go to the hospital, but did want to prosecute. We had a good case, plate number, vehicle type and color and she could recognize him. We took her to the station to talk to the detectives and turned in our report. Surprising to me the detective refused to follow up because he said the john just probably refused to pay her and for me to redo my report. I did just that, I ripped it up and wrote a new one including noting what he ordered me to do with the original and that he refused to accept what I believed to be fact. Of course the stuff hit the fan when I turned in the new report. I removed my statement about his actions only when he accepted the report and agreed to investigate it. Two things happened that day: 1) The Detective learned I was not going to back down. 2) I was determined to do my job no matter who tried to intimidate me and would stand up for a victim no matter who they were or what they did. I was getting burnt out, but I was still a straight shooter and a proud honest cop. The detectives were over worked, but this particular one seemed to be one who never went for warrants so he could close cases.

I went back on the street and did my job and completely forgot about that incident as that was my job and there were more crimes to work after that. A few weeks later, I received a subpoena to appear at Internal Affairs. I knew I didn't do anything wrong so I thought maybe they were looking for some information they thought I could help them with. Still I was a little confused because I didn't know any dirty cops. When I arrived at my appointment I ran into some of the guys who I knew from before including my old Precinct Inspector. Those that knew me knew I was an honest cop and greeted me with friendly chatter while asking me if I was transferring down there. As soon as I told them that I had been subpoenaed they made a quick U-turn walking away from me quickly. A Union representative met me and took me aside and told me my picture had been picked out of a photo lineup and that

I had been accused of beating up a prostitute and leaving her in a dumpster seriously injured. To that, I laughed and said that was nuts and it never happened. Still being naive enough that I thought if you told the truth and was forthcoming you would get a fair shake like I gave everyone. Big mistake again; I was told that I could have a lawyer present and I refused and told them I had nothing to hide and would answer their questions honestly. My Union rep. and I were then taken into a conference room and a recorder was set up in front of me.

I was handed two pieces of paper to read and sign and then they verbally gave me my Garrity warning, basically saying I could be fired. I then got the real shock when they gave me my Miranda warning that meant I could also go to jail. There were four of them and I was nervous at that point. They started asking leading questions like, "How many prostitutes have your arrested in your career?" I tried to do some quick math and figured 5-10 a month for about 3 to 3.5 years and said, "2-3 hundred probably." They seemed to light up and with a smile, one of them said, "You probably don't like them very much, do you?" I replied not knowing they were playing games with me that I had no personal animosity toward prostitutes I just did my job whatever it was and made a lot of felony arrests too. They then asked me what I thought they, the prostitutes, would say about me. I said that I never thought much about it, but I think some would say I was honest and fair. They then accused me of altering my daily log sheet. All the time during this interrogation, I was getting nervous thinking now I was being set up by someone and the Department was going along with it.

I sat nervously folding the paperwork in half over and over until it was the size of a quarter and put it in my pocket. When they were done, they told me I could leave and they would be in touch. As I was leaving, they were looking all over for something and asked me if I had seen my warning's paperwork. I sheepishly pulled out the little folded up, quarter size forms from my pocket and handed it to one of them, I with my goofy sense of humor was laughing when I saw the look on their faces when they saw how small it was. I thought it was my copy. I left that conference room with a bad taste in my mouth as I was sure they were after me and in a toss-up they were going to believe a prostitute before me and I was right. Even though I had a perfect record, no complaints, no write ups and a reputation of being an honest cop who didn't take short cuts, it didn't seem to matter. As I left the building the same guys, including the Commander, that greeted me when I came in, were now turning away like I had a disease.

I was told later by one of the guys that the Internal Affairs Dept. wasn't like it once was. They were in the process of breaking up crews and moving them from case to case during an investigation so only the Sergeant assigned to the case knew the whole case. That, in effect, added politics to the investigations as they controlled who the Sergeants were or weren't. The investigating officers only knew their limited parts of numerous cases and never all the information of a complete investigation. Paranoia maybe, but it made sense because the politicians hated us street cops and, unknown to many, part of the Internal Affairs job was to investigate crooked politicians and now they would have total control of who was supposed to investigate them. Guess what, the Feds were investigating the upper echelon of the Police Department and Mayor's office, but Internal Affairs wasn't, they were planting cash in businesses and vacant buildings and having scout cars dispatched to them to entrap officers. If the officers didn't make a report and put it in evidence as found money, they had them. The hand writing was on the wall and I think I was about to be sacrificed and it made me sick to my stomach.

I sweated it out for weeks thinking the fix was in then all of a sudden I received notification that my case was found unfounded. No explanation, no apology and no prosecution for those that falsely accused me. I later found out that it wasn't my testimony that saved me, or my folding ability, it was other prostitutes who testified under oath that it was untrue. Apparently they asked about altering my run sheet so they could at least get me on that. That didn't work either because at the exact time I was supposed to be beating up the prostitute, I was helping another prostitute who was robbed and thrown out of a car. She gave a statement on my behalf which also matched my run sheet. My report on her robbery and disagreement with the detectives in the police station, all more than covered the time span of the supposed incident they were trying to get me for. I was all for Internal Affairs policing the police and politicians, but it would have been nice if they were professional about it instead of using it to assist with the Administrations agenda of controlling investigations. I now knew honesty and hard work wouldn't get you by anymore; my kind, honest cops, had to watch their backs.

Healed Up / Scruples

I was starting to get used to my new partner, but had to keep an eye on him because he loved to pull tricks on everyone. I tried to keep everything very professional, and he liked to lighten things up. One night we were bringing in a prisoner and he asked him if he had any scruples and the prisoner asked, "What you mean scruples?" My partner told him it was little red dots all over your skin and the prisoner said over and over, "I ain't got no scruples." My partner then shined his flash light down the front of his shirt and said, "No, you don't have any scruples." He then told him if they thought he had scruples at the Precinct they would delouse him with a spray wand and it stung like hell. He told him to talk to the Lieutenant because the desk Sergeant wouldn't believe him and spray him anyway. He repeated to him that he had to insist to show the Lieutenant that his chest didn't have any scruples on it.

Now usually the way it worked was the Lieutenant hid out in the back offices not wanting to be bothered while the Sergeants had to do the desk duty and handle everything. If the Lieutenant was unnecessarily bothered, there could be hell to pay and that was exactly what my partner was setting up. I never pulled that stuff myself, but I kept my mouth shut and laughed my ass off when he did. I guess I was the straight man to his comic routines.

Sure enough, after the prisoner was dropped off we received a radio run back to #11-Busy. As we walked up to the front desk, all the inside officers had big grins on their faces, but the Sergeant went nuts on us. On the 80-Series we didn't have a direct supervisor who could make it miserable for us like they could on their shift guys; all they could do was bitch us out at the time.

The inside guys said our prisoner threw such a fit about not having scruples and wouldn't cooperate until the Sergeant got the Lieutenant to look down the prisoner's shirt. All the time he kept yelling that he didn't have no scruples and not to spray him. As we walked past the Lieutenant and Sergeants room to our Special Ops offices, the Lieutenant looked up with a smile and said, "Good one." Somehow my partner could get away with stuff that anybody else would be in trouble for. Working 7pm - 3am he could pull the same tricks on 2 different shifts, the 4-12 and the 12-8 midnight shift crews when he wanted to and he often did.

The new Administration eliminated the police manual and went to a general order book instead. Most likely because they made a lot of changes that weren't too popular, like the rules on Cowardice which before you could be written up and fired for like a military dishonorable discharge. We knew some of the new hires were outwardly avoiding or just going slow to dangerous calls and we didn't like it, but the new General Order's did not include "Cowardice." My partner, who learned and studied the General Orders as they came out, was pretty much an expert on them even more so than the supervisors. One day when a desk Sergeant told us we couldn't do something and my partner quoted General Order number so and so that said in effect, we could. The Sergeant didn't know what to say. As we walked away I said to my partner that it didn't sound right, and asked him if he was sure of the order and he said hell no, but the Sergeant doesn't know that. He had them jumpy as he was always right and that made it a lot easier for us to get things done.

Full Speed Ahead

I tried to put the past behind me and go full speed ahead with my new 80-Series crewmates. Both of my new partners liked to work and that was what we did. Some of the inside help weren't too happy with us as we brought in prisoners almost daily and they had to process them. Some of the most and longest wanted felons would be home for Christmas and the inside crew would almost beg us not to bring in a lot of prisoners on holidays. Of course we didn't listen to them or the bosses. It was the best time for us to get felons when they didn't think cops would get them during the holiday when with their families. But we did. Eventually we could get all 3 shifts a little peeved at us because they rotated shifts and we didn't.

That also made it possible for us to pull tricks on each shift. It was dangerous for them to leave the desk unattended when we were around, usually there were 3 or 4 officers and a supervisor manning the desk. Sometimes when food was brought in or there was a disturbance in the back, all the desk help would help or at least go and watch. That put us in motion; I would usually be on the lookout as my partner would pull something. One time, there was a 2-inch wide paint type roller that they rolled the black finger print ink on a piece of glass to finger print prisoners. My partner would quickly roll it on the ear piece of all the phones behind the desk that were also black. When the desk staff came back, the first officer to answer the phone would have a black ring around his ear. The best part was that sometimes the other officers kept quiet thinking that only his phone got inked. They were all laughing at each other until they realized, or a citizen told them that they all had black rings around their ears. That was when we made a quick exit laughing like hell and always looking for an opportunity to mess with the inside help, who usually took it pretty well. I almost always went along and even sometimes helped my partner with his pranks on other officers, but I always bitched at him when he pulled something on a citizen telling him he was going to get us in trouble. Somehow he was such a character that nobody ever complained.

EMS

In the early 1970's the City switched from using police car station wagons as EMS Ambulances to Fire Department Ambulances. It was a good move for us cops and the City as they didn't have to get five thousand cops certified at a great cost. They did the same thing with the new EMS recruiting as they did with us cops and recruited experienced Vietnam Veterans. They loaded up with Corpsmen and medics who had a lot of field experience and it showed. These guys knew what they were doing and weren't scared of anything. The only problem was these new guys were professionals medically, but still young. When they gave them top-heavy ambulances with lights, sirens and a license to go as fast as they could, they did. They had quite a few accidents and a few roll overs at first, but adjusted and they turned out to be good units that we trusted. Then, in the mid 1970's, like cops, the City started hiring less qualified Medical Techs for EMS and it was noticed. Some units took their time and would sometimes wait around the corner on a call for a scout car before responding to the call. We couldn't blame them as they were assaulted sometimes, but you couldn't beat the Veterans who put the sick and injured first. We also had scout cars that drove so slow to their priority 1 and 2 calls that we flew past them on the way to their call.

Dispatch was requesting a volunteer unit to relieve a scout car for lunch that had been sitting on a carbon monoxide suicide in an alley for hours. All the cars were busy and it wasn't usually an 80's series function, but we thought we would volunteer so they could get a break. We parked behind the car with the dead body and they went and picked up fast food at a drive through and were back in minutes. They told us EMS had pronounced him dead about 6 hours earlier and they had been waiting all day for the Medical Examiner to release the body. They thanked us for volunteering so they could get something to eat. Out of curiosity, my partner and I looked inside the vehicle and noticed that the guy was still breathing. We told the crew they better have the EMS unit return because their dead body wasn't dead anymore. As we pulled off and got back into service they were trying to revive him and calling for EMS to return. They were actually saying on the radio for everyone to hear, that their dead body wasn't dead anymore. If the public knew what affirmative action and lowering standards did to first responder's qualification and skill they might not like it. Unfortunately, we were living it and saw it get worse daily.

I can't remember how many times I advised a panicky citizen who's loved one was dying to also call a private ambulance, even with EMS on the way. We weren't certified and not allowed to convey people anymore. So whichever service got there first, EMS or the private ambulance, they would haul them. Most of the time it was the private ambulance service that showed up first. EMS was being used by some citizens as a taxi and hospital emergency rooms as clinics for minor non-emergency injuries and illnesses. EMS had to convey them, and hospitals had to treat them, and neither tried very hard to collect payment for their services. Unfortunately, by allowing EMS and hospitals to be used for non-emergencies, good people with true emergencies were left to wait and sometimes die because EMS didn't get there in time. I always wondered where the common sense was when the City allowed this to happen.

Detroit Lawyers

Our new Commander wanted our Unit 11-82 to spend as much time as possible on Woodward Avenue because of our knowledge and experience in that area. I had worked Woodward for most of my career and that was fine with me because we were still working felonies. I very seldom wrote tickets, but would stop someone to investigate them if they committed a traffic violation. If they weren't wanted or committing a felony, I would give them a break and let them go.

To be honest and from what I saw some lawyers pull on people to make a buck and their attitude, I wasn't crazy about them. I usually didn't pay attention to them unless they were directly involved with me and my duties. One night we saw a vehicle driving around and around very apparently johning for a whore; there was nothing illegal there, so I watched him until he committed a traffic violation. No big deal either, but if he was looking to pick up a hooker, it gave me a legal reason to stop him. I stopped him for failing to stop at a cross walk and he completely blew a fuse telling me he was a lawyer (big-big mistake), so I wrote him a ticket. When I handed it to him, he continued to tell me he knew people and I would be walking a beat as he ripped the ticket up and threw it at my feet. Of course I went back to my car and wrote him another ticket for littering and made him pick up the pieces. All the while being nice and polite because I could see he was trying to bait me into doing something stupid. I still had a baby face and he probably thought I was a rookie who could be intimidated. He was going to put me in my place as he was a lawyer and knew the law and told me so. He was getting loud and swearing at me as two women walked by. I quietly told him he shouldn't talk like that in mixed company pointing out the woman walking by and wrote him another ticket for profanity in public. When I handed it to him you could almost see smoke coming out of his ears, but he was quiet now. I told him I could do this all night and that I hadn't written a traffic violation in years. I also told him that without his attitude he would have been on his way with a warning. There were good lawyers that I respected even when I opposed them in court when they did their jobs, but a lot of them would sell out their clients for a quick buck or were actually inept. Looking back, I probably should have just given him a ticket instead of adjusting his attitude, but I just couldn't resist.

Breakfast Conversation at the Court House

We had a lawyer one time buy us breakfast in the cafeteria of the Recorders Court house. He sat down with me and my partners pretending to be friendly while sneakily trying to get information from us for his case. With all the arrests I had made I most likely had more court experience than he did at that point. We laughed and joked and said ridiculous things about the case in front of him knowing that was his objective. When I went to the court room and had to testify on the stand under oath, he dramatically asked about something and I would say, "No sir, it was just the opposite." He then got mad and said, in front of the jury, "That wasn't what you said at breakfast." I then smiled and looked at the jury and said, "We weren't under oath then, but we are now." We were a step ahead of him and not the rookies he thought we were. We wanted the jury to know the truth and not tricky lawyers spin. Some lawyers and even judges never see the victims when they were victimized and think it's a game of who wins.

If we had a weak prosecuting attorney we would try and help get the facts to the jury. For instance, I had a defense attorney trying to allude to the lack of lighting in an alley so that it would be impossible for me to see his client. The prosecutor wasn't responding as the defense attorney kept telling the jury it was 3am at night and his client couldn't have possibly been identified. So when he made a big point of asking me what time of the night was it officer, I just replied, "street lights," while smiling at the jury. The lawyer lost his composure and kept yelling at me and the judge saying, "I didn't ask that."

The jury smiled back and the judge told me to answer the question directly which I did, but the jury got the message and maybe more, seeing the defense attorney was playing games with them. I even thought I saw the judge crack a little smile. I was amazed that the prosecutor didn't ask me or anybody about the lighting conditions. I was also surprised that the defense attorney brought it up so many times. The people sure weren't getting their monies worth and you couldn't find very many lawyers who sued lawyers in this town. Doctors and everyone else yes, but not each other!

We couldn't do anything, but we saw lawyers asking people who were charged with drunk driving in the hallways of traffic court what they blew on the breathalyzer. Drunk driving in the 70's was .015 on the test and driving while visibly impaired was between .012-.015 automatically. When the lawyer had one defendant answer under .015 they would tell them they could get them off on driving while visibly impaired for "x" amount of money, if they pled guilty to it. Problem was it was always automatically lowered if under .015 with or without an attorney and the attorneys weren't doing anything but taking their money for nothing and the judges just let it happen. Again, there were good attorneys, but I sure lost trust in most of them, as I watched them work.

Escaped Hooker

I got a call when off duty from the day shift Lieutenant asking me how soon I could come into work. This was very unusual. If it was an emergency, I would just be ordered in. I asked him why he needed me in and he said, in a low voice, that they had a hooker escape and had to get her back ASAP before they all got in trouble. I asked him to call my partner in and I would be there within the hour. My partner loved overtime and extra money and would jump at it. We found out what happened when we got there. It seems that someone let her into the Commander's clerk's office to be nice because she told them she didn't have any money to make calls for bail. Of course everybody got busy and she was left alone to just open a window and leave. By the time anyone noticed, she was long gone and everybody was mad at each other and worried about how much trouble they were all in. As we were always pulling tricks on the inside help and they took it well; we figured we owed them. We told them not to worry that we would get her back. We went right out to Woodward and the second hooker we talked to told us she also worked in the Cass Corridor. We cruised around for a little while, and then bingo there she was. I pulled right up on the sidewalk drove down it to her and her eyes were as big as saucers not expecting to see us in that area. We put her in the back seat and my partner sat next to her as we didn't have a shield and couldn't give her a complete search as she was female. Still as we drove back to the station my partner was telling her everybody was pissed at her because they trusted her. I kept looking periodically in the rear view mirror as I drove, in case she caused a problem. I could have sworn I saw smoke coming from the top of her head, but thought no that can't be and kept driving. When I looked again a few minutes later, sure enough smoke was coming from the top of her wig and I noticed my partner was ashing his cigarette there. Naturally I yelled at him to cut it out but had to turn my head because I didn't want him to see me laughing as it did look hilarious in the rear view mirror. When we brought her in to the station all the inside help was ecstatic as no one was going to get in trouble and it only took us a couple of hours. I knew she wasn't going to bitch about her wig and the inside help didn't want it known that she had escaped. So, it was as if it had never happened and all was going to be forgotten. We were thanked by everybody and given the day off with pay. Not a bad couple of hours work and the hookers thought we were everywhere and knew everything after that.

Kicked my Ass

We received a call to East 7 Mile and the Chrysler Freeway on a large disturbance. As we exited our vehicle, there was a crowd of about 20 people with some armed with tire irons and ball bats surrounding a couple holding a baby. First thing, I drew my weapon and made everybody drop their weapons and back off. They were angry and about to attack the man who was yelling at the woman who was holding the baby. As we approached the couple, the man took a swing at the woman's face and she put the baby up in front of her causing the baby to be hit and driven into her face. The woman and the baby were both bleeding from their faces. My partner, who was a step closer than me, immediately grabbed him and he punched my partner knocking him down stunning him. I then grabbed him at both of his coat sleeves at the wrist to subdue him without getting punched. He was big and hostile and tossed me backward like I was a rag. As I flew backward in the air my arms straightened full out as I hung on to his sleeves with a death grip causing him to fall on top of me. We fell on a bunch of garbage bags breaking my fall but it still knocked the wind out of me. While he was on top of me I was worried that he was going to get my gun or bite me as we struggled until my partner got his wits together. My partner got a choke hold on him giving me room to get out from under him so we could both subdue him enough to get him handcuffed. Somebody must have called EMS as they pulled up just as we had him under control.

I had a cold and was sucking on a cough drop when the battle started and had bitten it into pieces. I still hadn't caught my breath back and was spitting the pieces out so I could breathe and talk. Some in the crowd were yelling, "Look that cops spitting out his teeth." I was trying to tell the medic I was ok and waving him over to the woman and the baby. Finally, I got my breath back enough and said, "cough drops." He then went to help his partner with the woman and the baby. When he came back, he helped get the garbage off of me from the bags that broke open when I fell. EMS conveyed the woman and baby to the hospital and we conveyed our prisoner to #11 all the while he was threatening to kill her and the baby. By the time we pulled into the police garage I was livid with him and when I tried to get him out of the back seat he started kicking at me. He landed a couple of good hits and that just made me madder. The only thing I could get a hold of was his hair to pull him out with and then he stopped fighting. All this time he was one tough dude. As we were walking in the hall to the lockup, I lightly kicked him in the butt and told him to get going. To my complete surprise after all the fighting, a gentle bump on the fanny made him start crying and telling everybody in the station that he could, "he kicked my ass," meaning me. He was way bigger and we were all a mess and everybody thought he was saying I kicked his ass in a fight on the street; continuing the myth of making me look like a tough little guy. As I was in the back doing my paperwork, everybody walking by or in the vicinity kept saying I stunk. I kept checking my clothes and running my hand thru my hair and didn't find anything. It was close to the end of my shift so the Sergeant who insisted I stunk, told me to just go home early. When I got home I stripped down to my underwear, washed up and still found nothing so I microwaved a couple of hot dogs. When I sat down to eat and was about to take a bite, I could smell crap. I ran my hand threw my hair again and ended up with dog shit on it this time. All I could think was if I could get my hands on the SOB, I would really kick his ass.

Pro Fight

We had a radio run to Walkers Lounge on Conant. When we pulled up a Sergeant's car was already there. The call was a large fight in progress and Sergeants usually worked alone so we really hurried in. The first thing I saw was a large man lying on his back on the pool table unconscious and bleeding profusely. Then I saw two large men half bent over beating on the Sergeant who was on the floor. My partner went after one who was about 270 lbs. I went after the other one who was 6'8" and over 200 lbs. Still there was no mace, no tasers in those days just large black jacks. I wasn't about to let this big guy get to a full stance and when he turned starting towards me, I stepped into him swinging the black jack from the floor to his head until he went to his knees stunning him. After a short wrestling match, I finally got handcuffs on him. My partner did the same to the other guy. Those who know about head injuries know they bleed a lot and we were all covered with blood and looked a mess. The Sergeant wasn't seriously hurt and when backup arrived we took off with our prisoners to Detroit General Hospital where they also have a lock up for detaining injured prisoners.

I was pissed again because I was getting tired of having to fight with these idiots so often. When I was doing the paperwork at the hospital detention area my partner and two of their officers were guarding the prisoners while they were being treated. I was grumbling under my breath and still mad at them when I noticed the two officers and nurses staring at me strangely and talking to my partner shaking their heads. I figured it was because my shirt was ripped, hair was messed up and I was covered in blood. My prisoner had 60 stitches put in his head and when they brought him to the lock up he was trying to talk to me. I just told him I didn't want to hear it and walked away, still aggravated with him for making me fight. I was in no mood for any bull shit. When the two officers assigned to the hospital asked me about it saying pretty big battle, huh? I just walked away saying not that big a deal and they walked away with their mouths open.

I should have known why the hospital staff and officers were looking at me and acting strangely. First of all, the big one I battled with was more than a foot taller than me and a lot heavier and he used to play professional basketball with the Detroit Pistons. Second, my partner who always was pulling something, apparently couldn't resist when the hospital cops and staff were commenting on what a battle those two big guys must have had with each other, he told them that they didn't fight each other; they pissed off my little partner over there and he did that to them. All the while I had smoke coming out of my ears while they just stared at me. They must have believed I was the toughest guy in town and a new myth was spread like the big guy who previously said "I kicked his ass." When my girlfriend found out what happened and who the prisoner was, she said she went to school with him and he was a real nice guy. I told her he wasn't so nice when I met him. Later I heard he used to be a nice guy, but got into the wrong crowd with drugs. Even so, pounding on a cop in front of another cop would get you thumped in the 70's.

A year or so later, while off duty, I went into one of my favorite bars, the Duchess Lounge, and sat at the end of the bar. The owner came over and asked me to come over to his table to meet a VIP. I went over and he introduced me to the people sitting at the table that were laughing and having a good time. When he introduced me to the VIP, who used to play basketball for the Detroit Pistons, I immediately recognized him as the one who attacked my Sergeant and I had to subdue. He wasn't on my list of nice guys so as we were shaking hands across the table I said, "You don't remember me, do you?" As he sat down, he said, "No." I then said, "I'm the one that put 60 stitches in your head a while ago." At that, the whole table went silent and mouths hung open in shock waiting for something to happen. I just gave him a dirty look and went back to finish my drink at the bar. I didn't want to cause a problem, but I didn't want to drink with him either. Most likely he was now on some kind of probation and shouldn't be in a bar, but that wasn't my problem either and if so, he hadn't learned his lesson.

I left the bar about an hour later and noticed him following me as I walked down Van Dyke toward my car. I walked past my car to where no other cars were parked to make sure he wasn't just walking to his car. Sure enough he started coming up behind me faster and no one else was around at 2am in the morning. I figured he must have been embarrassed and maybe teased by his friends. He was more than a foot taller than me and I still had an attitude toward him and the beer muscles were kicking in. I figured I was going to be in for a hell of a battle and decided I most likely would have to pistol whip him or hope he was drunk enough not to beat me to death. I always believed back then that I was good at what I did and had unbelievable luck when it was most needed. Just as he was about to jump me an old friend of mine, the party store owner/bar bouncer who I had given Luke to, showed up. He was on the other side of Van Dyke directly across from us. He was drunk and opened his car door, threw up on the street and yelled over to me while wiping his mouth off, "You need any help, Al?" He was 6'6" tall and big. At that point my adversary decided to turn around and head the other way rather quickly, most likely embarrassed again. I thanked my friend and waved goodbye. Only I could have luck like that; or was it luck?

Eight Mile Flare-up

It seemed most of the time that I volunteered to help out and do regular police work something happened like the fight with the crazy karate guy or the dead body that wasn't dead. I was good at felony arrest and undercover work, but didn't have a lot of experience at plain old regular police work anymore. We had a unit requesting a car to block traffic on the two right lanes on the East bound 8 Mile Road over pass over I-75 on a rollover accident. Again, we didn't normally do accidents, but it was days and we were right there so I volunteered – big mistake, again.

I parked our scout car blocking the two right lanes at the start of the rise of the bridge and grabbed a bunch of flares from the trunk. I started lighting them as I walked over the bridge and down the other side to keep traffic away from the accident. The fire department was doing a wash down to dilute the gas from the ruptured tanks and they were all causally standing around as I approached. I wasn't use to handling accidents anymore so I figured I would place my last flare about a hundred feet from the accident. What I didn't figure was there wasn't any wind and the fumes were just sitting there. When I lit the last flare, it caused a big ball of fire that covered all four lanes and went about 30 feet in the air. My partner and the fireman dove for cover as traffic just drove though the big flash as if it never happened. The fumes must have dissipated enough so no damage was caused, but what a sight. When the firemen and my partner got up and saw me standing there with a burning flare in my hand and laughing like crazy, they were not happy. They were all calling me a "Crazy Ass MF'er," like I did it on purpose. I didn't, but with my goofy sense of humor with no one hurt and nothing damaged, it was one of the funniest things you could see from my view. Afterward my partner, (The Character) who loved a good joke, thought it was pretty funny too after he calmed down. We laughed about it every time the story was told how Boudreau blew up 8 Mile Road.

You would think after a while I would learn to quit volunteering for things we didn't have to do but no, not me. I liked to work, so when I was in the area of another car's call and able to help out, I did. Even if it was not my expertise, I had to go. I ended up helping with two babies being born, sadly one didn't make it. Another time, I volunteered to stand by a decapitated head while waiting for the Medical Examiners assistant to pick it up so the crew assigned to do it could have a lunch break.

Guide Wire

One night my partner called in sick and that left me a choice of going home or going out on the street as a Corporal for a Sergeant. Easy choice, the last thing I wanted to do was drive a Sergeant around. I had enough of that back at #7 when I was a rookie. The Sergeant who wanted me to drive him around was a good guy and liked our unit because we were always in the middle of the action. So, I told him I would do it, but it wasn't my first choice. It didn't take long for a B&E in Progress run to come out and I headed for it. I made a quick left and then another quick left into the alley and right up a guide wire for a pole so that only the left rear wheel was still on the ground. Naturally when I looked over at him his eyes were big and his mouth was wide open in surprise as he was about six feet in the air. I couldn't help but laugh at the look on his face and what I just got us into knowing he would never make me drive him around again. He had to jump out of the passenger seat to get to the ground level and he started to laugh himself as this was almost impossible to do. When I called on the radio that 11-70 needed a tow truck, everybody had to drive by to see why the Sergeant's car needed a tow and they all had a good laugh. He was a great guy who had a good sense of humor. So, why not twist the story. Unknown to him at the time, every crew that came by asking me what happened, I told them, "That goofy Sergeant drove right up that guide wire." When we got into the station everyone was teasing him about it and he just smiled, laughed and pointed his finger at me in a friendly way. Good boss, good guy. He never did ask me to be his Corporal again.

Air Conditioning

We (80-Series Units) had received new scout cars last year and now the shift guys were going to get some new cars with new federal funds. We were probably the only City that had old beat up cars with broken windshields, dents, bad breaks and all beat to hell. Every city, except Detroit, had air conditioned cars and our light blue shirts looked dark blue as we totally soaked them with sweat.

The good news was that the new cars came with air conditioning paid for by Chrysler Corporation as a gift to the City. They were delivered just in time for the heat of the summer. The bad news was that as soon as they were delivered they were sent to the Chene Street garage where the City Administration had the A/C removed. They told the press if we had air we wouldn't get out of our vehicles or even roll down our windows. Same thing with mace, which every PD in the country had. The Administration said we would ride around spraying people.

We knew this Administration was anti-cop, but wished they would make up their minds. They didn't want arrests because that showed statistics of a large increase in crime and they didn't want us riding around in air-conditioned cars while doing nothing. All I knew was getting out of the hot car and making arrests in a cool breeze was better and without mace we could still forcibly subdue a resisting suspect with whatever force necessary. The people re-elected these guys with corruption and crime up and services and safety down. There wasn't much we could do about it so we just kept sweating and arresting felons.

No Prosecution

On October 10, 1976 I received my 6th Citation/Commendation for "Arresting two felons for armed robbery." While on patrol we were flagged down by three females who were assaulted and robbed at gun point at Oakland and McNichols. We immediately put out their description and type of vehicle. Then we made a quick search of the area. Sure enough we spotted them speeding away at Dakota and Brush and gave chase. We curbed them and ordered them out at gunpoint. We recovered the gun and the ladies purses with nothing missing. The sad part was and it happens all too often, after you risk life and limb and the complainants recover all their items and are made whole by the defendants (paid off), they don't prosecute. A good catch, but they had to be released to prey on another innocent victim who could suffer a worse fate. Failures to prosecute always disappointed me even when receiving an award.

Barricaded Gunmen

There was usually only one 70 (Sergeant) Unit on the street, but with the mass hiring's and affirmative action promotions sometimes we would have two. One day when one of the Sergeants was busy on the East Side of the Precinct with a barricaded gunman, as luck would have it, we received a radio run with the new female Sergeant (11-71), "A Barricaded Gunman with an 8 year old hostage." When we arrived the Sergeant had just pulled up and was talking to the grandmother of the child. Our Sergeant came from the Women's Division and didn't have any scout car experience. She was upset with this being her first command decision, but the good thing was she knew she didn't know what to do and was willing to let us take over. We had her and her Corporal watch the back so the suspect couldn't get out that way and also it got her out of our way.

In the 70's we didn't have enough cars to tie them up for hours on one call because people who needed immediate help wouldn't get it. Our usual mind set was to get it done quickly and safely as possible, but get it done. The grandmother gave us the front door key and she helped draw up a quick sketch for us of the interior of the house and where he was in the house. We had her call him as we snuck up and peeked into his bedroom window. He was lying on his back in a twin bed with a shotgun lying on his stomach pointed sideways away from the door and closet. We could see the young boy sitting on the floor in the closet out of the line of fire. We used the key and quietly opened the front door and approached his bedroom door that was slightly ajar. My partner quietly picked up a heavy wood kitchen chair that was next to the door and quickly threw it into the bed room door opening which shocked the suspect causing him to freeze for a moment. Almost immediately as he threw the chair, I ran in and yelled "Drop it" while pointing a 12 gage riot shotgun at his face. I knew, with a kid in the closet, as soon as he started to raise the gun, I would fire; luckily he didn't. He was so surprised that we were even in his house let alone that we had a shot gun inches from his face, that he slowly raised his hands as my partner removed his weapon. We handcuffed him, got the boy out of the closet, and gave him to a very happy grandmother who was crying and hugging us. The Sergeant was extremely happy and relieved and she let us know what a great job she thought we did. We smiled because we knew no other Sergeant would have let us do it our way. We would have been tied up for hours just like the barricaded gunman on the other side of the Precinct. She knew we called and peeked in the window, but she didn't know that we rushed him.

We didn't have a regular supervisor to give us our yearly service rating but working Special Ops the shift supervisors usually gave us top ratings that only went up to 90, not 100. When I got my rating the Lieutenant told me that the new Sergeant tried to rate me a 95 that didn't exist. She told him it was because she liked the way I handled a barricaded gunman situation. I ended up getting an 88 and the averages were in the 70's so I was happy. It is possible that some of the reason for the super high rating she was giving me was partly because I didn't make an issue out of how she handled her first barricaded gunman. She was the first female supervisor we had dealt with, but not the last.

After they got to know we were fair, but tough and gave them their respect as supervisors, they usually let us do what needed to be done, our way. Unfortunately, the poor guys working on the shifts under them weren't so lucky.

New Lieutenant / Court Time

We made a lot of felony arrests and mostly worked the night shift meaning we spent the days in court on trials making time and a half. My partner liked locking up predators and the extra money for going to court. He was married with a bunch of kids and needed the court time. I hated court, but liked locking up the bad guys. So my partner handled going for warrants and trials and I only went on the final trial when I had to; which was still a lot more than I wanted to. My partner, the forever jokester, started putting the name of one of the old time Sergeant's on some of our arrest reports, as a joke. We were on a long homicide trial and every day the Sergeant showed up at the trial making time and a half as he was working the night shift. When the prosecutor finally asked him what he did and what he could testify to, he said he didn't even remember being there. Right away I looked over at my partner who had a big smile on his face and I knew he had pulled something. When the prosecutor walked away the Sergeant told us he received a subpoena by the homicide section and this wasn't the first time. My partner, while laughing, said he just put the Sergeant's name on some of our reports as Sergeant at the scene for a joke. The Sergeant loved the joke and loved us after that, but didn't go back to court again. He picked up some pizza and beer for us at his apartment and we had a new friend. Most everybody by then thought we were a little bit nuts and we probably were at that point, but our Sergeant friend out did us.

Nobody usually wore their hat when on desk duty, but the Sergeant started wearing his hat inside, outside, and all the time. He was a good street cop and supervisor but started acting strange after two times being passed over for promotion to Lieutenant even though he out-scored minorities that were promoted.

One day we came right out and asked him why he was wearing his hat inside while on desk duty. He said matter-of-factly that he did it because of gamma rays, and took off his hat to show he had lined it with tin foil. He put it back on and told us we should do the same as the rays were bad this time of the year. We weren't laughing this time because this wasn't a joke; he was serious. Not long before that we had an officer commit suicide after studying for a year and then being passed over again for Sergeant after scoring high. He had watched other minorities promoted with way lower scores and it finally took its toll on him. Affirmative Action was affecting a lot of the guys in different ways and none of them were positive. About a month after the gamma ray incident, our new friend the Sergeant came in wearing his new Lieutenant's uniform. Everyone was happy for him and congratulated him on his promotion. He then went to the roll call room and held his first roll call as a Lieutenant. Later in the night, we heard that they had taken him to the hospital and he was soon retired as he had a mental breakdown. We found out that he wasn't promoted he just bought his own Lieutenants uniform, bars and all and fooled everyone.

I felt bad for him as he was retired on a disability, but still had to laugh as he went out in style and fooled everybody including us. If they weren't going to make him a Lieutenant, he would do it himself. Our kind of guy!

Still a Character/ Finger Prints

My partner was still pulling jokes and I loved it as long as they didn't hurt anybody and just gave everyone a good laugh. I would just tell him one of these days he was going to get us in trouble. We had been through a lot together already – shot at many times, fights with violent resisting felons, barricaded gunmen, etc. I actually enjoyed his antics, but always complained so he didn't go overboard and I didn't really know how far he would go.

When at the station, now and then, he would walk behind the front desk and put a couple of drops of skunk perfume in the trash can. Skunk perfume was sold by novelty shops and smelled like rotten eggs or very strong, disgusting passed gas. I don't know how they didn't catch on but he would do it 2 or 3 times a night and then not do it again for weeks. They would all be bitching about who stunk up the station and were pissed off trying to find out who was passing bad gas. The hard part for me was trying not to laugh. I usually went into the back where our offices were, as fast as possible, then collapsed in hysterics. With our reputation you would think somebody would have figured out that something always happened when we were in the station with a prisoner.

Sometimes we would get a citizen who demanded special treatment and just wouldn't listen to us. Usually they wanted us to take finger prints. Of course my partner had an answer for the ones who wouldn't wait for the detectives to do it. He kept a shaker full of baby powder and some scotch tape in his briefcase in the trunk of our scout car. He would shake it all over their house making a mess and putting scotch tape on different areas usually at the locations the person thought there might be prints. I just shook my head knowing he was making the citizen happy and immensely enjoying himself.

The detectives were so busy they never took prints on things like burglaries and such. Some of the detectives would make a comment to us with a smile about how their burglary victim told them the officers at the scene took finger prints already and they always knew it was us. I think the detectives got a kick out of the way we did things as they never complained either. When they needed someone arrested they usually came to us because we would get right on it until we got the guy. Working the 80-Series and not receiving regular radio runs gave us more time to hunt felons and that worked out well for us and the Detective Bureau.

Carter Elected

In late 1976 Jimmy Carter was elected President and that opened the spigot of money flowing into Detroit for the next 4 years. It was just in time for Coleman Young's re-election run. He was using the money as fast as he could to make himself a hero in the black community that was his main constituents. He stepped up his far left policies and race based politics. White's and businesses left Detroit in droves because of his rhetoric, crime and tax policies. On the other hand, he spent money on numerous failed programs like midnight basketball to keep kids off the street that the press pushed until the cutting and shootings started. Then it was quietly ignored. Same as the hiring of gang members for neighborhood watch security. Carter's Housing Urban Development (H.U.D.) was rebuilding the same houses over and over as the tenants didn't pay and then the neighbors stripped them for H.U.D. to fix and give them away again. The mini stations and all the officer's benefits and salary were paid for by Carter's federal money. Every park or City property sign had been replaced with a new one with "Coleman A. Young Mayor" on it bigger than the name of the building or department. The only thing that didn't have his name in large letters was the police cars because as soon as they put on the decals with his name, they were removed. We called him King Coleman and he called us White Occupation Troops. The Manoogian Mansion was available as the Detroit Mayor's residence during a Mayors term. The Mayors before Coleman and the Mayors after him chose not to live in the Mansion to save cost. Coleman Young chose to live there his entire 20-year reign and periodically refurbished it. His river side area wasn't big enough for a private pool so he took some land from the City Park next to the mansion to satisfy the zoning ordinance and put in a pool.

At that time, City workers were banned from talking to the press and he packed the City payrolls with supporters with high salaries. Of course the only raises cops got were from court ordered arbitration and we always were paid less than that of other Cities. He was packing the Police Department with less qualified officers and supervisors as fast as he could. In 1977 they hired and promoted a record number of officers. Of the over 1200 hired, 1100 were minorities and the standards had hit rock bottom. They were no longer individually investigated, but pushed through a controlled oral board type system and it showed. His first term, our arrest where up each year, but somehow the prosecutions were down with each year. We had a shortage of street cops and he had over thirty body guards; the past Mayors had only six. We had a fixed wing air plane supposedly for picking up out of state prisoners, but that rarely happened. Most of the flights weren't police related and a lot of the flight plans were bogus when checked. The Mayor was good at separating the races for political gain and retribution instead of rebuilding the City. The new hires from the Mayor on down had an entitlement mentality and were fully taking advantage of it legally or otherwise. Normally when a citizen wanted to report a crime, you took it. It also showed statistics of where crime was happening and if you got lazy and didn't take it you could catch hell. With the new attitude of the City and supervisors not wanting crime statistics up, officers weren't pushed to take reports if the complainant wasn't injured or there wasn't a good likelihood of an arrest or prosecution. Even with that agenda, crime soared and the tax paying population declined. Even our police dogs were affected; they were trained in "Bark & Hold" instead of "Bite & Hold" like everywhere else. A strong message was being sent that perpetrator rights were more important than victim rights in the Big "D" because the Administration wanted to show they were fixing past racial injustice. The problem was the whites just left and poor and middle class blacks were the victims and we saw it first-hand daily. We were still at the beginning of the big downward slide. The homicides solved were at 70+ percent, but later went to be 70% unsolved. The gangs and black organized crime were fighting over the narcotics trade that was being taken over from the Italian Mafia. Henry "The Blaze" Mazette the black godfather, with my old gambling (numbers) conspiracy cases crime boss, Edward "Big Foot Eddie" Wingate who had early ties with the Mayor, had obtained their own international connections for drugs. Yes, our new president, Jimmy Carter, didn't have a clue and our Mayor and his people would play him like a fiddle for their own gain, with a lot of federal money coming in without any restrictions or accountability.

There wasn't much us street cops could do about the upper level corruption, but that did take the spot light off of us so we could do our jobs better. A lot of department cops also served in combat in Vietnam and lost close friends. When President Carter gave amnesty to all the draft dodgers who ran off to Canada while they fought, it didn't go over well. In the mid to late seventies we had the Triple Crown of losers - President Carter who didn't have a clue, Governor Milliken who was a wolf in sheep's clothing and Mayor Coleman A. Young, who was full of hate and would bite off his own nose to spite his face. Well at least they were a bi-partisan bunch that sped up the downfall of a great City and drove the middle class blacks and whites out under their rein.

We were backing up a scout car that had a radio run of a man on the porch with a rifle. As we stopped our vehicle two houses and across the street from him, he started shooting as we exited our vehicle. We both took cover behind the trees directly across from him as he went back into the house. We notified radio we had shots being fired and a barricaded gunman situation. Twenty-four hundred responded that they were almost there and to have everybody hold their positions. Twenty-four hundred was the roving inspector and was in charge of everything out on the street when he was out there. Bad news for us was that we had to sit and wait instead of handling it our way quick and safe, then move on. Because of that, it could turn into an all-day thing. That is not the way we handle these situations, but it was the City's new way and that lasted for 40 years until they finally realized people died. It went back to our way in 2015 and they let us cops go get-em before someone else was hurt or killed.

As the Inspector (twenty-four hundred) came flying around the corner almost on two wheels with his tire's squealing we couldn't believe our eyes. It was one of our Precinct inspectors who usually kept a low profile because he was usually half drunk. He wore a toupee and every time you did see him his hair line was up or down, never the same. Here we were taking cover behind a tree from an active shooter and as he came around the corner we could see though his open driver's window his toupee flapping up and down from the wind. We looked at each other and started to laugh like hell at the sight we were witnessing. As he pulled up right in front of the shooters front door, we quickly stopped laughing and started yelling and pointing to him as we left our cover to get his attention. He finally realized where he was and pulled off around the corner.

We were in the best position to keep the gunman contained until all the Precinct units were ordered to leave the area, including ours. The Tactical Mobile Unit was to take over the scene on his orders. We were amazed that we had to leave and had to expose ourselves to the gunman to get out of a position that someone would have to take a risk to get into. It was the best spot to keep him from being on the loose. What do we know, this is the new way of doing things and they somehow think every situation is to be handled in the same way no matter what the circumstances are. We did what we were told and left the scene. Nobody could get back into our original position because he kept coming out and firing shots when they tried to get back to the spot. He then got into his vehicle with no one able to stop him. Now they had a mobile gunman on their hands driving all over putting everybody, including the public, in danger. You never let a gunman on the loose like that, but in this case, they got lucky and he surrendered. Oh for the good old days before mass promotions of the unqualified. Still we had a good laugh and the inspector kept a low profile until he was fired for running over a fisherman in his boat while off duty and drunk on Lake St. Clair cutting his victim's fingers off while he was fishing.

Minority Supervisors

There was a big difference between affirmative action promotions and minority promotions. One group was qualified and one group wasn't. The minorities who hired in before the standards were drastically lowered and worked the streets to gain valuable experience made good supervisors and knew we were out there taking risks to protect those that needed us. The affirmative action group usually took the inside jobs avoiding real police work at all cost and doing their studying for the promotional exam while on duty. Some, who were connected, even attended classes while on the payroll. Even with that advantage, a lot of them hired in the mid-seventies still couldn't pass the promotional exam, so separate promotional lists were created.

There were two lists: Blacks, Females and White Males. So in effect a white male was only promoted after minority officers had been promoted on each round. A white male would have to write in the 90's to stand a chance to even get on a promotional list. The minorities were promoted to every other spot while writing in the low 70's and that was with extra pre-test classes. Knowing you weren't on a level playing field and competing for 30 slots from thousands of competitors and no time to study was frustrating for many. Most of us knew we weren't going to get promoted to Sergeant and Lieutenant was even worse odds. So we just kept working the streets trying to earn and keep the respect of each other and the new supervisors who we had to work with from then on.

It took over twenty years to reverse the City's affirmative action promotion policy and most likely that was because the white officers were then the minority. Most of us didn't even bother to take the test or study for it any more. Personally, I liked working the street and didn't want anything to do with being a supervisor. I felt bad for all the good hardworking cops who did want to move up the ranks and couldn't because of their skin color or sex. I found reverse discrimination (Affirmative Action) just as bad as discrimination. I also found lowering the standards in certain occupations to be extremely dangerous in many ways. Even in 1977 you didn't need a crystal ball to see what this was going to, and already had started to, do to Detroit and its Police Department. Whites had no future and most blacks didn't want to be cops, so you weren't going to be getting the cream of the crop in applicants, especially in mass hiring.

From 1970 to 1974 my first four years the minority officers had it tougher than us because their family, friends and neighbors didn't like cops and didn't understand they were trying to help their communities. Some of them, who were hired and promoted because they earned it, weren't too happy to be looked at as affirmative action recipients and they would let you know it. After 1974 the Administration was trying to divide the police department by the races and they weren't totally successful, because like the military in combat we street warriors black and white had to depend on each other first to survive.

The others would take the easier way of avoiding trouble on the street and staying out of our way. So what really happened was the cops, black or white, who earned respect by proving themselves, were tight with each other. The dead beats were just dead beats that should never have been hired. Sadly, we were getting more dead beats with attitudes as time went on and we all know what that led to.

We had rookie police women barely out of the academy grabbing car keys and announcing it was their turn to drive before they even knew the streets or how addresses ran. Some of them carried .357 and .44 Mag. revolvers and couldn't shoot them if their lives depended on it and it did. After quite a few incidents of not being able to handle their weapons, the department finally issued a general order that you had to qualify with the weapon you carried. They had to be taught that the senior person on the vehicle was in charge and responsible for both of their actions. It wasn't because they were female or a minority; it was because of the lack of experience and part of a learning experience that everyone went through. I was glad that I was always in units that you had to earn your way into, instead of putting up with those who thought things were owed to them. There were good police women on the street and they knew they had to learn and prove themselves by their actions and they did. The female supervisors on the street had a different problem. They were in charge and had little, if any, street experience. Some were smart enough to at least listen to and take advice from the experienced senior officers. We tried to help them as discreetly as possible to get the job done and not to embarrass them. Still some in their arrogance and to show everybody they were in charge, made some big screw ups that in the end caused them embarrassment and lack of respect from the troops. Not to mention court cases and evidence would be ruined if not handled properly.

We had a female Sergeant insist and make officers at a homicide scene move a dead body out of the rain which totally destroyed the homicide scene. There was another situation with a dog gone mad and the Sergeant instead of capturing or shooting it if necessary, ordered the officers at the scene to hit it with their black jacks to render it unconscious. Anybody with a brain would know you don't usually just knock out a dog or even a person with a hit on the head. Of course, the apartment ended up a mess and the dog didn't survive after being bludgeoned by the officers with black jacks. They were trying to write the officers up, but the Sergeant had put in her report that she had ordered them to do it. Naturally the investigation ended there. Usually they would listen to us as we didn't work directly under them, but as time went on it got worse for the shift guys who did work under them.

One night we brought in an unruly prisoner who was street smart and had to be made to do everything including being handcuffed, get into and out of the car and even walk into the station. When he wouldn't sit down in the lockup room for the doorman we sat him down forcefully. He was smart enough to resist without fighting and making everything difficult. We had a new affirmative action Lieutenant working the desk who took umbrage with the way we sat the prisoner down and rushed back into the lock up demanding loudly that we stand him up. We stood him up, took off our hand cuffs, gave the Lieutenant a dirty look and then whispered to the doorman to be careful that the prisoner was violent. We had a reputation that we not only didn't rough up handcuffed prisoners, we didn't allow it. We made a lot of arrests and our commander who also was black knew how we worked. The Lieutenant, kind of, apologized to us the next day when we came in and told us he didn't know the prisoner was so troublesome. One of the desk officers later told us that after the Lieutenant apologized to the prisoner for our behavior, the prisoner spit in his face, slapped him and called him a Nig.... It shocked the hell out of him and apparently he was so upset he got called into the Commander's office who straightened him out. After that he had a complete turnaround with us and I suspect the Commander had a lot to do with it.

Female Partners

In 1977 the shifts were flooded with new female officers, but we didn't have any females or rookies in our units. Pre 1977, we were mostly all male officers on the street and even hearing a woman's voice on the radio was strange to us. When they had a serious run we would back them up just like we did for everybody, but we sure didn't want to work with them anymore than working with any rookie. Our unit went from one serious call to another and we didn't have time to teach or protect an inexperienced partner, that could get us or them killed. So when one of the shift Sergeants, who was a friend, kept asking me to take a female rookie partner out on the street, I finally said ok because my regular partner wanted to go home sick. I called dispatch and told them to shut down 11-82 the felony car, and put us on as 11-3 a regular scout car. I advised them I was working with a brand new female rookie. I hadn't worked a regular shift car since I was a rookie and never had worked with a brand new rookie, or a female. I was very apprehensive because I never had to worry too much about keeping my partner safe and memories of Danny Ellis who was killed protecting my rookie classmate at #7 who selflessly worked with us. I really didn't totally understand the extra chance he was taking at the time, but now I did. I just wanted to get her through the shift alive and in one piece. I was so nervous with the situation, even as a single party boy I didn't think about trying to impress her as I had heard she was single and from a famous family and happened to be a total knock-out.

She seemed intelligent and very professional, wanting to learn and that took the edge off a little. I was still going to be cautious as I didn't know what to do with a rookie. It didn't take long as our first radio run was "family trouble, man on the porch with an axe." I don't know if she was scared or not, but she gave me a big smile like this has to be bull shit and then told dispatch we were on the way. I always took everything on the street as possibly worse than better, but this run on the day shift could be phony. Still taking no chances on the way there I told her not to get out of the vehicle. I told her to have the radio mic in her left hand and her gun in her right hand and to call for help if needed, then protect herself. We pulled up one house away and sure enough there was one big angry man with a huge axe on the porch. I ordered him to the ground at gun point; to my relief, he dropped the axe and let me handcuff him. When I looked back at my partner, I couldn't have been more pleased because she did exactly as she was told. She took it serious and had the radio mic in her hand with her door half-open and her gun in her other hand. I knew then she would be a good street cop because she wasn't afraid and was smart enough to learn anything could and would happen. She did turn out to be a good street cop.

The public also had a hard time adjusting to uniform police women working the street. We had another run to Van Dyke and East Outer Drive, "A rape just happened." When we arrived a young 18 year old girl was alone in a Doctor's office; she was the receptionist and everyone else was out to lunch. I quickly got a description and was putting the info out on the radio. I thought it would be easier on her to give the details to a police woman instead of me. To our surprise she said she didn't want to talk to her, but wanted to talk to the police officer, meaning me. I could see then that the public hadn't adjusted to uniform females yet.

It was especially tempting for some of the married guys who all of a sudden had a bunch of young attractive women working with them who looked up to them, causing a lot of hanky-panky. Some of the Sergeants were using them as Corporals to drive them around, which was ridicules as new rookies were usually not allowed to drive right away. It took quite a while to learn the streets and how the addresses ran. One of the guys actually created a contest that they bet on which supervisor or crew knocked up a new female rookie first. It didn't take long for it to happen as one of the new married Sergeants was to be a new father. Even some of my old married partners got into big messes by dating them. Most of us single guys avoided them like the plague dating wise as we saw what a soap opera was going on. I was confronted by one who asked me, "What's wrong with us that you won't go out with us?" I just laughed it off saying dating a co-worker, especially a cop, was a bad idea. My real thought was that it was just nuts and dangerous for both parties.

From 1977 on, it would never be the same as the mass changes that started in 1974 were coming into effect. Later studies showed that the female officers started trying to imitate the male officers, trying to be macho and sexually open like males. This caused a lot of problems at work and in the home life of the married cops of both sexes. Whenever there was a Precinct event where the females could dress up and be seen out of uniform, they would be dressed as sexy and hot as they could be to show they were still women. Nothing wrong with that except male, macho cops took advantage of the rookies.

Rubber head and the Moose

My neighbor was a beauty school drop-out and used to give me haircuts on my front porch. He would never accept any money and just told me to buy him a beer sometime. He hung out at a small local bar on Harper Ave. that wasn't my kind of place, but to pay him back for the free haircuts I told him I would meet him and buy. Unknown to me, he had a couple of enemies who were always up there. I walked in with my new civilian roommate and walked straight to the back of the bar where he was sitting. We sat down and I ordered beers for us and then all of a sudden two large men came walking toward us very fast. I turned to look just as the biggest one hit my neighbor so hard with a right hook that he flew off his stool. He landed 3 or 4 feet away. As I kept turning and saying "Hey," he immediately hit me with a left hook knocking me up against the bar. Then his body builder buddy threw my roommate over the pool table and against the wall. Both, my neighbor and roommate smartly stayed on the ground. The big one whose nickname was Moose and an ex-heavy weight boxer, continued to punch me like I was a speed bag over and over. I was knocked silly, but afraid to go down as his buddy was next to him and dancing back and forth like he was trying to get close enough to get in a hit or two. My neighbor and roommate were able to get out of the bar while I was being pounded. I was telling them very calmly, per later testimony, to "calm down, I am a police officer," numerous times. I somehow saw a gap between the two of them and quickly moved through it to get behind them and out the door. Only the body builder followed closely behind and attempted a spin type karate kick at my head which I ducked. He attempted a second kick and as he spun my roommate, who also took karate, kicked his foot out from under him. The body builder then gave chase after him as he took off. I was battered and bleeding from my lips and dizzy, but my senses were coming back. I saw a phone booth and called 911 as my neighbor and roommate showed up safe and sound. I was pissed, but not as pissed as I got with the new civilian 911 operator. I told her I was a police officer who with 2 other civilians, had just been assaulted and injured by 2 men who were still at the scene. She asked me numerous questions like my badge number and where and who I worked for which was fine and if I needed an ambulance which I told her no. She then told me if I wasn't that injured to go into the 15th Precinct and make a report at my earliest convenience. Wow, no wonder the public lied to get a scout car out to the scene. I repeated that the perpetrators were still at the scene and I needed a scout car and a supervisor right away. She again told me I needed to go into the station to make a report. I told her, no problem, I am going back in the bar and make the arrest myself even if I have to shoot somebody to do it because my request for a car was denied and I hung up. I was livid and told my friends to go home and started back to the bar pretty sure she would send a car now at least to protect the perps from getting shot. A few minutes later a supervisor and a scout car showed up and we went into the bar to make the arrest. With the 911 operators delay they had enough time to get away. Luckily we had good witnesses still there to give statements.

When I went home that night I must have had a concussion because I had a hell of a headache and kept throwing up. I didn't remember identifying myself as a police officer over and over as all the witnesses said or calmly telling them to calm down without fighting back. The first few hits must have caused it because I remembered everything else and the only visible damage to me was two split lips. The next day the detectives from #15 wrote up a warrant request for John Does with a physical description until we could get actual names for an assault and battery of a police officer warrant. Then I was surprised to learn I had to get the new Commander of the 15th to sign off on it. It seemed that I had fewer rights than a citizen who had been assaulted. I was even more surprised at his interrogation of me accusing me of being drunk in a bar and starting a fight. I didn't like it, but told him I just walked into the bar and hadn't even took a sip of my first beer when I, and my friends, were sucker punched and it was the first time I was ever in that bar. I could see he didn't believe me so I told him it was all in the witness statements and I knew none of them. He then said in a threatening manor, I'll call your Commander who is a personal friend and see just what kind of officer you are. I was disgusted with this Commander, but happy he was going to call my Commander. After his call, he told me my Commander told him to sign off on the warrant as I was a good officer who had never gotten into any kind of trouble on or off duty and he ok'd the warrants. Still I couldn't understand how anyone with any common sense could believe a drunken officer who started a fight would come in and try to get a warrant that could possibly get him fired; so much for the intelligence of some of our new Precinct Commanders. With the support of my Commander they were able to go after these guys.

When we found out their names and addresses, The Cruiser of #15 started visiting their houses. They complained to my neighbor that the Big Four was after them and they ended up turning themselves in because they were scared to death of the Big Four arresting them the hard way for assaulting a cop. They were both found guilty, fined and put on probation with attending AA for a year. I later learned what set them off. When my neighbor entered the bar before I got there he showed them a rifle round and told them the next time they would see it, it would be in their head. Now I knew there was more to it.

With the size of these guys and one being an ex-heavyweight boxer pounding on me some of the guys gave me a new nickname and started calling me "Rubber Head" because I didn't go down when pounded or receive serious injury.

The only reason I didn't go down was fear of being kicked to death, so I continued bouncing off the padded bar edge back into him over and over. Now my partner (The Character) who spread the stories of me before battling with big guys had another story to embellish about the little cop.

Years later, I was introduced to a large young man as I was sitting in the Duchess Lounge. When the young man heard my name was Al and I was a Detroit cop he asked me if I knew anyone named Moose. Like a dummy I said yes and that I had a problem one time with a guy nicknamed Moose at a bar on Harper Avenue. He then told me that Moose was his Dad. I thought, "Oh, shit," this is going to be a big, big problem. I have had fights on duty and off duty and it always seemed to be with the big guys and this kid looked real tough. Me and my big mouth, will I ever learn? He really surprised me as he told me his Dad was a violent alcoholic who used to beat him and his Mother when he got drunk. He thanked me and shook my hand. My luck still was holding or like I said before, which I truly believe looking back, someone up there was watching out for me. He said after his Dad went to AA he stayed sober and completely turned around his and their lives. It was good to hear about something bad turning out good for once. I hope the other one changed directions and straightened out too.

Gino's Bouncer

We responded to a disturbance call at my friend's bar and bowling alley on Van Dyke and East Outer Drive (Gino's Falcon Show Bar) one morning when it was closed. I met the owner by the side door who excitedly was telling me one of his night bouncers had flipped out and was trying to get him to go with him. He said the bouncer was saying the world was going to end and he was inside busting up the place. My partner stayed in the car while I was talking to the owner. He didn't know what kind of problem was developing and cancelled the car that had the call. The bar owner was a big tough guy who knew how to take care of himself so if he couldn't handle the bouncer I knew it would be a problem for us too. I wished my partner wouldn't have cancelled the car because now we inherited the problem without backup. In the 70's we prided our macho selves and wouldn't call for backup unless absolutely needed. With the layoffs and shortage of cars at the time we tried to handle everything without tying up other units. When we went inside the bar, we saw he had smashed doors into kindling wood and was totally flipping out and screaming that, "it was all ending." We tried to calm him down and when he wouldn't I told him if he didn't he would have to go to jail. He approached me and said try it as he put his hands behind his back and turned around for a second to challenge and mock me, not expecting me to be able to handcuff him. I was ready with my handcuffs in my hand which he didn't see in the dark bar, and I clicked them on him before he could pull his hands apart. It was part fear, part experience and part luck on my part. He really got angry when he realized that I got cuffs on him that fast and he twisted, turned and resisted all the way out to the scout car. We had him in the sitting position, but he wouldn't put his legs in the car and kicked at us as we tried to put them in. I was out of breath from wrestling him at that point and tired of fighting with him, so I cracked him under his knee caps with my flashlight and in went his legs. On my way into the station he was still ranting and raving about the world ending and wouldn't calm down. I don't know why, maybe out of frustration, I told him, "You should be on TV-2 so everybody could see how you're acting." All of a sudden he said no TV, no TV-2 and sat back quietly and calmed right down. When we pulled into the police garage and started to take him out of our vehicle he started to pull away and resist again. Hoping we didn't have to wrestle with him again I said to him, "You want TV-2" and he stopped resisting and said no, no and calmed down again.

When we took him inside we told the new desk Sergeant and the doorman not to take his cuffs off as he was violent. We went into the back to do the report and see what they wanted to do with him as he was having some kind of a breakdown. A few minutes later the report clerk came into the back and told us our prisoner was tearing up the print room and throwing everybody all over the place. We ran back to the print room and found him in a corner with 3 or 4 officers around him trying to control him. I walked past them all and whispered in his ear, "You want TV-2" and then loudly told him to sit down. He immediately sat down and everybody was looking at me wondering what I said to him. I told the desk Sergeant he would be smart to get handcuffs back on him and walked away. They ended up cuffing him and sending him to Detroit General Hospital for observation without any prosecution. When asked what I said to him, I told them that I said that, "I would kick his ass again" and just left them shaking their heads. Sometimes weird things work and I learned to keep trying things; whatever it took.

Pimps & GM Executive

Not all the prostitutes on Woodward had pimps. The ones that didn't usually had to play cat and mouse with the pimps unless they were rag nasty and the pimps weren't interested. Pimps, just like in the movies, were violent predators who would beat, rape, and sometimes terrorize the hookers with lighter fluid. Some of the young girls were picked up in suburban rock-n-roll bars then wined and dined until hooked on drugs, then threatened and put out on the street to work. Others, who were doing a good business on their own, were forced to work for the pimps. A lot of hookers were transients and moved from City to City by crime organizations. After working most of my career on Woodward Ave., I did my job, and got my cases against the hookers, but felt sorry for most of them who didn't rob customers or cause other trouble. Whenever I could, right or wrong, I went after the pimps in full harassment mode. We shook them down every time we could and tried to bait them into taking a swing or doing something stupid. We embarrassed them in front of everybody and threatened them in private. The hookers loved it and quietly supplied us with some private information on the pimps, like where they lived and most important where their Mama's lived. Even pimps were very touchy about their mothers and they thought we were crazy enough to mess with their family so it was good to have that information. I had been undercover on the street so often and so long that for me to bully a bully or mess with a pimp put me dangerously close to a gray area. The pimps never challenged us and responded with a meek yes sir, no sir and I really didn't know what would happen if they did challenge us. Most likely something bad and I think they knew; we were ready for it.

There was a General Motors executive who was found tortured and killed in a field in Ferndale near 8 Mile and Woodward. He had been cut, burned and tortured for hours. The media was all over it and neither Ferndale nor Detroit wanted the case because of the media attention it was getting. In between police calls and our normal duties, we put out the word to the hookers we wanted to know what happened. The next day one of the hookers said she knew him and his regular girl who had a nasty pimp and they were both bad news. She was scared, but would talk to homicide if protected. She told us that the victim had been telling everybody he just inherited a lot of money and was now rich. Well that was a good motive to torture someone and maybe bleed him to death accidently. We heard later that his wife had just inherited money, not him. My theory was the pimp and the hooker tried to torture him into giving them money he really didn't have access to and he ended up bleeding to death. They dumped him in a field in Ferndale, but it was unknown where the murder actually happened. The sad, frustrating thing was neither City would talk to our hooker because they kept arguing it wasn't their case. If either City cared enough to get real time information they just might have found out where, when, and how it happened right away. Both Cities had our information, but the information was never acted on and it just disappeared into the woodwork; because neither City wanted to take it on. I couldn't help but wonder if it was because it was an election year and crime was up, especially homicides that they didn't care to follow-up on our calls. Busy as we were and without the time to get more involved, we had to move on knowing a big opportunity was missed to solve s major crime.

Off duty 1977

On duty, I was living one life working the gun car in uniform going from one felony to another felony. Off duty, I was living a different life but similar to when I worked undercover. I got to know the people who lived that life style when I worked the bars and clubs and I became a part of it. I did have a little taste of normal life when I had my children for a weekend or was with my new girlfriend who did live a normal life. She was young, quiet and what I called a real trooper because I took her to places that would have scared the hell out of most people. I took her to biker bars, gay bars, tough rock & roll joints, illegal after hour's clubs, go-go bars, and all black private he-she show bars, etc., etc. She quietly took it in as an educational experience. She trusted me and didn't judge other people's life styles while in their place and everyone was friendly and accepted her. She had a normal life and kept busy with her work and school. Even though we weren't exclusively dating she was already the rock in my crazy life and somehow seemed to understand and accept me. We spent time together with my kids and took them on trips up North and enjoyed holidays like a family. She didn't try to be their mother, just their dad's girlfriend and their friend and we all got along fantastically. One day I decided to get a dog and we picked up a Doberman puppy together and called her Doobie. People were surprised that a cop would name his dog Doobie, but it wasn't what most people thought. At the time, Dobie was a common name for a Doberman and I wanted something different and since I always liked the Doobie Brothers band, she became Doobie. She picked up my personality, was friendly and easy going, but could and would kick butt if requested or be pretty intimidating. She was good with the kids and very protective of all of us giving warnings when a stranger was to close or threatening.

I was starting to get a taste of normal life again after years of big City street living and constantly under duress. I did, somewhere way back in my memory, remember a little bit about suburban living, but that wasn't going to last. The kids went home, my girlfriend went back to her normal working life and I hit the streets again 24/7 cop until the next time we got together.

Special Operations Ends

The Mayor was re-elected, budgets cut, cops laid off, crime spiked, Judge Del-Rio was charged with misconduct and the other radical judges were releasing felons as fast as we brought them in. President Jimmy Carter's first chunk of money had almost all been spent and midnight basketball, gangs in charge and being paid for as neighborhood watch, were all failures. The attitude of the criminals on the street was "we are in charge now." This was the monster the mayor created and he couldn't control it. They promoted so many affirmative action Sergeants it seemed like there was at least one Sergeant for every 3 cops. They tried to lay off white males with higher seniority and keep lower seniority affirmative action hires until the courts stopped them. Our unit, Precinct Special Operations, was eliminated with the elimination of Precinct Narcotics, Eighty-Series, and moving the Thirty-Series (B&E Car) to the Detective Bureau (#11-I0S) while cutting it down to one unit on steady nights. Morality was also moved to the Detective Bureau. It made no sense to us breaking up their most successful and dedicated teams who worked together like a fine tuned machine producing great results for years. Instead of being rewarded for the work and sacrifices they were just dumped without any notice or warning. Special Ops made more arrest and lost more officers killed, wounded, or injured, in the line of duty than all three shifts combined.

I was sad to see it go, but proud that I spent most of my career working it in one form or another. There were no dead beats only guys who were willing to pay the price for each other and do their job above and beyond what was required of them. Everybody in it had enough seniority to get off of the street and into a safer position, but volunteered to make a real difference in a tough, dangerous City. I was wondering what I was going to do, at this point, I was burned out on working undercover and hadn't worked a regular shift car since I was a rookie a long time ago. I didn't want it to end and I wasn't ready to slow down and have to work with anybody who wasn't full speed ahead. I also wasn't a ticket writer; I was a hunter looking for felons just like the rest of the 80-Series crews. We still had some good supervisors and the newer less enthusiastic officers were being laid off. The shifts would be shorthanded, but filled with more old Special Ops officers with street experience. I still wasn't crazy about writing tickets and doing normal Police work, but that wasn't all bad. Maybe some of us could be working together until they called back the ones who were laid off and maybe, just maybe, I might be ready for a normal assignment like a one-man report car or an inside position.

CHAPTER 8

Bravo Series - Unmarked Felony Car

11-9 Bravo

WITH ALL THE NEGATIVE CHANGES happening there was some good news that was totally unexpected. Coleman Young ran on demagoguing S.T.R.E.S.S. and the Big Four on his first election, but now, right after his second election win, with crime up and the streets controlled by thugs, he reversed his decision. The Precinct Cruisers (Big Four) were brought back. The only difference was it would have a Sergeant as its Crew Chief instead of a senior highly experienced officer in charge. Of course the Sergeant in charge didn't last long because most to the new Sergeants didn't have enough working street experience to be in charge of a crew that was experienced. So it went back to its original form with a real Crew Chief and its history as a unit that could and would handle anything that needed handling. Six senior highly experienced officers usually large, tough and intelligent were assigned with four working and two off duty daily. The driver was in uniform and the other three wore suits and ties or sport coats. They were supplied with big brand new black Chryslers and a long history to live up to.

With the Cruiser Crew picked, even though I wasn't the smallest cop in Detroit anymore, I still wasn't big enough for the Cruiser Crew. I figured I was going on to one of the shifts and I was all right with that. Before being placed on a new assignment, I was called into the Commander's office and wasn't sure what it as about. I knew I hadn't done anything wrong and I did get along well with him, so I was curious. When he told me I was to pick a crew for the new Bravo Series Car if I wanted it, I was pleasantly surprised. He told me it would be a felony car with uniform officers in an unmarked car handling only priority 1 and 2 radio runs. It would be steady nights working 7pm - 3am to overlap the shift change at midnight. Basically we would be doing almost the same thing that we did on 11-82 mostly working Woodward Avenue that was in 11-9's area, but could work the whole Precinct. We would be 11-9 Bravo working with the Cruiser (Big Four) and B&E Car on felonies without a direct supervisor. I told him I did want it and he told me that 11-9 Bravo and the Cruiser would be working for him and to let him know if we had any problems directly. I requested that my second on 11-82, my old partner (The Character) which he approved. He then suggested a young officer's name for our third man which, of course, I agreed with and he turned out to be a good honest hard working cop. We had a good crew and the only difference I could see was we were in an unmarked car and there was only one Bravo unit instead of three 80-Series Units. We still let Reverend Lund ride with us sometimes and used our hookers and connections for leads on felony arrests. We started what we called a "Want Book" as there weren't computers in the cars at that time. It was a large journal type book that we kept updated with pictures, Id's and information on felons we arrested and cross indexed with who they had been arrested with and their other associates. Then we would know how and where to get a hold of them and their cohorts quickly.

I spent a lot of off duty time with pictures of some nasty looking people working on the "Want Book". The "Want Book" idea came from the old Precinct Support Unit (PSU) that I spent my advance training in right after the academy years ago and it was still a great idea. PSU was like a mix between the Cruiser and Eighty-Series Cars. They were felony cars painted all black and had uniformed serious, experienced, go-getters working them. They did their homework to make a lot of good felony arrest. It later was turned into the S.T.R.E.S.S. Unit that also made a lot of good arrest, but was politically demagogued by the media and politics. Looking back, I can see now that my whole career was emulating PSU as they had my total respect.

I looked up to them and didn't have the chance to be a part of them since they had been eliminated before I had enough experience. Just like what was happening now to Precinct Special Ops, before the young go-getters have a chance to learn from them. I also always looked up to the Precinct Cruisers (Big Four), but being the smallest cop in Detroit for years, I never thought I had a chance to be a part of it except as a fill in once in a while. Now being able to work with the Cruiser and B&E Car was going to be a pretty good deal in my book.

Unmarked Vehicle / Stop & Searches

Our vehicle was a plain 4 door Plymouth with a police radio, hand held spot light, siren, and a little blue light with a magnet that you could put on your roof if needed. There wasn't a gun rack so our shot gun and M1 Carbine was kept in the trunk with our large bullet proof vest for raids. We were pleasantly surprised when we were called to meet Downtown Narcotics to be their uniform assist on raids in our Precinct. Our Special Ops Narco Crew who had been transferred downtown hadn't forgotten us. We had friends and co-workers who transferred downtown to Homicide, Organized Crime, and most other units that we volunteered to help anytime they wanted us to. One of our new connections was a State of Michigan Parole Officer who was looking for a felony absconder who had friends in our Precinct. We kept periodically checking the area for him until after about 2 months we spotted him and after a foot chase arrested him for violation of parole. Our new parole officer friend liked the way we stuck with it and wrote a nice Letter of Commendation to our Chief of Police to be put into our records. This was my 2nd letter of Commendation. My 3rd Letter of Commendation came from Chief of Police Hart a few weeks later for "Persistence and Diligence in a Felony Arrest".

Most criminals know a 4-door Plymouth could be a Police unit but still it let us get a little bit closer to them and that helped. It got a bit dicey going from point-A to point-B in a hurry and we knew if anything serious happened, it would be our responsibility. So there were advantages and disadvantages to an unmarked vehicle. We didn't write traffic tickets, but could, if necessary and carried tickets with us. I always found it humorous when someone decided to try to bully us or act out with a little road rage until we exited out vehicle while in uniform. One day we were driving on a side street at 15 mph which is the speed limit in front of a school when the guy behind us kept speeding up and almost hitting our rear bumper. He was attempting to get us to speed up and when we didn't, he sped past us giving us the finger while almost hitting a dog. We then hit the siren, pulled him over and gave him a 6-point reckless driving ticket while he whined about not knowing we were cops. Apparently he thought it was fine to try and intimidate everybody else. I usually didn't write traffic tickets, but that was the exact type of attitude I liked to adjust.

We only made traffic stops when the violation would give us a legal reason to look for guns or a person wanted on warrants. If they didn't stop, we would have to have a marked unit stop them for us, but they usually did stop and we made a lot of CCW motor vehicle arrests and got guns off the street. My partners loved going to court in the morning and getting overtime and I liked locking up felons and sleeping in the morning. We were always shaking down cars and suspicious people. I don't know how many guns we got off of the street, but I know it was a lot of them. Most of the time we didn't have any problems with the searches as we gently, but firmly, talked to the subject's as we patted them down and always made sure we had a legal stop and not just random stops.

I used to tell them that I wasn't going into their pockets but was going to pat them down for offensive weapons for their safety and mine, while I was investigating them. In most cases, they cooperated with me. By talking through it before they realized what we were doing, we were done. We found a gun or we didn't, and knew whether they were wanted on warrants or not. If they were clean, we told them we were going to give them a break on their initial violation and let them on their way while we joked around with them. Usually they were happy not to be going to jail for something as the ones we stopped usually weren't the hard working innocent residents. We were after guns and not little packets of heroin that might be in their pockets. That would have put us out of service for hours taking the dope down to central narcotics. Half of the people out on the street at night in our area were drug users and could be easy pickings. We wanted and hunted hold up men, burglars, shooters or violent wanted felons. Our function was also to respond to and back up the regular units on priority or dangerous type calls. At the midnight shift changes we would be the only unit out there for emergency calls until the midnight shift started so we tried to make ourselves available for dispatch.

Arab Markets

My partner (The Character) was still pulling tricks and jokes when he could. We had come to respect and made friends with a lot of the hard working Arab store owners who were in some of the worst parts of our Precinct. We would stop and have a pop or bag of chips with them while joking or just shooting the bull. They liked that we were looking out for them and understood their plight of trying to make an honest living in a tough neighborhood while assimilating to their new country. My understanding was that the Police in their home countries weren't so friendly or honest. Unfortunately, some of their son's and grandson's assimilated and entered into illegal professions.

My partner was usually chewing on something, munching on chips or Frito's. If he wasn't he was chewing on a tooth pick and more times than I can count, he would end up choking on pieces of one. Cops are a strange bunch and instead of being concerned or helping, we usually would just laugh and shake our heads until he choked it up or swallowed it. We became pretty hard on each other sometimes when we were doing dumb things. I used to use a nasal spray more often than I should have and sometimes my nose would just start gushing blood after an adrenaline rush from a phony call. My partners would shake their heads and tell me I better quit that shit before I bleed to death. It wasn't that we didn't care for each other; I think it was we lost patience with anybody who did dumb things including us. We also developed a strange sense of humor that I don't think a lot of people understood who hadn't seen or lived through life like we did. We saw the worst things imaginable on a daily basis and laughed whenever we could pull any humor out of a situation. Maybe it was a laugh so you didn't cry type of reaction. I don't know for sure, but most of us developed it and did a lot of laughing with and at each other. Sometimes after shaking a car load of guys for guns or wants on felony warrants, if they were clean, we let them go. I would then notice their rear license plate was covered with a Frito's bag. Of course, my partner (The Character) would have just finished eating a bag of Frito's that he just got at one of our party store friends places. He would have that sheepish grin and say nothing. I would just shake my head knowing those guys would be getting pulled over again as soon as another scout car saw their covered up license plate. I always wondered if any of them ever figured out how a Frito's bag got on the license plate or why they kept getting stopped.

The Tree

We responded to a radio run "Marx & Minnesota a man firing a gun." We had been to so many of these runs that it was almost like clockwork for us. We pulled up lights off driving slowly and closing our car doors quietly a half of a block away and walked quietly toward the location. We heard a shot and headed in that direction toward a S.E. corner house. We were quickly approaching when the suspect saw us and started firing at us. As usual that's when the chaos begins even when you're experienced. The only thing between him and us was open space and a two-inch wide tree that we both started doing the bump to get behind it for cover. We laughed at our silliness and then immediately charged toward him as that was the only real option. That apparently surprised the hell out of him and he quickly jumped inside his house. There still wasn't anywhere or anything for cover so we were plastered against the side of the house as he was trying to get a shot down at us. The angle downward put us just out of his range. As long as we pressed tight to the aluminum siding, the window he was trying to get a shot at us from was too high for him to shoot us. We notified dispatch that we were under fire and pinned down against the house. We couldn't get in and we couldn't back away because there just wasn't any cover anywhere. I was already getting cold and remembered being stuck lying in a cold wet snow bank for hours at another barricaded gunman years before and didn't want to go through that again. We started talking to him through the closed window and not being trained negotiators, simply let him know how it was going to go down with us. We told him if he gave up we would only kick his ass, but if he didn't we would kill him for shooting at us. After we had charged him while he was shooting we figured he most likely believed we were little nuts. He then charged out the rear door and my partner knocked him off his feet and I kicked him until we could remove his weapon. Another barricaded gunman situation handled quickly and mostly safe as I only broke a few bones in my foot. It turned out he had already been convicted of eight violent felonies and one was for murder. I was awarded my 7th Citation/Commendation for "While under fire displayed a calm & professional manner which resulted in the apprehension of one dangerous armed felon;" which meant, I got an extra day off with pay too. Well as any hard driven Inner City cop knows, after you almost get killed again you could really use a drink. The problem was when we left the hospital the stores were closed and neither of us had anything to drink at our houses. I knew my girlfriend had beer in her upper flat so I called her and she said no because she had to get up early in the morning. My partner (The Character) egged me on to tell her that I was injured and to play on her sympathy and it worked. I limped up her steps with my foot all wrapped up, playing it to the hilt while drinking all her beer then after, admitting my foot injury wasn't that bad. It was a good thing for me she was so easy going and didn't hold it against me even when I deserved it.

Suicides

We responded to attempted suicide calls as sometimes they could be dangerous and turn into a suicide by cop. I saw far too many of them that showed the victim had changed their mind, too late. On one such case the victim had blown out the pilot light of his oven, turned up the gas and put his head in it. It was apparent as his vomit trail led to the phone where he called 911 for help, but died before we got there. Sometimes the act was for attention and once put into motion went too far and sometimes it was quick and final, but messy. We took them all very serious and sometimes they wanted to take us with them. Another suicide attempt we went to the victim put a 22 cal. hand gun with low grain ammo near his temple and shot himself. As we entered he was holding his head, rocking back and forth and saying "my head, my head, it hurts." I kicked the gun that was lying at his feet away and pulled his hands away from his temple expecting a mess. I was amazed and shook my head as I saw he missed his temple. He hit the bone next to his temple and it was all black and you could see the small caliber round just under the skin. That was one of the goofiest attempts that I had seen and when the cop behind me said in amazement, "Wow, I'll bet you got a headache." We then stepped back and let EMS take care of him; I was on the verge of actually laughing at a suicide attempt hearing what the cop behind me said. Maybe, just maybe, we were out here too long and tried to find humor in almost anything.

We responded to another call, "Man with a rifle threatening suicide." As we pulled up his mother said he was in the basement with a rifle. He heard us as we entered and fired a shot up from the basement through the living room floor just inches from my foot. We had two choices, pull back and have a barricaded gunman situation or head for the basement steps. That was an easy choice for us as we learned to go forward instead of backward, if you can, and to keep the situation contained. We were at the bottom of the closed in basement steps and he was 10-15 feet away. He had the barrel of the rifle against the side of his head with his thumb on the trigger. We were trying to talk him down when the Sergeant and his Corporal ordered us back and they took the positions at the bottom of the steps. The Corporal that day was the Corporal because no one would work with him because he was an idiot. The Corporal whispered to the Sergeant that he could take him by rushing him which was stupid because he had not lowered the gun. It appeared he was going to drop it and give up and the Sergeant wasn't dumb enough to let him charge him. Right after the Corporal said he could take him someone on the stairway behind me immediately responded and said, "Take him." Of course the Corporal thought the Sergeant ok'd his request and he charged the victim who was putting the gun down. He knocked a couple of the victim's teeth out in the struggle with the Sergeant totally shocked because he didn't give the order. I don't know who said to take him, but it was almost a total disaster. Some statistic show cops committed three times the number of suicides as the general public does and some deny that statistic. I only know in the 1970's ten Detroit officers committed Suicide and I knew three of them personally. I, like most people, who weren't directly affected including physiologist, don't really understand until they are directly affected. Classroom theories help, but it can't be explained in books. You have to be there to really understand it.

Bubble Yum

We came into work one night and our silver unmarked car hadn't been brought back from the City garage where it was for minor repairs. We worked 7pm - 3am and the 30-Series car worked 8pm - 4am so we borrowed their blue unmarked car and hit the street figuring we could switch back later. When I was driving, I had to keep an eye on my partner (The Character) so he wouldn't get us in trouble. This particular night he was chewing as usual on a bunch of Bubble Yum. When I turned onto John-R Street from McNichols heading north I saw a sudden movement. It was his arm throwing a big piece of chewed Bubble Yum out his window in a quick movement while still looking straight ahead. To my chagrin, and total amazement, there was a Middle Eastern man sitting in his car with his arms on his driver's door window frame just staring into space. He was in deep thought or just day dreaming when a thud was heard and the Bubble Yum struck him in the upper forehead sticking there in his hair line. I quickly sped up and made a left turn while yelling at my partner and complaining again to him that he was going to get us in trouble. He just shrugged and innocently said, "what, what." I couldn't help but laugh because of the look on the guy's face of shock and surprise. I could imagine him trying to get the gum out of his hair after he realized what happened. We continued on patrol until 8pm when we were called into the station because the 30-Series wanted their car back. So we went in and switched cars with them and then continued working.

A few days later they were in the station bitching to some of the guys that they just got chewed out for throwing gum in some guy's hair and they didn't even do it. We made a quick exit knowing if we laughed, which we did, they would know it was us. It seems the guy came into the station with his hair full of Bubble Yum and said two white cops in a blue four door Plymouth police car threw gum in his hair and then took off. By then we had our silver car back and they had their blue car which got blamed. We decided to wait a few weeks for them to calm down before we confessed to them while laughing and teasing them about it for years. They were good cops and took it well that (The Character) struck again and they ended up the victims.

Devils Night

Devils night was a big night of mischief and arson fires in the City. We caught a group of teenagers with their pockets full of raw eggs on the north side of McNichols and John-R. Instead of getting tied up with a misdemeanor violation, we just broke the eggs in their pockets. Usually the teens from Detroit on the north side tossed eggs back and forth with the teens from Highland Park who lived on the south side of McNichols. With their eggs broken, we started to leave and I figured with no ammo (eggs) the battle would be over. Then, as we were getting into our car, (The Character) tossed some eggs over the buildings into Highland Park and a few minutes later, as we left; they returned fire with their eggs. My partner (The Character) was incorrigible, so I just laughed and drove off.

The arson fires were a different story, they were dangerous. The City down played the numbers of them and tried to portray them as greedy land lords burning their own buildings, or just dumpster fires. The truth is like the crime figures the City was cooking the books and skewing the numbers and those on the front lines knew it. Landlords couldn't get and didn't have fire insurance for one, and the City wasn't even counting the smaller fires like dumpster and small buildings (garages). Scout cars were pulling in one overhead door opening, volunteers were switching the used fire extinguishers for newly filled ones and then they went out through the opposite overhead door with newly filled ones in their trunks.

It was like a production line all night long and most of the minor fires were left to burn themselves out. That was just our Precinct and there were eleven others doing the same. Other Police calls went unanswered or delayed for hours. We still went from one emergency to another, as the shift cars ran from fire to fire all night long. It was a grand ole time for the low life's who took full advantage and most of it went unreported by the local media. The national media reported it, but really didn't know the real story of just how bad and dangerous it was. This was just the beginning of the murder and arson capital as it became nicknamed and we weren't allowed to talk to the press by this Administration.

Ransacked

The guys in #11 started to experience the decline of the Precinct as #11 was changing to look like old #7 or #10 when I worked there as a rookie. It was becoming a high violent crime area, with decay and animosity toward the Police that bordered on hate. It was getting as bad as the inner City Precinct's, even though it bordered the suburbs on the North (8 Mile Road). The 15th on the East was starting to get nasty too. Same with the 12th Precinct on the West side with Highland Park and Hamtramck to the South of the 11th. When I first came to #11 a few short years before, it was mostly Polish law abiding citizens who liked and respected cops. The main crime areas were Woodward Avenue, the projects, and the Harper & Van Dyke area that we called "The Hole." That used to belong to old #7 when I worked there years before. There were good and bad patches throughout the other area's that were changing almost monthly. My partners who hadn't worked at other Precincts were surprised by what was happening. I was used to the dirt, neglect, rats and cockroaches in homes we were sent to. In old #7 there were no good areas and #11 was rapidly heading there.

My partner (The Character) had a knack at criticizing someone while acting innocent or naïve. He would say to a complainant who had a break-in or a family disturbance, things like, "Wow, they really ransacked this place," when it was apparent it wasn't ransacked at all, it was just filthy and not taken care of. I always cringed when he did it, but no one ever seemed to catch on that he was commenting on their housekeeping. I was taught when at a call to never sit down or touch the phone to your ear and to keep moving so cockroaches wouldn't get on you. Now, years later, the cops who worked in the better Precincts, were learning that too.

While we were scratching ourselves, (The Character) and I would tell some of the guys assisting us with a lock up or conveying one of our prisoners that we thought the prisoner had body lice and they should let us know if we need to go the hospital. Of course the guys we did that to spent the next hour or so walking around scratching themselves thinking the worse. It was kind of like when you looked up into the sky like you were seeing something interesting and everybody else looks up too. Before you knew it everybody thought that they had body lice until the bosses told everybody that they didn't have them. By then we were all laughed out. We still had some decent areas, but spent our time in the higher crime areas as that is where we were needed most and there were more and more of those areas in the City.

"The Hole," Harper and Van Dyke area, was one of our most desolate areas with more vacant lots than houses. We had one scout car that broke records recovering stolen cars from suburban malls that were dumped their daily. The way it worked was a group would take the bus to the mall, do some shop lifting and when ready to leave, they would steal cars and bring them back to Harper and Van Dyke area to sell or strip. Stolen cars from suburban malls were recovered there every day. We didn't know it in the seventies, but that area was a future look at what Detroit neighborhoods were to become. It was no place to accidentally pull off of the Ford freeway I94 that ran through that area.

Farm a Lot

One of the car companies, with a lot of publicity from the media, plowed up vacant lots in neighborhoods and supplied the good people who lived next to the vacant lots with plants and seeds to garden it. This had been tried years before in #7 and people ended up fighting over it when the produce was ripe. Well the same thing happened again. After the older hard working couples planted, watered and weeded the gardens all summer, the lazy neighbors were steeling the produce when it was ready to pick and assaulting the older people that maintained the lots if they tried to stop them. This time it was even worse, as some of the older couples actually shot at and hit some of the thieves. It was one heck of a mess for us. We learned a long time ago in urban farming the scare crow needed to be armed.

Broken Axle / Sergeant Phones

Our unmarked car was an old detective car that was really beat up and was way up there on miles, but it got us around. One night a scout car crew had gotten into a chase with a burglary suspect and we headed over to help them out in case he bailed and there was a foot chase. That was exactly what happened. They lost him, but were able to put out a good description. A few minutes later while cruising through the alley with our lights out, we spotted him and drove quickly toward him before my partner could exit the vehicle. I was basically chasing him with the car as he was running on foot. My partner was trying to also get out on foot to chase him, but I never slowed enough for him to jump out. The suspect was running on the sidewalk. I was a little ahead so I made a quick left to cut him off, as my partner was starting to open his door and was off balance. The suspect was faster than I thought and as I completed my turn instead of being in front of him I was heading fast right at him. He was trapped between the vehicle and a brick wall. I had to hit the brakes or I would have hit him and the wall and most likely seriously injured him. I had misjudged my speed and distance and was stopped when my two front wheels, while braking hard, hit the curb. It broke both front A-frames causing the vehicle to come to an immediate stop, I was relieved that I didn't hit the suspect. The front of the car was only inches away from him and I am sure he expected to be hit. His eyes and mouth were wide open in shock. My face was right up to the wind shield as we looked at each other.

When I looked over at my partner he was almost on the dashboard because he was off balance when we came to the dead stop. The look on his face as to what just happened kicked in my weird sense of humor; with the relief that I didn't hit the suspect, I just started to laugh as the suspect started running again. He got away, but I'll bet he had the heck scared out of him as I know it scared us. As we waited for a tow truck my partner (The Character) didn't find it funny and was bitching at me that I nearly killed him.

In the 1970's, before the 1985 Supreme Court changed the law, an officer could shoot a fleeing burglary suspect as a last resort if he was getting away as one of the five Capital crimes. I don't think squashing one against a brick wall with a car would have qualified though, but I'll bet he didn't know that.

Nothing slowed down (The Character). Our old Precinct Special Ops office was next to the Lieutenant and Sergeants offices and we still used it. The walls between them were wood on the bottom and glass on the top, then open above that. You could see and hear into all the offices. On phones in the 1970's you could unscrew the mouth piece part and remove a little metal piece that looked like a flying saucer. With that piece removed you could hear, but the party on the other end couldn't hear you. When I walked into our office (The Character) was ducking below the glass part of the wall with his finger on his lips and waving for me to get down where we couldn't be seen. I ducked down with him and heard a Sergeant on the other side of the wall trying to explain to someone who he was and that he was investigating the citizen's complaint that they filed. The Sergeant was talking louder and louder and getting madder and madder because he wasn't getting the person on the other end to understand him. As we peeked over the wooden part of the wall after a few minutes we saw him open the desk drawer where (The Character) had put all the inner mouth pieces and he realized why the other party couldn't hear him, but he could hear them. He looked around and saw us peeking over and laughing at him and he smiled back. We had good old bosses still around and he was one of them. He just laughed and put the piece back in while pointing at us as we walked away cracking up.

Broken Black Jack / New Guy

We were responding to an "Officer in Trouble" call and as we pulled up there were 4 or 5 people tussling with two crews (4 officers) in the Nevada Projects. We and other officers were running toward the wrestling match and saw an officer swing his black jack at a suspect who was on top of a cop, just as one of the other responding officers was arriving at the pile up and was directly across from him. The officer arriving suddenly stopped and fell backwards, out like a light. The officer who had swung the black jack was looking at the limp piece of leather in his hand wondering what had just happened and with a goofy look on his face. The suspects were quickly handcuffed and everybody was trying to figure out how one officer had a big knot on his forehead and hadn't even reached the battle yet. The officer with the black jack was looking around for the end of his black jack. Of course we were laughing as no one was seriously hurt and we were far enough away to see what happened. The stitching at the end of the old black jack had worn away and the lead insert flew out like a projectile straight across to hit the approaching officer in the forehead as it was swung. Sometimes if too many people are involved in a scrum they can actually hurt each other and from a distance you can see the whole picture. It probably wasn't too funny to the officer with the knot on his head or the officer who put it there, but to us it was a hilarious sight like the Three Stooges would have done. Nobody ever seemed mad at us as we laughed at almost every crazy thing that happened, even when it happened to us. I think most of the guys thought we were over the edge anyway.

My partners were off and they scheduled me with a big new guy. We usually never worked with rookies and he was a big kid 6'4" and was pretty intelligent and excited to work the Bravo Car. I remembered how honored and excited I got when I had a chance to fill in on #7 Cruiser when I was a rookie. I figured with his size he could take care of himself. I didn't have much experience with brand new guys so I just told him to do what I told him to do and ask his questions later. Most of the night we responded to priority 1 and 2 runs backing up the cars that got them. I explained as much as I could about the Precinct and how to handle situations.

Just before midnight we got a run, "B&E in Progress Occupied Dwelling." On the way I explained to him there were no other cars on the street as it was shift change. I told him to go to the back corner of the house so he could cover the rear and one side of it. I was going to go to the opposite front corner to cover the front and opposite side so there was no escape. Then if it was a good B&E, I would let dispatch know and enter the premises. I must have scared the shit out of him because as I approached a broken basement window I could hear voices inside and got a weird feeling that someone was behind me. When I turned around, that great big kid was almost glued to my back startling the hell out of me. He was all excited and kept saying he heard voices. I gruffly & quietly told him to go back to the back and don't let anybody get out, I was going in and then I notified dispatch and they put out over the radio that we had a good B&E in progress.

I looked into the broken out basement window and saw it was only kids. I tried the side door that was unlocked and went in and handcuffed the kids together as another scout car from the new shift coming on duty arrived. I never told anybody else about it, but I teased the big guy for years about trying to hide behind a little cop. He always just said, "yeah, a crazy one too." He turned out to be a good street cop who was smart enough to get promoted to Sergeant as soon as he was eligible even with the stacked deck against him. After a few years, he finished law school and quit the job before he burnt out; like I said, smart kid.

11 Year Old Kills

Some kids growing up in the violent streets of Detroit never have the chance to be kids and would kill just like an adult. Some other kids are just that, kids and the problem was you didn't always know which ones you were dealing with. We had to be careful and understanding. Some of these inner City kids were tough as nails before they even hit their teens and suburbanites didn't even have a clue. It was totally different out there in the suburbs. There was a call of a Burglary in Progress and a perp was kicking in a front door. The 10-year old got his father's shotgun, racked it and took off the safety while pointing it at the door. He then told his 8-year old brother to climb on a chair next to the door and unlock it. As the perp knocked, the door opened and the 10-year old shot and killed the perp. The kids were excited and happy that they killed a B&E man with no regrets for taking a human life. They did what they had to, but it was sad that this was the world they were growing up in. It was survival of the fittest.

We also had an 11-year old boy who shot his little brother in the face with a shotgun killing him and making quite a mess. The kid had peed his pants and had a faraway look in his eyes as he was in shock and couldn't say a word. Other times, I've seen kids dancing around a dead person like it was party time with the adults egging them on. Some were taught that victims were losers and the predators were the winners. Guess what a lot of them chose to be later and usually they ended up being the real victims.

Ren Cen Hookers / Y.B.I.

With the layoffs we were shorthanded on the streets, but the guys who were working the streets were more experienced and motivated. Still calls went unanswered and it took a long time before citizens in the neighborhoods could get a car, if ever. When they did they were hostile because the crime was long over and the perp gone. Citizens quickly figured out they could get quicker service if they lied and said it was a shooting or a serious crime in progress, even when it wasn't. We went from one phony call to another all night long with real ones in between. So we were surprised to find out that this Administration had already assigned a mini-police force to Ford's Renaissance Center that was still being built. With the tax write offs, giving them free City services, it would never be profitable and in fact took more cops off the streets. Pure politics as Ford, most definitely, could use their own security sources. The reason wasn't just a new building, Ford was supporting this Administration with campaign funds and vocally. Before it was even completed there were arrests for prostitution, robbery and assaults including stabbings, and one homicide. They actually changed the design during construction to build a step type wall on the street side to keep the locals out and crime down inside for their image. They took from what few cops that were on the streets and moved some downtown to fool the public and the media about how safe the City was. Even so, it was never profitable and didn't revive downtown; it only helped the City to decline faster and used its valuable resources. The Renaissance Center and later the People Mover were and are financial losers.

Around this same time, but yet receiving none of the same press coverage, Young Boys Incorporated (Y.B.I.) was taking over the drug trade by using juveniles to sell and transport drugs, because they couldn't be prosecuted. They also got their own international supply of heroin eliminating the Italian Mafia. They were smart and had connections and were winning the drug wars on the street out-doing the other gangs. They dressed sharp with John Dillinger type derby's to show who they were. They mostly worked the west side and downtown so we didn't have much to do with them unless they were traveling through our area. It was curious to me as our Mayor also was known to wear a John Dillinger type derby on occasion. I later heard his favorite niece Cathy Volson was married to Johnny Curry who was big into the drug business. I didn't think much about it at the time as I wasn't working Narcotics or dealt with Y.B.I. or the west side gangs. Later my opinion was maybe somebody should take a look at their political connections, but I knew the Feds had already failed and the City wasn't going to do it. Maybe the Mayor just liked derby's and didn't know the meaning (gangsters) and the media, well, it wasn't part of their agenda to find out.

Pig – Copper Cruise

One of my co-workers got divorced and kept his large house in the settlement. We decided to rent out four of the six bedrooms to others from our two houses and I moved into his bigger house with Doobie. It had two fire places, family room and large swimming pool. We split the rent from all the others, with them paying the utilities. In effect I was basically almost living for free at the time. The good or bad thing was, depending on how you looked at it, with all young single cops it turned into a party house kind of like the movie "Animal

House" with constant action (without the mess). You had to lock yourself in your room and refuse to come out to get any rest.

Now I was not only living a crazy life on duty and off duty, but my home life was just as nuts. We were all hard working and hard drinking guys who kept going forward to keep from remembering the horrors of the past experiences we all had on the job. There was no brake or wind down and normality like the married guys had. Looking back, it was like a rollercoaster ride that never stopped and we didn't want it to. Having a safer job or slowing down off duty would give us too much time to think and that would have accelerated the burnout.

My old Sergeant from #7 and Northern District Morality who came to #11 also had a pig farm a few hours up North. One night, after I was partying all day and night and with only a few hours' sleep, I felt something pushing against my arm that was hanging off my bed. I looked with blurry eyes and saw a baby Arnold the pig snorting at me while pushing my hand with her snout. That's how I met Copper Cruise our new pet pig. My old partner

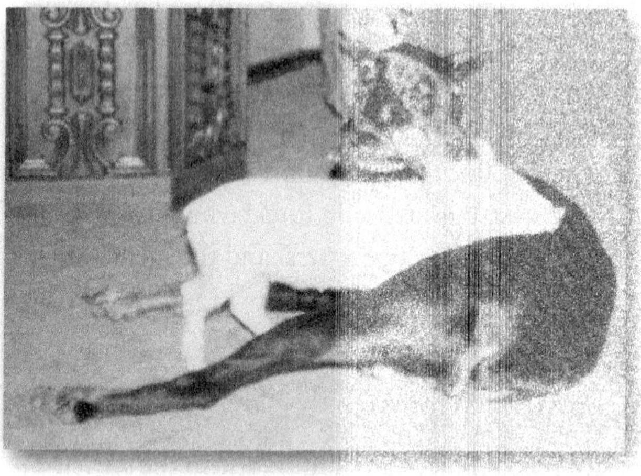

drove up North to the Sergeant's farm and brought a real baby pig back and left her at our house. The dog loved the pig and it was immediately house trained and started acting like a dog. Pigs really are smart and it fit right in this crazy animal house we lived in. She went everywhere the dog went and they usually slept curled up together with the dog protecting the pig like it was her pup. It went for car and even boat rides out to the Islands on Lake St. Clair to play. Neighbor kids would knock on our door so they could play with her in our yard. She was even used for the Police field day celebration. She loved her kiddy pool and the big pool sometimes. Pigs are really clean, but don't have sweat glands and that is why they play in the mud to keep cool, but they prefer clean water. She chased the ball or ran around shaking a rag like a dog and she came when called. She sat on the couch and it appeared she was watching television for hours. She roamed around during parties greeting and playing with everyone. She was part of the crew and the only thing she didn't do was go to work with us. Our work was still done seriously. Unfortunately, pigs grow fast and we had to give her back to the Sergeant after only one summer with us. The Sergeant promised to make her a breeder instead of the other options. She had numerous litters, but never forgot people. When some of the guys went out to visit her she would always leave the herd and run over to them still acting and playing like a dog. She was one happy pig and lived a long life. The Doberman too!

Courts / Terrorism / Guilty, Guilty, Guilty

Domestic terrorism ramped up in the mid-sixties and went wild in the seventies with the police and government their main targets. The main goal was revolution by force and each group had its own agenda. They all wanted to be in charge and rule over everybody else as they saw fit. Riots, bombings, snipers and ambushes were their outward tactics, but worse were the stealth tactics through the anti-cop and supportive media, kind of like what is starting all over again now. The (R.N.A.) Republic of New Africa, B.P.P. (Black Panther Party), S.D.S. (Students for Democratic Society), Black Muslims now called Nation of Islam, Weatherman (offshoot of S.D.S.) and many others under the guise of civil rights, tried to gain power and take over. One hundred and eighty-four people were killed and over 600 seriously injured in the 70's. In comparison, 54 people were killed in the last 35 years by domestic terrorism.

The court system in the late 70's was quite liberal too. Not all, but a lot of them were activist judges who were releasing people who had been convicted over and over on previous felonies by believing them over the cops, victims and sometimes eyewitnesses. We were arresting the same predators who were basically one-man crime waves that were tearing the City apart and speeding up the white flight. It wasn't only the Mayor and his Administration that was openly anti-white, it was Detroit's court system too. We saw, first hand, the changes from early 70's to late 70's where some judges appeared to rule on cases with racial history in mind instead of law and facts. Totally amazing to me was they weren't helping the City's victims, they were victimizing them again and again by giving breaks to the guilty thinking they were making up for what they believed were past wrongs. Neither black nor white victims had a chance and most of them left and we couldn't blame them. I watched neighborhood after neighborhood change with whites leaving and blacks trying to find a safe place to live.

My partner and I were at Recorders Court on a week-long homicide trial and I was exhausted and not happy. We worked every night from 7pm - 3am on 11-9 Bravo then had to be in court by 8:30am everyday all day. It was hard to stay awake and we went out into the hall to take a break every once in a while like everyone else including the jury. Naturally my partner (The Character) had to get into something and started saying guilty, guilty, guilty over and over as the jury was going back into a courtroom. Not a good idea and I, like normal, said you are going to get us in trouble and like usual he just laughed. We were then called into that court room and completely chewed out by the judge who told us he would find us in contempt and jail us if we even looked at the jury again. I was tired, pissed and didn't want to spend any time in jail and let him know he went too far this time. As we were leaving for the day we got on the elevator and as luck would have it, a bunch of the same jurors got on with us. I looked at my partner in fear of what he was going to do and one of the jurors said "Hi, officer, how are you today?" He looked back at me with a big grin and to my relief said nothing and kept looking forward.

Lucy & Ethel

My girlfriend was spending more and more time at my house with me and our dogs. Her dog, Henna (Irish Setter), and my dog, Doobie (Doberman) loved playing together and my neighbor's dog, Shotzee (German Sheppard) would come over to my house and just walk in the front door that would sometimes be left open for him. My neighbor, Nancy, had a little boy about 4 years old who would come over to my house wearing a helmet and carrying a stick and would tell me his name was Brian-Al and he was a Policeman too. Debbie and Nancy ended up being lifelong best friends, going on vacations together, having lots of laughs and some crazy experiences. Separately they were totally different, but when they got together, you never knew what they would get into. Eventually, Debbie and I moved in together into a large 3-bedroom upper flat in the Gratiot and 6 Mile area. Nancy and her husband rented the lower flat. I took a panel off the wall that separated the basements so Debbie and Nancy could visit each other through the basement. When doing laundry at night, Debbie would slip through the opening and knock on Nancy's kitchen door and visit over a cocktail or coffee while the washer was going. Same with morning coffee in PJ's and robes; they could be found in the kitchen reliving the latest escapade or making plans for the next. The living arrangements and their antics brought the memories of the old I Love Lucy Show; I sometimes called them Lucy and Ethel. Debbie would always give me a look of disapproval, but I meant it in a good fun way. They could write a book themselves as Nancy ended up married to Pat a Lieutenant at my Precinct and Debbie married me and they ended up being two of the best Cops wives ever and still are. They still sometimes do their Lucy/Ethel thing, but in a more normal environment in suburbia.

CHAPTER 9

The Precinct Cruiser (Big Four)

Unexpected Opportunity

To my great surprise when the Sergeants were pulled off all the City Precinct Cruisers, it made an opening on our Precinct Cruiser (Big Four) and I was personally requested to go on the car. I had always looked up to and respected the Cruiser and its history all the way back to the Purple Gang days (1930's). In 1976 the height and weight requirements were completely dropped so more females could be hired for street duty. With the change there were now other cops my size (5'7"). The Cruiser was still manned by large experienced men who had more than proven themselves over the years to get on the Cruiser. They weren't huge like the old days, but still usually over six feet tall and pretty tough guys. They were respected by law abiding citizens and feared by thugs and law breakers who they actively hunted. Their skills and street smarts were learned over years of street work. There was only one Cruiser working each Precinct; twelve in the whole City. For me, being on the Cruiser (Big Four) was the pinnacle of a serious hard working street cop's career.

The media pushed the agenda, without checking facts, of some radical groups like the Republic of New Africa (RNA), Black Panthers, White Panthers and Anti-Cop Street group's, that the Cruiser (Big Four) drove around harassing and beating innocent black teens without any evidence of wrong doing from made up third hand stories. The fact is the Cruiser didn't go after misdemeanor arrest or minor violations, let alone waste time on anything that wasn't a felony or serious incident. The Mayor, Coleman A. Young, and most of the command officers were black and wouldn't stand for any harassment of innocent black youths by a special unit like the Cruiser (Big Four) on their watch. They made sure a complaint or accusation was more than thoroughly investigated.

The Cruiser crews were racially mixed since the early sixties and when brought back in the late 1970's they were completely mixed with half black and half white crews. They had a reputation that you didn't want to attract their attention in a negative way or you could pay a price. That was earned years ago and continued throughout the existence of the Cruiser. Yes, they were tough, but fair and took no crap from anybody. They worked exclusively for the Precinct Commander through the crew chief who was like a top Sergeant in the army with only two in each Precinct. With the Cruiser back on the street again, a lot of felons were going back to jail and innocent victims welcomed having the Cruisers back.

I felt honored to be the fifth man on a six-man crew and most likely the smallest, once again. I was proud when citizens actually shook our hands and told us we were missed and encouraged us to, "Go get em!" That was what renewed our spirit and drove us on. Like anything else, most Cruiser Crew members, but not all, took their assignment seriously. Some got the assignment because of connections and liked the attention and perks, air-conditioned car (the only ones in the City), plain clothes, and freedom to basically supervise themselves. Of course, those types would get weeded out by a good Crew Chief and Precinct Commander in a short time.

Our new Commander was a serious cop who wanted the Precinct cleaned up under his watch. I knew most of the guys on the Cruiser and they were experienced and all street-wise, except one. My first day on the crew, I was in the back seat with that one guy and as we were pulling out of the police garage he was playing with his gun and pointing it all over. I was amazed at his ignorance and attitude and was looking at him in disbelief. While pointing his gun at me, apparently trying to be funny or trying to intimidate the new guy, he said to me, "You don't like this?" I looked him in the eye and told him, "If you point that at me again, I'll kill you." I hoped to make him wonder if I meant it and to put his gun away. I didn't play games or put up with dangerous gun play.

He started laughing until the Crew Chief said, without even turning around, "He's not kidding." With that he sheepishly put his gun away while giving me a strange look. After that, when we were on the crew together, I ignored him letting him know he didn't have my respect. The rest of the crew did their jobs in a professional way like I was used to when I worked on Special Ops 80-Series units and they were good guys. It was their crew and I was glad to be a junior member of it. We backed up street units, handled our priority runs, and made good arrests. I figured with my informants and street experience, I would be able to eventually add to the expertise of this crew.

Fingers in the Door

My Crew Chief was quiet, but had a reputation of somebody you didn't mess with because he was a man of few words, but would act quickly if provoked. There was a story about one of the new rookies blasting his boom box in the basement locker room. It was said he politely and quietly asked the rookie to turn down the volume to which the rookie just laughed at him and turned away. He then matter-of-factly fired one shot from his .357 Magnum knocking the boom box off the top of the rookie's locker scaring the hell out of him. He then quietly and calmly changed clothes and left while the other officers in the locker room cracked up and another legend was born.

I had never worked on the same unit with him before, but we came across each other as he worked undercover Precinct Narcotics in Special Ops at the same time I worked in Special Ops. We went on a lot of raids together and respected each other's work habits. One night after lunch we were all getting back into the Cruiser and the Crew Chief sits in the right front seat. Everyone was talking at the same time while getting in the car and my door, the right rear, didn't usually close right so I had to slam it closed. I didn't know that the Crew Chief had reached his hand all the way back into my rear door frame as he adjusted himself in the front seat just as I slammed my door.

He calmly and quietly told me to open my door under his breath. Being new on a cruiser crew I hadn't learned yet that you do what the Crew Chief says without question because usually there was a reason for quick compliance. He asked me again to open the door and I was asking why, and then I noticed his hand was shut in the door and I finally opened it. His four fingers were squashed almost flat so the driver called in clear from lunch, and to make us busy to Holy Cross Hospital with an injured officer.

I felt really bad that it took so long to open the door so before we left him at the hospital to go back on patrol, I told him I would pick up a case of beer for him and we can go to choir practice after we got off. When we went back to the station everybody was asking us who got hurt and what happened. Of course, I couldn't resist a chance to screw with those that kept asking. On the radio we said we were going from lunch to the hospital so I started telling everybody he was ok and just had choked on a chicken bone. Well that cracked everybody up. Then the Sergeant on duty told us it was almost time for our shift to end and we could just shut down the crew if we wanted to. We did and there was a case of beer that we had picked up for him just sitting there so we decided to have a few. After a while a scout car brought him back to the station to the teasing from the inside help about choking on a chicken bone. When he came over to the closed library where we usually had choir practice all the beer was gone and we were drunk and laughing about the chicken bone joke. He was disappointed about the beer being all gone, but wasn't mad and thought the joke was funny, even if it was on him. Cops have a strange sense of humor that looks weird to civilians because we laugh and tease about each other's predicaments and minor injuries, but we love each other like brothers knowing we would do almost anything for each other.

Suddenly in Charge (Crew Chief)

After a few months working the Cruiser, I had a weekend off. When I came back, I was called into the Commanders' office and he told me the entire crew, except for me, had been removed from the Cruiser and sent back to uniform shifts. He said I was now the new Crew Chief. He didn't go into any detail of what happened and I never asked why and it was never mentioned by the guys. I assumed the top four pulled something unacceptable to him as they never complained and he probably gave them a break by just putting them on shifts. The one guy who liked playing with his gun wasn't with them, but he was dropped too because, most likely, it was known that he wasn't Cruiser material. It was a complete shock to me going from the bottom seniority of the Cruiser to the top in one sudden quick movement. I liked them and felt bad for them, and thankfully, none of them ever showed any animosity toward me.

The Commander proceeded to tell me what he expected a Cruiser Crew to be in no uncertain terms. He was an old timer who remembered the old Big Four and the true history. I could see by what he did that the Cruiser in #11 wasn't going to be anything but the best. He told me to hand pick my crew and that it should be half black and half white. He wanted no trouble and more good arrests without unnecessary injured prisoners or citizen complaints. He told me I would be responsible for everyone on the crew and would answer to and work directly for him, as the Precinct Cruiser directly represented him. He told me, as the Crew Chief, he would back me up completely. I liked what he was saying and I felt the same about the Cruiser and respected its history.

As I left his office feeling up to the challenge by his speech, it didn't take long for me to realize what just happened. I was now responsible for a crew of six and had a history to live up to instead of sitting in the back seat and letting others make the hard calls. The entire old crew was gone and I had to put together a good crew from scratch. I realized that it couldn't be done by friendship; it had to be done by who deserved to be on the Cruiser and would benefit it. For the next few days as I put together a list of crew members, I suddenly became the most popular guy in the Precinct. The word was out that I was going to fill five spots on the Cruiser and a lot of people wanted the job. I knew after I picked the five I would be the most unpopular guy by the ones who didn't get the assignment, especially by my friends who thought they were a shoe in. I wanted my Cruiser to be the best one in the City so I picked five guys who, I thought, would make it the best. Luckily for me my friends, who were good cops, understood why I did what I did and there were no hard feelings.

My first pick might have surprised some, but I knew he was one of the best hard working cops in the Precinct even if he liked to screw with people for a laugh. I picked my second man from Special Ops, my old partner (The Character) to help me build and train a crew that would honor the Cruiser's history. I figured as the alternate Crew Chief on the Cruiser (Big Four) with its history that responsibility would slow the tricks down. I was right and he stepped right up to help build what I have always thought was the best crew in the City. I picked four more, easy going, but tough, large (over 6 feet), serious officers who liked to work. They knew it was an honor to be a member of a unique unit that had a history to live up to and a chance to be even better. I told them what the Commander wanted and expected from his new crew and that nobody will be in our way so we can even do better than expected. We didn't have a Thompson Sub Machine gun sitting in our rear deck window opening like old time Cruisers did, but we did have a lot of varied experiences, an explosive expert, a sniper, and a karate expert. Everybody brought something special to the Cruiser and we all were on the same page of cleaning up our Precinct. We already had a Want Book, informants, and connections in Narcotics, Homicide, Armed Robbery, Sex Crimes, State parole officers and other Precinct Detective Bureaus which we had worked with when we were in Precinct Special Operations. I picked well, only one had to be replaced and his replacement was a better fit. We all got along and worked together like a well-trained team. Everybody had extra assignments, like keeping up the Want Book, checking teletypes for crimes, checking with the Detective Bureaus for wanted persons or taking care of the vehicle and our equipment daily before heading out. We carried four large bullet proof vests, tear gas gun, 2 riot shot guns, 2 M1 carbines, axe handles, gas masks, extra ammo and had access to a sniper rifle, if needed. Individually, we carried 9mm automatics, 44 cal. & .357 Magnum revolvers, Kel-lites and black jacks. We drove a large black Chrysler with a large engine with lights and siren hidden in the grill and Detroit Police in gold lettering on both front doors with no other markings on it. The Chrysler went like hell, but we had to be careful because with four guys and a lot of equipment, it was hard to stop when you got going. I only drove it a few times to see what it was like because Crew Chiefs usually sat in the right front seat and were not supposed to drive. The vehicle itself was the driver's responsibility. We were human and not perfect, but one hell of a Crew who made a big difference with a lot of good felony arrests while enhancing the reputation of the Big Four of Detroit.

Hitting the Streets

As we were pulling out of the station ramp, I would simply ask the crew, "What do we have tonight?" They would let me know what was new on wanted felons whom we hunted nightly or the latest on newly committed felonies. I would then direct the driver to where, or who, I wanted to start on in between responding to priority 1 runs or shaking down suspicious cars or persons for guns or felony warrants. We averaged between 15-20 felony arrests and got numerous guns off the street each month which was a lot of arrests for any one unit.

We weren't hesitant about making a felony arrest of a crime that happened in our City, even if he was an hour or so away. We wanted predators to know and worry about the Big Four coming for them. The looks we got in suburbia, especially by the older folks who remembered the Big Four, was amazing. Those that knew who we were would sometimes wave and smile. It happened often on 8 Mile Road the Northern border between Detroit and the suburbs. In a lot of situations, the image and reputation alone stopped violent actions.

The Cruiser (Big Four) had a reputation, but some of it was false and put out by people who just parroted others with an agenda. Rumors and false stories were spread by those that never had contact with the Cruiser (Big Four) or knew anything about it or the history of the unit. The Cruiser (Big Four) never worked exclusively on prostitutes, gambling, or liquor violations, which are misdemeanors. That was the responsibility of the Vice Squad or the

Precinct Cleanup Crew. The Cruiser (Big Four) worked on organized gangs like the Purple Gang who ran the Vice Organizations that were running illegal vice activities, not the activities themselves, and who committed violent felonies. The Cruiser (Big Four) didn't harass innocent black teens who were just standing on the corner. They did move white or black persons off a corner when they were committing minor crimes like drinking, gambling or harassing people, before it turned violent.

The crews were de-segregated in the early sixties and before that the City was mostly white. Most of us knew the stories and that was what most of them were, just stories, with no proof of fact. Many of the stories supposedly happened when there was no Cruiser Crews working and sometimes when they didn't even exist. Either way, we never corrected the false claims of mass harassment because it made our job easier to control the uncontrollable type of situations. Innocent, nonviolent, decent, law abiding people had nothing to fear, but violent lawbreakers who chose to challenge the Cruiser crew (Big Four) would get an attitude adjustment really quick. The biggest proof of that fact was Mayor Coleman A. Young who put the Cruisers back on the streets in every Precinct and he personally knew how the Big Four operated. The four of us were outnumbered a lot of the time and the reputation evened up the odds. With all that said, like everything else you run into a bad fit. Even after hand picking my crew, I had to let one of them go, who was a good cop on a two-man car, but his image of and actions on the Cruiser (Big Four) were not acceptable to the reality of the Precinct Cruiser.

Football Player

While on patrol with my new crew we were pulling up to a stop sign at E. 7 Mile, when to my utter surprise a huge kid was bent over trying to pull the stop sign up and out of the ground. His buddies were egging him on and it actually was coming out some. He was about 6'7", and close to 250 lbs. and in his late teens. My driver that day was (The Character) and he wasn't surprised when I bailed out and rapidly went face to face with the kid yelling, "What the hell is wrong with you?" My partner then told him he was going to jail if he kept that shit up. My partner (The Character) was used to me battling big guys and just stood next to the Cruiser smiling. My two new partners were still sitting in the back seat of the Cruiser with their mouth's hanging open as their little Crew Chief was raising hell with a really big kid and ready to do battle if necessary. They were caught off guard by my actions at first, but then they quickly got out of the car thinking this might be one hell of a battle. They would soon learn I wasn't intimidated by anything or anyone and I was going to seriously enforce the law no matter what, or who was breaking it. Secondly, they were going to learn we work with those who cooperate with us as we weren't there to flex our muscles and harass anybody. The big kid apologized and said he was just showing off for his buddies as he was the starting defensive end for the Iowa Hawkeye's college football team. He was a nice kid making a minor mistake who realized it. We wished him well on next Saturday's game and I think he and my crew all learned a lesson on how we were going to work. With (The Character) on the same page it was going to be a lot easier building a good crew. I always wondered if that kid made it to the pro's as I think he had the size and right attitude or, if some street punk killed him.

Biker Club Key

Most of the Motor Cycle Clubs had enough sense to keep clean where their club houses were and did their dirty work somewhere else. We had one of the many clubs in the Precinct that had previously shot at officers from their club house years before. Knowing that, we kept a close watch on them. One warm sunny day a couple of the club members were out in front of the club house illegally drinking beer. We could see that one had the club's keys on his belt. As we searched them and proceeded to advise them that they couldn't drink alcohol on a public street, one of the crew members snatched his keys. He was drunk enough not to even notice. We told them to keep their drinking inside and hoped he wouldn't know what happened to the keys. We periodically checked to see if the same pad lock was on the large steel door grate. Our thought was that if we had another barricaded gunman shooting at cops from the club house, we could get in. It wasn't exactly by the book, but it was done and may save lives later.

It didn't take long before a problem arose when a suburban Police Dept. requested a Detroit unit to assist on an arrest at the club. We responded and were told that one of the bikers was wanted on arrest warrants and they chased him into the club as the door and steel grate was closed on them. We knocked and advised them if they didn't open the door we would forcefully enter. The door had the same old rusty pad lock and we had the key. I figured it would be best to keep the key a secret and instead send a message that it would be a problem for them if they didn't cooperate with the Cruiser (Big Four) in the Precinct where their club house was. We then called for a tow truck that hooked up to the steel grate and proceeded to rip the front of the building off around the grate and door. We then walked in with the suburban officers and told them to take their wanted man. The suburban officers and the bikers were all in utter astonishment to what we had just done. The four of us just calmly entered our vehicle, waved and left with the message sent that the Big Four was in charge of this Precinct.

Ass Chewing / Maine Melee

After a couple of days off, the Commander wanted to see me immediately. Being called into the Commanders office is not usually good and it wasn't this time either. He was chewing me out about something my crew did while I was off. It was minor, but I wouldn't have put up with it and they knew better. I just said, "But boss, I was off," and that really fired him up. He said, "I don't give a shit" and told me, in no uncertain terms, that it was my crew and I would be held responsible for them while I was working or not and that I was to take care of problems before they got to him. I was probably too easy going with my crew, but now I knew the Crew Chief position wasn't like being a senior officer on a scout car who was responsible for the unit only when working. A Crew Chief was responsible to completely handle the crew whether there or not.

I let the crew know if anybody tried to pull something that was unacceptable people would be replaced, even if I wasn't there. We were all learning and we had a lot of extra space to do what needed to be done, but we all had a special responsibility to do it right. The basic chain of command was the Crew Chief only answered to the Commander and the cruiser crew answered to the Crew Chief.

I was also very protective of my crew and wouldn't put up with shift supervisors pulling my guys off of the Cruiser to fill in on other shifts so their less seniority officers had choice days off. When they did that, I was authorized by the Commander to change it back and I did every time they tried. With the layoffs at 25% I understood why they did it, but my orders were to run a four-man crew nightly and my guys with higher seniority gave up having weekends off to do that.

We really bonded after being in a large chaotic battle. We received a radio run that there was a "large disturbance at an address near Maine and Carpenter Streets on the Hamtramck border." When my uniform driver knocked on the front door a rather large man came rushing out knocking him to the ground. The other three of us immediately went to his aid and a flow of other men came out of the house attacking us. While we were all fighting, one of my partners was able to get on the radio telling the dispatcher that we were in a large fight and we were losing. Macho as we were, I was extremely pleased he didn't say, 'Officer in Trouble', as that would be an embarrassment for a Cruiser Crew (Big Four). In the chaos, with all the fighting going on, it put a big smile on my face. It was what some would call an old fashioned donnybrook without weapons; one big fair fist fight. I finally got my opponent on the ground and as I was holding him down I could see scout cars pulling up one after another with lights and sirens blaring waking up the whole neighborhood.

As each scout car crew exited its vehicle they were immediately in physical combat with other neighbors coming out of their houses. The responding units kept calling for more cars until all of our cars and cars as far away as #7 and #15 also responded before it was finally under control.

I don't remember how many arrests were made, but our paddy wagon made numerous trips and our cell block was over flowing. When we got into the station the front lawn and lobby was full of angry wives and mothers who appeared to be about to take over the station and the shift Lieutenant was inside going nuts. We went into the lock up and when talking to the prisoners we found out they had called the police for help at noon and were pissed that we showed up 12 hours later at midnight waking them all up.

We heard from the others that they had a big family reunion with relatives from as far away as Poland and were woken up by the Police fighting with their relatives. With no one seriously injured and no weapons involved and basically the City's fault for dispatching us 12 hours late as if it was still in progress. We could understand some of the anger.

As we were talking to them and they were yelling out to their family members to go home, and telling them it was a fair fight. We agreed with them and we all started laughing about the big battle we just had that someone called it the Maine Melee. The Lieutenant in charge and the inside help were going crazy with the big mess that we brought in. So we suggested that if they promised not to sue, we would promise not to charge anybody and let them go as it was a mistake and a fair fight. I was pleasantly surprised when the frantic Lieutenant agreed and released everyone and told them to go home while giving us a look of relief. It was an unusual end to a possible International problem as a lot of them were here from Poland on vacation. We kept our word and they kept theirs. Whenever we drove by Carpenter and Maine, the small Polish community on the border of Hamtramck, they gave us a friendly wave and a smile. I don't know if the battle was historic in Poland or Hamtramck, but it became legend in the 11th Precinct and it totally bonded my crew.

State Cops

In the late 1970's the Motor Traffic Bureau was cut back and the State Police took over. The Motor Traffic bureau consisted of elite, well trained, riot control, motorcycle & traffic enforcement units that patrolled the Detroit freeways. My understanding was that the State gave their officers double seniority credit to get enough volunteers to work Detroit's freeways. At first the State cops would show up to some of our shootings or holdups in progress calls as they monitored our radio frequency. After getting shot at a few times they weren't so curious or were told to stay on the freeways. Either way, we saw less & less of them unless it was an officer in trouble call. They kind of reminded me of me when I was a naive lily-white rookie from the suburbs, but more so because some of these guys seemed right off of the farm in Northern Michigan. They told us we were crazy for working in this war zone and we told them they were nuts for driving up and down a freeway all night long. We were all cops, but from totally different worlds crossing paths.

Naked Hooker

We were driving North on Woodward when our driver spotted a good looking hooker who was drunk and staggering down the street. When she spotted us, she turned down the first side street. My driver started to slow down and I told him to leave it and keep going. The rest of my crew, in the back seat, kept yelling for him to turn and follow her. So, he turned as I was bitching at him knowing this could only be trouble and as he was going slowly by her she fell and a couple of porch lights went on with a few people coming out and waving us down. Now I was really pissed that we had to stop and tie up a four-man crew on a drunken hooker and I let the crew know it. I was stuck now and had the two officers in the back seat put her in the middle between them and told my driver to head into the station for our misdemeanor arrest. All the way into the station I was bitching at all of them for wasting our time on a drunk hooker when I noticed the two officers in the back seat were smiling and paying no attention to what I was saying. The hooker was wearing a loose wrap-a-round dress with nothing under it. As she wiggled around in the back seat, it was coming off. They weren't touching her, but were enjoying the show until she started peeing all over the back seat, on them, and herself. Maybe they should have listened to this old vice cop who knew almost anything could happen when dealing with hookers and sometimes even worse things happened. They were both trying to get away from her and wanted the driver to stop so they could get out and away from her; they weren't laughing or enjoying themselves anymore. I told the driver to continue on and told them they started this mess and now they're going to have to finish it. I was laughing now.

By the time we pulled into the police garage she had gotten completely naked and was covered with pee. Both officers bailed out the rear doors almost before we stopped and they weren't very happy. She crawled out the back seat and rolled around the dusty, dirty garage floor while laughing and covering herself from head to toe in dust that stuck to her everywhere. She looked like a ghost from an old comedy movie. To make the lesson learned stick, I told them to take her to the lock up and see what the desk Sergeant wanted to do with her. Neither one wanted to touch her, but knew they had to get her up front somehow though the long hall way. I told them I didn't care how they did it, but "Do it." They put on their leather gloves and proceeded to pick her up by her hands and feet and placed her in the wheel barrel that was in the garage and rolled her up front as she was laughing and enjoying her ride. I then told the driver, who started all this, to clean up the car. As this was all going on a young State Police crew was coming into the garage with a prisoner of their own. The look on their faces was priceless as they apparently couldn't believe their eyes as they watched a naked lady being wheeled in a wheel barrel. When they got her up front and into the lockup area no one wanted anything to do with this situation. It took a while, but with her being non-violent and cooperative, we didn't want to just lock her up and the Sergeant didn't want her in the station. We figured we would take her to the Salvation Army Harbor Light substance abuse service center if they would admit her. They agreed to take her if we could get her there. So I had my officers put her back into the wheel barrow and wheel her back into the garage and put her in the paddy wagon with a blanket and take her to Harbor Light. As they were wheeling her down the hallway to the garage the very same State Police crew was bringing in another prisoner and couldn't believe their eyes as she was wheeled right past them again. I laughed and thought welcome to Detroit boys the City that will make you laugh and scare the heck out of you minutes later. I know my crew learned a lesson and understood that the situation could have been a lot worse; we weren't out here for fun and games. A little humor is fine to ease the stress of the streets, but wasting a four-man felony crew's time like that wasn't acceptable. Off duty I got into all kinds of goofy situations, but on duty, I was mostly all business and serious about my crew and our reputation.

Off Duty

I had moved out of the animal party house I shared with my cop buddies and in with my girlfriend into a 3 bedroom upper flat in the 6 Mile and Gratiot area with our dogs and cat. It gave me somewhat of a normal life. I still spent most of my time working the Cruiser or with my street friends and bar owner buddies in the bars and clubs like when I worked undercover. I never drank on duty, but off duty I did and usually for free on the owners because they knew I would help them out if they had any problems in the bar. It was almost like a second job working undercover, but when I took action I didn't make a report or arrest unless I had too. I learned my lesson years ago about the mess you have with off duty arrest and just put into my mind not to identify myself as a police officer. Right or wrong, I was not going to end my evening because some idiot robbed or assaulted someone in my presents. The places I was frequenting were pretty rough. I had chosen to work the streets right from the beginning of my career and did so without a break

I was fidgety and nervous when off duty during quiet normal times. For some strange reason, I had to be out there or something bad might happen. Maybe I worked the streets too long on and off duty to even know what normal was anymore. All I knew was that I was street smart and a survivor, but had trouble turning it off. I had no intention of getting promoted as I was a working street cop and didn't want to supervise. Even if on the street you were there to supervise, not work the street, and that wasn't for me. I was at the pinnacle of my working career and a Crew Chief of a Cruiser Crew, there was nowhere else for me to go to be so completely involved in the action.

It was my life and I didn't realize it, but I had put the Police Department almost first in my life. I loved my kids and was happy they were all living a happy normal family life and my girlfriend who lived a normal life in spite of my wild and crazy existence. She accepted me and my job and was my rock. It reminded me, looking back, of what a normal life used to be for me before I tasted the addictive excitement of living on the edge daily where I thought I could help those in need. The problem for me was I couldn't stop or go back to "normal" for even a short time. I wasn't able to let it go and just be off duty.

If I saw someone picking on someone who was weaker, smaller, or older, even off duty in a bar, I would sometimes actually bully the bully by moving next to him and challenging him. Other times when I saw a bar bully sit next to another bar bully I knew something was going to happen between them and that would be ok if they took it outside. That happened quite often in the bars on Van Dyke; being so used to it, it was almost entertainment for me. Yes, I was out on the streets too long and didn't realize it at the time.

The Holdup

One night I was sitting at the corner of the bar of one of my favorite spots, The Duchess. It was a go-go bar with a pretty rough crowd and I knew most of the people who worked there. The security camera monitor was right in front of me and I would glance at it when I saw anything unusual happening in the parking lot while shooting the bull with the owner or employees. I looked at the screen and saw a guy walking toward another guy who was getting out of his car. The first guy pulled out a gun and started shoving and hitting the guy who was getting out of his vehicle. It looked like an apparent carjacking or robbery. I got up and told the owner to call 911 and tell them there was a hold up in progress in the parking lot. I drew my gun and held it behind my leg and walked out of the bar toward them staggering and acting drunk until I got close enough to put my gun next to his head and cock it. I ordered him to drop it, which he did, and then to the ground spread eagle. I retrieved his gun and the victim ran into the bar. I knew I had to hold him until help arrived and couldn't search him for another weapon without putting my gun away. With my street experience and the look of him, with his eyes darting all around, I had the gut feeling this guy was street smart too. We both knew I couldn't shoot him as I already had his gun, so I planted my left foot near his head and cocked my right leg back while holding him at gun point. Sure enough he rapidly rose up to run and I kicked him with my right foot directly in the face knocking some of his front teeth out and then put him back into the spread eagle position while letting him know not to try that again. One street boy just met another street boy and he knew it, so he didn't try to get up again.

When the scout car showed up I told them that the victim was in the bar and handed them the gun. The scout car crew knew I worked at #11 and I told them they had enough witnesses as it was watched on the security camera. They didn't need me as I was off duty and the suspect thought I was just a person coming out of the bar. After searching him they put him in the back seat of the scout car and made him hang his head out of the window so he wouldn't bleed in the car. While I was talking to the officers, he was calling me a punk while lisping without front teeth and I just couldn't help myself and had to respond back with a lisp, saying, "yeah, I'm the punk" while laughing at him. Long before, I had lost any pity for violent predators like him and only felt for the victims.

It turned out I was right about his street smarts as he had a long violent record and would have gone on to prey on someone else if not stopped. I forgot during the excitement that the parking lot was under surveillance and when I went back in the bar the bartender had turned the TV monitor so everyone could watch. I thought "oh crap" if just one bleeding heart saw me kick him instead of trying to just hold him down until help arrived, I could catch hell for not making a report. Again my luck held as everyone was excited about the outcome as they watched it live on the monitor. I heard that one guy actually raised his arms up and yelled, "He scores," after the kick like it was a football field goal. They knew that they could have been the one approached in the parking lot. For me it was just a few minutes on duty while I was off duty and I just went back to what I was doing, socializing. In my world, I was easy on him because I took a chance getting that close to him. I could have ordered him to drop the weapon from a distance and if he didn't, I would have been forced to shoot him; like most cops, we really don't want to kill anybody. Extra risks were taken by doing it the hard way, even if some thought that it was brutal. Those that complain are not the ones you would ever see helping anybody any time, but are good at doing a lot of Monday morning quarterbacking. Their attitudes change when they are at the business end of a predator's gun. On or off duty, and even retired, I will always protect the victim's rights over predator's rights and would hope that most people would feel the same.

Last Chance

Around 2am in the morning we were cruising North on Woodward Avenue approaching 8 Mile Road and turned into the parking lot of the Last Chance Bar. The patrons were exiting the bar at closing and there was quite a crowd and usually a potential for trouble there. As one couple was walking toward us the male pulled a .38 caliber revolver out of his waist band, pointed it in our direction and fired a shot directly at us that just missed our windshield traveling over our vehicle. He then, while staggering and apparently high or drunk, put his gun back in his waistband as we were exiting our vehicle and drawing our own weapons. He re-drew his gun and was waiving it about in our direction. With the large bar crowd behind him we held our fire and kept ordering him to drop it. The female with him was yelling to us that it was just blanks. He then put his gun on a trunk of a car and, as it was still in reaching distance, we approached rapidly so he couldn't grab it again. As we got close he then started swinging and kicking and we had to take him to the ground to subdue him. While we were doing that the female attacked our uniform driver from behind as a hostile crowd started to form and get closer. Even on the Cruiser (Big Four) in the 70's, you got your prisoners, evidence, and without hesitating left the scene before the crowd got out of control because it could get really ugly, really quick. It turned out her so called blanks were real live rounds.

I later received my 8th Citation/Commendation for "When faced by an armed subject, exercised great discretion affecting his apprehension without injury to anyone." It was harder to be written up for an award on a four-man crew or a felony car as that kind of action was the norm instead of the exception, but it seems if you didn't return fire they liked that more. Kind of like they get the first shot.

Tow Truck Killed

We were heading west on 7 Mile Road and passed a scout car going the other way. We waved at them, and then we saw a man in the parking lot of a gas station walking toward another man who was pumping gas from a tanker into the gas stations underground tanks. The first man had a shot gun in an apparent hold up attempt. We immediately pulled into the station and the suspect ran behind a tow truck. As we exited our vehicle, he knelt behind a tow trucks upper bed edge and angled boom & boom supports for cover and started firing at us. My partners had a .44 Mag. and .357 Mag. revolvers and a 15–shot 9mm automatic and I had a .357 Mag. revolver. We got 3-4 shots off each with the revolvers while my partner with the automatic fired 12 shots as the suspect fired 3 shotgun rounds. We had to fire double action so it shows just how different and faster an automatic fire's in the same amount of time by just touching the trigger over and over.

I was standing in the open with no cover and could see each blast from his shotgun that seemed to be pointed directly at me. My partners were on both sides of me returning fire and each of their weapons had different sounds. I fired three rounds as I ducked backwards trying to escape the shot gun blast. There was nowhere to go and I was sure, with him only 30-40 feet away, this was going to be my last action and yes, everything was in slow motion. My ears were ringing and without a breeze I could smell all the cordite smoke that was just hanging in the air around us. The tow trucks tires were hissing and its glass windows were crumbling by the hits. The tanker driver who was pumping gas had run and jumped the freeway fence. The suspect threw out the shotgun and raised his arms in surrender as my partners ran toward him. I holstered my weapon and started patting myself down all over as I knew I had to be hit somewhere.

I had heard gunfire in my general area numerous times not knowing for sure if it was directed at me or my partners. This was the 10th time that I did know gun fire was directed in my direction. I couldn't count how many times that I had weapons pointed at me. If I wasn't completely sure before that someone up there was taking care of me, I was now. By looking at the gas station it could have been completely blown up by the gunfire and it was a miracle that no one was hit. It turned out when the suspect attempted to rack the fourth round in the chamber and the previous round jammed the shot gun that is why he surrendered. He also had a pistol but wasn't able to get to it because he was wearing coveralls.

The scout car crew that we had passed moments before the shoot-out came back saying it sounded like world war three had just begun. They found the tanker driver, who ran quite a way down the freeway, scared to death that the whole corner was going to explode.

The rounds I fired, were in a two-inch group about one inch below the thick steel edge of the tow truck's bed right in front of where his heart was and it saved his life. I fired at him to try to make him stop firing at me, not to kill him. We cop's, just like most humans, aren't made to kill, but we will if we have to. I have known a lot of officers who had been shot at and had weapons pointed at them while holding their fire when they didn't have to at great risk. Other officers have been killed doing the same thing by not wanting to kill. I am pretty sure there was one gas tanker driver who had one hell of a story to tell his friends.

The next night when we came to work we got teased pretty badly about killing a tow truck. Someone put a toy tow truck on our dashboard like they used to put Japanese flags on a plane during World War II each time they shot a plane down. Tough crowd, we almost get killed and the guys tease us, that's how it was in the Big "D" during the seventies. While laughing, the Commander jokingly said to us, "What the fuck are you clowns trying to do blow up a whole neighborhood?" Usually after a harrowing experience that everyone survived, there was a lot of nervous energy released by teasing and joking about it after.

Prowlers

Quite often, by the time a radio run comes out the crime is over and the perp is long gone and your function is to help the victim and do the paperwork. After helping physically and psychologically injured victims daily from rapes, robberies, burglary, etc., etc., you get very pro-victim and anti-predator. People, who haven't been victims themselves, really don't understand what these people go through and how it sometimes affects them for years making them fearful. I think if the public had seen victims as they were being victimized they might not be so pro-criminal rights for those that commit crimes over and over. There might truly be more victims' rights. We see it daily, year after year, and know the politicians and media play it down while making a bigger issue out of law breakers being treated badly. I don't condone violating anybody's rights, but society, being so easy on criminals, encourages bad behavior and those on the front line with the suffering victims, see it play out over and over. One example that society and the courts treat as minor is home burglary, which is considered a property crime (non-violent). We lock the same perps up multiple times and usually they cop a plea to "entering without owner's permission," which is a misdemeanor. They then can just do it again until someone shoots them or they kill or rape someone. When a victim is burglarized, even if they weren't home at the time, it affects them psychologically trying to live there knowing a thief was in their home going through their things. It is such a personal invasion that they cannot feel safe in their own home ever again.

We got excited when we actually caught someone in a burglary in progress. I learned as a rookie to treat a prowler run real serious as they turn into burglaries quite often. For us, coming face to face with them instead of picking up the pieces after the fact was an exhilarating experience that didn't happen every day. It was better than a hockey player scoring the winning goal after triple overtime to win the Stanley Cup. It was the same when catching a holdup man or even a murderer during or right after the fact.

Murder

I also learned driving slowly, with lights out and sometimes the wrong way down a one-way side street, while watching and listening very carefully, you could catch law breakers who were looking the other way.

One afternoon we were doing just that when a "B&E in Progress" run was dispatched and we were only a few houses away. We saw a male and a female with two kids come running out of the rear of the address that dispatch put out and enter a vehicle that was parked in front. The driver was looking behind his vehicle toward where oncoming traffic would be coming from and didn't see us driving up on him from the wrong way on the one-way street. A few seconds later another male came from the rear of the same address and approached the driver's door while we were only a few feet away.

All of a sudden, one shot rang out coming from the driver striking the last man right between the eyes killing him instantly while he was unarmed. The driver then saw us and put his vehicle in reverse and went around the corner onto Nevada Street then took off down to the Chrysler freeway service drive at a high rate of speed. My two partners who were in the back seat immediately exited our vehicle to control the homicide scene while my driver and I gave pursuit with lights and sirens until we curbed the vehicle on Margaret Street and arrested the occupants. My driver back tracked our chase route and found where they pitched their gun and preserved it for prints to which the driver's prints were later found. In the meantime, my other partners preserved the scene and took eyewitness statements from several people who also stated that the victim was unarmed when he was shot. We had a perfect case of homicide right before our eyes with four officers and two separate neighbors all seeing the victim shot and killed while unarmed and the suspect attempting to escape and ditching his weapon. I was so happy and proud of the way my young Cruiser Crew handled the complete case so professionally that I could hardly contain myself.

When the TV news trucks arrived and asked to interview me, they wanted to set up a scenario (they do that often to set the agenda) of a young police officer seeing a man shot and killed right before his eyes. I may have looked young, but I had been in this war zone many years and saw a lot of violent crime and, at the time, I was just pumped at the job we just did and wasn't going to play their game.

I remembered as a rookie being told not to trust the TV press because some have agendas that usually aren't completely up front and honest. So I did what I had learned and gave them an interview while telling them when he was hit, he went down like a water buffalo and using MF'er every other word. After they walked away shaking their heads a radio station reporter, they usually get pushed out of the way by the TV crews, politely asked me if I would tell him what really happened in a radio interview. He was laughing because he was street smart enough to read my hostility about giving a set up on air interview to the TV people. I gave him the story of what happened and how it was swiftly and correctly handled. On my way home I heard the interview on my car radio and was quite pleased with it and joked later that I had a real DJ's voice.

I was at this time hard as nails on the outside, but I did feel for the victim who was killed, but like everything I had seen and experienced, it wasn't wise to think of the past if you wanted to keep going in this business. Weeks later during the trial at Recorders Court, one of our famous activist judges dismissed the jury half way through the trial and decided to hear the case himself. We were shocked because, 1) he could do that, and 2) that he found the defendant not guilty even with all the eyewitness testimonies and evidence. Most of us over the years had seen activist judges play God and do what they wanted in the radical 70's, but we never thought it would happen on a homicide that was witnessed by four police officers and independent citizens. The rumor was the defendant had friends in high places and the victim didn't. It wasn't too hard to see why some cops just got burned out trying to do the right thing. I received my 9th Commendation/Certificate for "In recognition of efficient and valuable service."

Slow Times / Socializing

The beginning of our shift, when working 11am – 7pm, could sometimes be a little slow, especially at times when we didn't have court. We were usually busy and being slow led to boredom and we would mess with each other when bored. One of the guys was kind of a clean freak and if anybody even touched the outside of his water glass or one of his eating utensils at lunch he would wipe them off or request new ones. He was a great guy, but of course when we found out, we just had to tease him like everyone else on the crew. I had the driver take us to the State Fairgrounds while telling everybody I wanted some horse shit to throw on him. I got out and looked around while he was bitching at me. I picked up a clump of old leaves telling everyone it was horse shit and threw it on him. He was twice my size and mad. He chased me all over but, luckily I was faster than him. The rest of the crew told him it was just leaves while we all laughed and enjoyed our foolery. Another time while leaving the station after an arrest I had the driver stop and I went into the bathroom and came out with a half wet paper towel holding it by the dry end by two fingers like it had been dipped in the toilet. It hadn't and was just tap water, but he took off running with me chasing him with everybody cracking up until I pitched it and told him it was just tap water. Another time, when he was the driver we got a flat tire. The vehicle was the driver's responsibility but he didn't want to take all the equipment out of the trunk to get the spare tire. I made the mistake of laughing at his plight and walked toward the police garage when something hit me behind my right ear knocking me to my knees and I thought I had been shot. When I realized that I hadn't and saw a flashlight battery lying next to my hand and he had a great big grin, I knew he had bopped me with it. If you're going to put it out, you have to be able to take it and sometimes we got a little rough with each other.

One morning we were just coming through the car wash and the workers were drying our windshield. One of my other partners was driving that day and my clean freak partner was in the back seat. The driver kept pulling my hair near the back of my head in short quick jerks when I looked the other way. He knew I didn't like my hair pulled so he was messing with me. I kept telling him to knock it off which he didn't. So, I just socked him between the eyes breaking his sun glasses in half. As soon as I hit him I felt bad that I broke his glasses and started to apologize until he laughed at me telling me they were already broke. When we both looked out the windshield the guy who was wiping the car dry had frozen with his eyes big and mouth hanging open in shock watching us fighting. We laughed even more figuring he probably thought with the Big Four's reputation for fighting, that we fought with each other when there was no one else to fight with. (The Character) by now had slowed on his tricks and antics and was seriously studying for the next Sergeants exam day and night, but every once in a while he couldn't resist using the skunk perfume. All in all, we were a pretty serious bunch while on duty and worked well together.

We did have a couple of outings together, one was a New Year's Eve party with our wives and girlfriends where us white guys were taught the freaky-deaky dance that had caused a lot of violence country wide, which was a blast for us. One male had a female dancing right behind and one right in front of him to the music while touching and in unison. That dance had caused quite a few shootings in Detroit as it was so sexual.

Another time the Commander gave all six of us the night off together to go to a ballgame at Tiger Stadium. My one partner who drove had a purple ghetto van with murals painted on the sides and it looked like something out of the sixties. My future Mother-in-laws boyfriend was a great guy and went with us, but didn't have much experience with ghetto cops as he was a tee-totaling naive suburbanite. That night he had the time of his life and stories to tell of a world he didn't know existed. I had worked in and lived in mixed communities for years, but never had really socialized with a majority of persons of color very much. I had, after years and years of losses, slowly pulled away from most everybody and turned somewhat into a loner and not very comfortable around people most of the time.

After a few drinks and enjoying watching our suburbanite having the wildest time of his life, it was more fun than the ballgame. On the way to the stadium we stopped at an all-black liquor store in a tough neighborhood and I went in and bought a bunch of booze. As I was leaving a couple of guys were following me out and making comments saying something about a little white boy and I thought they were going to rob me or jump me. They followed me right up to the van and when the side door slid open and two big black guys got out with shoulder holsters they stopped in their tracks, totally surprised and turned around quickly. After a wild ride and passing a bottle of Jack Daniels around, my suburban friend was drinking too and was fitting right in with us nuts and having a great time.

While the seven of us were sitting and enjoying the game we noticed people moving away from a group of 5 or 6 drunken rowdies who were swearing and rough housing with each other a few rows in front of us. After watching families sit near them and leave in disgust, a couple of us went down and asked them to calm down a little. They all stood up challenging us and said what are you going to do, call security, and laughing. They apparently thought there were enough of them that they could do what they wanted. My partner said no, you guys are going to hope security shows up quick as he waved at the rest of the crew who were now standing and waving back. I was glad they decided to calm down as there was no bluffing on our part. Later when a couple of them were getting sick, every time they threw up we would stand and yell "RALPH" until they stopped to the delight of the fans around them. We had a great time and my Mother-in-laws boyfriend told that story over and over for years about his time with Detroit's Big Four at the ball game.

Snow Storm

We had a large snowstorm and most of the City streets were unusually empty around 2am. We had just checked Woodward Ave. and we were surprised that the hookers were out, but no johns' or vehicle traffic. We approached East 8 Mile Road and a vehicle came through the intersection at a high rate of speed and we immediately gave chase on East bound 8 Mile Road. The wind and snow was blowing so hard even with our big Chrysler carrying 4 large guys and a trunk full of very heavy equipment was hard to keep on the road. At 70 mph or so we still needed all four lanes to stay on the road drifting from the far right to the far left lane and back. As a kid I used to like to drag race and was kind of a speed freak driving fast cars like GTO's, Corvettes and large engine cars. Speeding around the streets was fun when young and naïve, but not fun when forced into a high speed chase when you or others were vulnerable for serious injury. Luckily there wasn't any traffic on 8 Mile at that time during the storm. He didn't stop until he slid into a pole at Gratiot Avenue about 9 miles East of where we started. As we slid to a stop, I was the first one at his driver's door and as I opened it he came flying out swinging and kicking.

All you needed when someone made you chase them and get your adrenaline up was them to start fighting. We went to the ground pounding on each other until my partners got there to help hand cuff him. On the way into the station one of my partners of color was looking at the suspect's driver's license and commented that the only white boys who were stupid enough to fight with the Big Four were either from the Cities of Hazel Park or Roseville and he was naturally a Roseville boy. As they were laughing at that, I asked them what's wrong with Roseville; I'm from Roseville (knowing it was a tough little City). There was dead silence for a minute as they just stared at me and then started laughing. They said "that figures" alluding to all the times that I had been in the middle of a violent situation. I laughed too because they didn't know the half of it.

Nikki's Lounge/Sniper/Gun

When off duty, I sometimes went to a bar at 6 Mile and Davison called Nikki's Lounge. Since I spent a lot of off duty time in the Precinct, I got to know the people, good and bad alike, in the bars. One night a scout car got a radio run to the bar, "Man on the roof with a rifle, shots fired." We responded and were told by the Sergeant in charge of the scene that it was now a barricaded gunman and they had the building surrounded. As he was trying to figure out how to get up to the roof, I told him we knew how and would go in if he would have everybody hold their fire. There were two apartments above the bar and I had been up there before. There was an alcove between the two apartments that you could climb from one to the other by opening the windows on each side. My crew and I went into the bar and up the back stairs into the vacant apartment, through the alcove and into the occupied apartment. The window was unlocked so we opened it and one by one the four of us, in single file, quietly climbed in and walked through a bedroom. There was a young couple sitting in bed watching TV as we quietly walked past them. I looked at them and held my finger to my lips signaling to be quiet. One of my partners pointed to a large baggy of pot that was sitting on their dressing table and I let him know to forget it by whispering loud enough for the couple to hear "pipe tobacco" and kept walking. At the rear of the apartment was a small emergency door that went out onto the roof. We went through the door and were able to come up behind the suspect who was looking over the edge not expecting anybody to be behind him. We hand cuffed him and left the same way we had come in with the couple still sitting in their bed in amazement as we put the prisoner through the still open window in the alcove and left as I said thank you to them as if they gave us permission, which they didn't. I was pretty sure they wouldn't complain because we ignored the marijuana and got a man with a gun off of the roof.

Nikki's had a trivia night contest one night a week that involved the customers and they gave out prizes to the winners. One night, while off duty, I was sitting at the bar and they had just passed out question cards for a Trivial Pursuit game when there was a scuffle at the front door and someone yelled, "He's got a gun." I was sitting at the far end of the bar and by the time I got to the front door the man with the gun was running east on McNichols (6 Mile Rd.) and entered Phil's Bar at the next corner before I could catch him. Phil's Bar was well known as anti-cop and we have had officer in trouble calls there before. I was well aware of it and my adrenaline was already up. I pounded on the locked door yelling police open up and after a few minutes they opened the door and I entered the darkened bar with the door closing behind me and locking automatically as it was buzzer operated. As I was looking around I saw the gunman sitting at the bar breathing hard. I slowly walked toward him and a crowd started forming around me. I thought, oh shit, I stepped into it this time. I knew they weren't afraid to kick my ass and then lie about it which was the norm with this bunch. I asked him where the gun was; as my first agenda was to get the gun off the street before someone used it. He hadn't used it at the scuffle in Nikki's and ran instead and that was a positive. He said, "What gun, I don't know what you're talking about," as I searched him. I told him if I had to find it he was going to jail, but if I had an idea where I should look, I would just take the gun. After a few seconds, he said you might want to look behind the jukebox. I walked slowly through the crowd, slid out the juke box and picked up the gun. Unbeknownst to me at the time, someone from Nikki's called 911 and told them there was an officer in trouble at Phil's Bar with a man with a gun. Of course with that bars history, multiple cars responded. As I was buzzed out of the bar, I saw scout cars screaming up over curbs with officers exiting their cars with shotguns and hand guns drawn. I was impressed, but also surprised because I thought I had to handle this alone. The car that had the radio run was shocked when I handed them the gun and told them to put it on evidence as "found property" and notify dispatch that everything was under control. The scout car crews just shook their heads as they left. They knew I got into more than just finding a gun at Phil's Bar, but knew it was handled. The crowd at Phil's Bar was smiling as I was keeping my word instead of letting the situation get worse. That is how I got street respect and let everyone know I was straight up and kept my word, but it took full scale effort on and off duty.

When I walked back to Nikki's Bar there was some back slapping and a beer and shot of schnapps sitting there for me with the prize I won on the Trivia Pursuit contest that I didn't even enter. Now I had street creds from all three bars at 6 Mile & Davison, Nikki's, Phil's and the Caravan (a country bar across from Nikki's). One night four guys jumped me and our morality crew as we were leaving the Caravan and walking back across to Nikki's. We were working undercover at the time and after adjusting their attitudes without ever identifying ourselves, we just left leaving them bleeding and wondering what just happened, but the owner and bouncers knew.

All three bars had different clientele and all tough crowds. So it helped to have a fair, but tough attitude. I had learned and learned it well that you never bluff, back down, or show fear to man or animal, but to always give them a way out if possible. Like the Marines do when outnumbered or losing, "Charge," or in sports, "The best defense is a good offense." That has always worked for me even if I got a little bloodied sometimes.

Buddy's Battles

In Detroit at 6 Mile and Conant is the original Buddy's bar and restaurant which was and still is known for its square pizza that is the best in town. Buddy's cliental came from all over the metro area because of the quality food and friendly environment. We didn't usually have trouble at Buddy's, but on this particular night I had a three-man crew instead of four, and Reverend Lund, our Police Chaplin & friend, was riding with us. Around midnight when they were closing we got a radio run to Buddy's that there was a "disturbance in progress" and because of the shift change no one else was available. When we entered the Manager and staff pointed out two large men who refused to leave and were swearing and threatening to fight the staff. The four of us surrounded them and explained this was a restaurant that closed at midnight and they were not going to serve them and they had to leave. One of the men calmed down and seemed to understand that he wasn't going to get anything more to drink. The other one jumped up and started causing a disturbance so my partners each grabbed him under an arm and escorted him out by force with the Police Chaplin following. That left me alone with the other one who seemed to have calmed down. I walked behind as I escorted him down the rear door steps. As we got to the bottom my partners had already gone out the door and it closed, he then turned around, grabbed me by the throat with one hand, lifted me up off of the ground and started punching me in the face with his other hand, totally flipped out and screaming. As the back of my head was bouncing off of the cinder block wall, I was starting to lose consciousness and the only thing I could reach was my Kel-lite (steel flashlight). I was able to strike him several times in the only place I could reach, his head. I had been taught not to hit anybody in the head unless it was the last resort because head injuries bleed more and makes battles look worse than they were. Well this was a last resort and the only option I had. He was a big boy, over 6 feet and 225 lbs. or more. I was alone, getting my ass kicked and worried about passing out and losing my weapon. I don't know how many times I got hit or how many times I hit him, but I know I kept hitting him until he stopped choking and punching me and finally slumped down on top of me. After the crew placed the first guy in a responding marked unit for conveyance, the Police Chaplin opened the rear door of the bar and saw both of us laying their totally covered with blood. I was a little groggy and light headed when I stood up and the Police Chaplin was yelling to my crew to hurry up, Boudreau's been stabbed. I quickly sat down trying to slow my heart beat that was pumping even harder now. A couple of waitresses started wiping blood off of me to see where I was stabbed as the uniform crew took out my assailant who was still bleeding profusely. My partners who were concerned were also looking and asking me where I was stabbed. After most of the blood was cleaned off of me, and it was apparent that I wasn't stabbed, my partners started yelling at me, "You little asshole, you're not stabbed" and I was yelling back at them, "The Rev said I was stabbed and I believed him." While we were all bitching at each other the waitresses walked away shaking their heads in disbelief at us that after all that happened we were goofy enough to be arguing with each other. They thanked us and were all a buzz about the excitement that they had just witnessed that didn't usually happen there. For us it was almost the norm. His punches were glancing blows as I turned my head, but I had a few bumps on the back of my head, but nothing serious for a guy whose nickname was "Rubber Head".

It was the last day of the month and we got off at 3am to start the next day at 11am for our 11-7 day shift. The next day we were getting ready to hit the street when one of the front desk officers came into the back and told me not to go in the front. He said a big guy was talking to the desk Lieutenant and he had the back of his head shaved with 60 stitches in it from last night's fight at Buddy's. Of course as soon as I heard that I wasn't going to hide in the back and let him tell the Lieutenant only one side of the story. So I went right out there and if he wanted a rematch, I wouldn't get sucker punched this time or at least I would tell the true story and embarrass him. As I walked up to him he turned toward me and to my surprise he put out his hand to shake mine and apologized to me. He said he was drunk and had just caught his best friend in bed with his wife and had lost it. He told the Lieutenant that there were no hard feelings and that if the officer hadn't taken him down he might have killed or seriously injured him. My luck had held again as I was also vindicated because the desk Sergeant wanted me to change my report the night before and say I had hit him with a black jack instead of a flash light. I refused to lie even if there was a complaint as I did what I had to do at the time. I knew the Sergeant was just trying to save me from a biased Administration, but still I wasn't going to perjure myself. He didn't want to file a complaint or sue, just to apologize; so I talked the Detectives into just charging him with the misdemeanor of disturbing the peace instead of assaulting a Police Officer. It was unusual for injured prisoners to admit to their actions and not make false claims for law suit purposes and I for one appreciated someone taking responsibility for their actions and I hope his life got better.

We left the station and a little while later we received a radio run to Buddy's on a "Disturbance". We all looked at each other wondering if he returned there because two runs, in two consecutive days, never happened there. It was a good family type bar/restaurant. I hoped he didn't return as my trust in my fellow man had just been raised up a notch from a very low point. When we arrived the place was packed as it was lunch time and I was relieved to see he was not there. There were two men who were pushing and swearing at each other causing a disturbance and the restaurant clientele were angrily pointing them out to us. When we approached, one guy sat down, and the other guy started swinging at us. We quickly blocked his blows and put him on the ground and started handcuffing him when a female sitting next to the other man jumped on my back swinging at me giving the guy on the bottom an opportunity to nearly break free to start swinging again. My uniform driver knocked her off me and handcuffed her and we gained control and hand cuffed him. The dining room was a mess with tables and chairs all over the place, but no one was injured just bumps and bruises unlike the bloody mess of the night before. After we placed him in the back of our Cruiser I was standing in the open door way of the rear seat getting his side of the story when a car pulled up and the driver got out and went at me trying to get the prisoner out. I was alone with a prisoner I was detaining and was being rushed by another guy. Luckily for me our driver saw him and was on him immediately; helping me again. It turned out the man and female we arrested were married and she was out with her boss, the man who sat down when we showed up, and they were having an affair. The witnesses told us the woman and her boss was taunting the husband about it when he confronted them and a shoving match ensued between them and that's when we entered.

I felt bad for the husband, but after swinging at us he and his wife had to go to jail. The boss who thought he was in the clear was laughing and seemed to enjoy the whole situation while arrogantly telling the angry on lookers whose lunch was disturbed to mind their own fucking business. When I told him to stand up and turn around and that he was under arrest for disorderly conduct he stopped laughing and someone in the crowd started clapping and the whole restaurant joined in, as we removed him. As we were taking statements from the employees one of the witnesses told our uniform driver that was a pretty good fight, but you should have seen the bloody one last night. The driver told her he did see it and pointing at me and said, "He was the one in that one too," which caused a few mouths to hang open and dead silence for a moment before we all had a short laugh about the two unusual battles in less than 12 hours. As far as I know there were no problems at Buddy's for the rest of my career and we ate lunch there quite often and our food bill was usually taken care of.

Cop Shot

I wasn't there, but it was around this time there were two officers, one male and one female working an Accident Prevention Unit. Their function and expertise was in traffic enforcement and serious accident investigations like fatal scenes. They usually don't handle priority type radio runs. Like all street cops who had worked the streets they would back up regular units or sometimes volunteer to handle the run if they were close or all the cars were busy due to being shorthanded because of layoffs. In this case, they volunteered to answer a family trouble run. When they arrived the subject attacked the male officer and while beating on him, got his gun and shot him twice while the female officer was unable to disarm him and finally had to shoot and kill him. The male officer survived, but both officers suffered the effects of the incident while taking on a dangerous call that they didn't have to, but did. Most officers usually could get a little safer assignment after they had paid their dues working the streets and answering dangerous runs.

My old partner, who was also my roommate for years, taught me years before the sounds of incoming gunfire. He always teased me about working dangerous assignments when I had enough seniority to work something less dangerous. Like most of the guys I worked with, he was a combat Marine in Vietnam and had started out in a violent inner City Precinct paying his dues. He then transferred to a steady day shift one-man Accident Car that wasn't supposed to be as dangerous as specialized units. He responded to an accident report on Van Dyke and the driver was waiting for him at a small neighborhood bar. When he walked in by himself he walked right into an armed holdup in progress and surprised the holdup man. Due to his quick reactions and street smarts he got the drop on him and arrested him. He was awarded a Departmental Citation which is one of the higher awards the department gave at that time.

There were no safe assignments on the Detroit Police Department just some that didn't put you in violent situations over and over. One-man report cars and supervisor units weren't supposed to respond to violent types of runs by themselves, but they did when a citizen needed help and they were the closest or only unit available. On duty, off duty or by yourself, you were always in harm's way because you were taught to react to violent crimes in progress and we all just did it even without bullet proof vests, mace, tasers, radios, or backups. You could never let your guard down even for a second no matter what assignment you worked.

Bank Robbery Stakeout/Terrorism

We had a local bank robbed and as usual procedure the Fed's show up after all the action and take over the investigation as it was a Federal crime. Not all but most of the Feds seemed to have an attitude of superiority with their college degrees and looked down on us street cops. I don't know about all cops, but the guys I worked with who were usually in the thick of things and full of street experience, didn't trust them. Others, like me, looked down on their lack of street knowledge and naivety of how things work in the big City. We got a tip from one of our informants that the holdup man hung around a blind pig near the bank and he was spending big and bragging to friends about being a bank robber. Out of courtesy and normal procedure, we notified the FBI and gave them the location of the blind pig. They wanted our informant's personal information and bitched about it when I wouldn't give it out. In my book, the Fed's already had a bad track record with me.

We parked in a dead-end alley across the street from the blind pig that was overgrown and full of garbage so we could watch the front door without being seen. There was no foot traffic near us to give us away and we sat there for hours and our guy hadn't shown up. Everybody was tired, bored and hungry and one of the guys said, boy I sure could go for a pizza then another one said yeah and a beer to go with the pizza. A few minutes later, to our surprise, a kid came walking up the alley behind us carrying a large pizza and said, "Officers, I got a phony order here; do you guys want a free pizza?" We thanked him while laughing in amazement and one of the guys joked that the beer would be on the way any minute. We all grabbed a piece and were strangely looking around at each other waiting for someone to take a bite first. Then one of the guys said, "Its ok, I wrote down his license plate number." It was sad that we all had gotten so paranoid that we, if even for a second, thought someone was trying to poison us instead of just being nice. Trying to stay alive in our environment meant not to trust anybody, but each other, whether it was the FBI or a pizza delivery boy we always had to be careful. The bank robber never showed up and we were later told by the informant that he got nervous and left town when he heard strangers were trying to get into the blind pig. I wonder who?

They must have had some FBI agents who were street wise as they had to infiltrate quite a few national terrorist organizations in the 1970's. The R.N.A. (Republic of New Africa), Black Panthers (B.P.P), S.D.S. (Students for Democratic Society), Weatherman, White Panthers and Black Muslims (known today as the Nation of Islam), were very active and quite violent in the seventies. Some are still active today, but have changed their M.O. to being stealthy and using the press and public opinion to get to their agenda of control. For us that are lucky enough to still be alive, we are watching history repeat itself with terrorist activity and crime increasing nationally and internationally. In 2016, as I write this, I am hoping the public and media wake up before too many innocents suffer. It is still a strong memory for us who were on the front lines daily then. Just ask an old seventies cop.

Deputy Chief Arrested

Early one Saturday night while on patrol, we responded to a one-man Sergeant unit calling for the Cruiser because he had a man in sight who was carrying a gun. He put out his description and location and we were right around the corner at Van Dyke and Davison. We observed a large male carrying a sport coat with a gun on his left hip before he put his sport coat on while entering a hall party. The party was packed and I didn't want a shootout in a crowd that large. My uniform driver and I hung back until my two black partners could get right next to him on both sides in case he went for it. Being the only white faces in the crowd, we drew immediate attention. As we approached, we told him to keep his hands away from his waist. Strangely he just laughed and started to turn away to walk off and my partners had to grab him and remove his gun as he was pulling away. I asked him if he had a permit to carry a concealed weapon and he said he did, but not on him because it was expired and we should know who he was.

As we were putting the handcuffs on he was angrily and loudly saying he was a Deputy Police Chief. We hurriedly got out of the crowd that started to get loud with some anger toward us and with some laughter toward him which made him madder. My thoughts were to affect the arrest before we had a mini riot and clear the area as a Deputy Police Chief wouldn't need a permit to carry. His badge and ID card would be all he needed and it was mandatory for him to immediately show it when investigated. He was bullshitting or being arrogant by not cooperating with on duty officers. Either way he was going to jail now because he did not have proper ID. He was ranting and raving about having our jobs and we just killed him with politeness knowing he was baiting us. The Sergeant who called for us was visibly nervous about this arrest and left the scene. I knew we could be in a political buzz saw with this Administration and let the crew know the arrest was legal and proper, but we could pay a price for it. After deciding that no one is above the law and that we weren't going to be intimidated, into the station we went with our prisoner to process him.

When we got to the station the Lieutenant in charge was going nuts. He was already getting calls from the Mayor's office. Our Deputy Police Chief (prisoner) turned out to be a Civilian Deputy Chief which is a Mayoral appointee and not Certified Police personnel. They are required to obtain a permit to carry a concealed weapon unlike trained Police personnel who were moved up the ranks. The Lieutenant and the original Sergeant were in full panic mode telling us our ass was grass and we stepped into it this time and to remember what happened to #12 Cruiser when they just stopped the Mayor's cousin (they were all put back in uniform) and they did nothing improper. Our arrest was legal, but naturally the Mayor's office had intimidated everyone including the Detectives who wouldn't request a warrant from the prosecutor's office and he was released at the station.

He then wanted to write us up and press the issue, but we hadn't violated any Department rules or laws. To prepare my crew, I told them that he probably had enough political power to punish us anyway by having us at minimum put back in uniform. To my surprise, one of the officers on my crew who was actually the one that put the handcuffs on him told us not to worry, we all did the right thing and he had just called his uncle. I was amazed and asked him who his uncle was because when I hand picked him for my crew it was because he was a good, hardworking, honest cop, I wasn't aware he had an uncle on the force. He then told me his uncle was a real Police Deputy Chief who was appointed by the Chief of Police and was not a political civilian appointee. His uncle was connected from the Chief on down with a reputation of being an upstanding cop who worked his way up to his position.

My luck had held again when doing the right thing even against the political powers and the Lieutenant, Sergeant, and Detectives who bailed to political pressure were looking a little silly now. The Civilian Deputy Chief was now told he had no authority to write us up or change our assignments. He was told as a civilian he would have to make a citizen's complaint against us like any other civilian if he wanted to pursue this, but nothing done was improper and it would be found unfounded. I didn't know it at the time, but we created a big battle between the professional command officers of the Police Department and upper echelon of the Administrations civilian appointees to the Police Department. It wasn't the first time or the last time I stirred up stuff because I enforced the law no matter whom or what you were. Hard headed yes, but also fair and equal no matter if you were a Deputy Chief or a street hooker that had been robbed and assaulted and refused your right to prosecute. With all of the guys that I had the honor to work with I truly believe we were of the same mindset and work ethic as to be honest and fair even if it made things harder for us sometimes.

Biker Wake

The Tactical Mobile Unit (T.M.U.) had basically surrounded the area around St. Cyril and Van Dyke Streets and escorted hundreds of out of town bikers into that area for a wake of a high ranking national biker. Dispatch and our Precinct roll calls had advised all units from #11 to stay out of that area as T.M.U. would be handling any calls there. T.M.U. was a great unit with good cops, but I wondered why in the world the Command Officers would exclude the Precinct officers who knew the area and had working relationships with the local biker clubs.

The biker clubs in our Precinct knew and respected us and no way was anybody going to tell us to stay away from a possible problem in our Precinct. Technically no one told us to stay out and we weren't about to show the same weakness as the department was showing in our and most likely their view. The last time the Department held everybody back was at a concert downtown and people were robbed and raped while the street cops simmered with anger while being held back. This was our Precinct and we were the Precinct Cruiser (Big Four) and were going to lay down the law to the bikers about any problems between them and the citizens wouldn't be tolerated.

I personally knew a lot of them from on and off duty situations, good and bad. I showed them respect and they returned it as I gave them a fair shake even when arresting them. We had a pretty good working relationship and I wanted to keep it that way. So we went in with our big black Chrysler and no one seemed surprised or hostile in the least. They were actually quite friendly as a group and when I asked for the person in charge they brought about a couple of guys who were reasonable. I asked them if they had been advised by anybody from the Police Department yet and to my amazement they said no, but the Department had blocked traffic on their way in. I told them to police themselves and not to cause the locals to call or we would have to police them and that the City had the Tactical Mobil Unit in the area. We all shook hands and they did police themselves after we left. We made a point to cruise around in the area every once in a while to show them and the locals we were still in charge of our Precinct. The Cruiser (Big Four) had a reputation and history to live up to and keeping us out of our areas would diminish that. We weren't going to let that happen. We still had occasions of people approaching us on the street welcoming the Big Four back, especially the old timers who were preyed upon by the predators.

I don't know how the other Cruisers worked in their Precincts as there were 12 Cruisers City wide, but I did know most of them took their assignment as an honor and privilege. I neither saw nor heard of any real reports of documented abuse, just repeated third party hearsay stories. A friend of a friend heard some innocent person was "hassled for doing nothing because he didn't have proper I.D." We never corrected the stories mainly because a tough image in a tough neighborhood in a real tough City actually helped us do our job with less violent behavior from those who we investigated. Even some police officers who never saw it believed it happened. All I know is I filled in on #7 Cruiser, worked on #11 Cruiser and was a Crew Chief in charge of #11 Cruiser and we didn't hassle innocent citizens, but we sure took violent predators to task when needed and they were documented in the arrest and daily run sheet reports. We didn't have the time, interest, or inclination to make enemies out of possible future informants or willing witnesses of criminal activity and as some say that's not hearsay, that's right out of the horse's mouth. In my years on the Cruiser with a large amount of arrests we had exactly zero citizen complaints. Force was met with force with only enough to affect the arrest and stop the resistance. A lot of times our reputation going back to the 1930's Cruiser was enough to control situations when we were outnumbered. The Cruiser, just like most anything else, had evolved since the 1930's when it was developed to handle the Purple Gang and violent gangsters like them.

MDT Terminal / Blue

In 1979 we went what was high tech for us as they installed MDT computer terminals in some scout cars. I had them put ours in the rear seat compartment because we usually had a four-man crew or at least three on every shift. The officer in the back seat was assigned to run any suspicious license plates and everybody we had contact with to see who was wanted or their past criminal histories. We could even communicate with dispatch or other units, kind of like today's e-mails or text messages.

Before the MDT computer terminal, we had to switch to another radio frequency and wait in line as other units also were running checks. Once a suspect knew we were running a check on them it could get dicey if it took too long. The N.C.I.C. (National Crime Information Center) and S.O.S. (Secretary of State) was immediately available with the MDT. We rode by biker club houses, known houses of illegal activity like blind pigs, and dope houses and ran plate numbers as we went by. When we got a hit on wanted felons or a felony car we would sit on it and arrest the wanted suspects. Most misdemeanor warrants, if minor, and the subject wasn't in the vehicle at the time, we wouldn't waste the time of a four-man crew sitting on it, but if moving we would shake it down

The MDT Terminal was a great help, but our 'Want Book', that we spent hours and hours over the years off duty keeping up, still was invaluable. We even had units from other Precincts sending us messages asking for information on where subjects lived or who they hung out with or if we had info. on the subject they had in custody. A little bit of new and old technology worked well.

We had a lot of tricks in our bag of tricks like hunting hard to get felons on Holidays. That used to make the inside crew mad as hell at us. Like I said before we were all workaholics and in my case, I was 24/7 involved and knew nothing else for years. We researched, talked to informants and found out anything we could on the hard to get ones. One felon whose nickname was "Blue" was doing a good job eluding us. So on Christmas night we snuck up and listened by his Mother's side door near the kitchen where most phones were in those days. We had obtained her phone number and one of my partners made a call from a pay phone (no cell phones then) and asked if Blue was there while he acted high and a little out of it. As soon as we heard her say hang on I'll get him, we walked right in and arrested him as he was coming to the phone. It might sound a little crude to some, but to get the violent smart repeat felons off the street you had to be street wise yourself and be a little crude as long as you kept it legal, which we did.

The laws were a little different in the seventies, but they were already being changed to protect and help the predators and remove protections from victims. Looting, arson, rape, murder, and burglary were considered to be capital crimes and they could be shot if trying to escape as a last resort by a police officer, but that law was changed in the 1980's. Now the deck is even more stacked against a victim by the system. The victims don't want to get involved in the system just to be victimized again. Criminal rights are important, but a victim who didn't choose what happened to them should have a little more weight, not less!

Broken Neck

We started off our shift one night with only 3 men on the crew and then one more had left sick. That cut our usual four-man crew to just two of us and dispatch assumed there were four when they dispatched us to a shooting with a large crowd in the street fighting. It was shift change which meant there were no backup units on the street, just us. As we arrived we saw two groups of men with about 15 to 20 on each side of the street dashing back and forth attacking each other with bats, crowbars, rocks and anything they could fight with. One was lying on the lawn and had been shot in both legs. Normally this type of run was what the Cruiser (Big Four) was designed for, but today we had a half crew and a hell of a mess to deal with. I advised dispatch that we had a good shooting and two crowds fighting with each other and we would need more units when available. I grabbed a shotgun knowing that usually will get people's attention, being we were so outnumbered. Dispatch then advised us that another shooting, "a fatal," was being called in only a few houses south of our location. We were in the middle of Omira Street and the two groups had pulled apart with us in the middle separating them when one side decided to rush the two of us. One big black uniform cop and one small white plain clothes cop with a shotgun. My uniform driver was huge and a body builder and he caught a hold of the first one that got to us in a head lock. I then racked the shotgun as loud as I could while squatting down and pointing it left and right while yelling and screaming in the crazy man act that I used when being the first man in on Narco raid's.

Sudden loud and crazy action usually caused people to freeze and it was working in this situation too. The problem was it usually only worked long enough to gain entry when doing it on a raid, but in this situation, we were alone in the middle of the street. After a minute or so the shocked and surprised crowd started coming toward us again. My partner swung the guy he was holding in a head lock to the side and I heard a loud crack. I stood all the way up lowering the shotgun and started yelling at my partner saying, "You broke his neck you asshole." He was yelling back at me, "I did not you little ass." He let go of the guy and he took off back into the crowd apparently ok. We were both arguing and both groups had stopped fighting and were staring at us crazy cops in amazement as more units pulled up to help us handle the commotion.

The shooting victim we had lived, but the other victim, 5 houses away, was just coming home from work and was hit by a stray shot in the head and died immediately. It turned out the two extended families from each side of the street had been fighting for years and this day it came to a head. Looking back our little argument in the middle of the street during a violent confrontation while totally outnumbered bought us enough time for help to arrive. During those days, I still hadn't realized just how nutty things we did were. All I knew was at the time this was normal to me and not unusual behavior and usually worked.

Family Trouble

On Fleming just north of East 7 Mile Road, we responded to a radio run, "family trouble, one has a gun." We pulled up one house south of the address and approached the house and saw a woman walking down the front porch steps with a child. As that was happening, a man came to the door pointing a rifle in her direction. We all drew our weapons, but were unable to fire as there was another woman and child right behind him in the house. I ran toward the woman and child and pushed them to the side and out of his line of fire as we all attempted to take cover. The other woman and child escaped out the side door during the commotion in front.

He was visibly drunk and pointing the rifle at us as we were ordering him to drop it. We didn't have good cover and were all exposed to him. When he pointed the rifle downward we quickly rushed the front door with our weapons pointed at him. Our sudden charge caused him to drop his rifle and we took him into custody for felonious assault. I received my 10th Citation/ Commendation for "When faced by an armed subject exercised great discretion in effecting his apprehension without injury to anyone." In my book all we did was eliminate a barricaded gunman situation again the easy way before it got out of control and innocent citizens were put at risk. Like I said, and always believed, a good offense is the best defense. We were there to take risks and go forward not backward when we were needed. All of us on this crew were like-minded so we knew we weren't going to be the only one to charge.

I truly believe our type of actions limited harm to victims, but I know it also put us and perpetrators in a more dangerous position. Our priorities were in favor of the victims and to control the situation as soon as possible so no one else would be victimized. I have seen and heard of situations where innocent citizens were raped, shot, and assaulted while law enforcement hesitated, negotiated, or waited the situation out. That wasn't going to happen on our watch! I don't mean to blindly rush in like cowboys, but look, listen, stay calm and use your experience during chaos to take advantage when possible instead of over-thinking and non-action. We knew the risk we took and that was what we cops were there for.

Cadillac Room Biker

One afternoon we backed up a scout car that had a police run, "An assault just happened on north bound Van Dyke and 7 Mile Road." The victim had been pulled from his car while sitting at the red light after only looking at the man in the car next to him. He had been beaten viciously about his head and face. The witnesses at the scene gave us a good description of the perp and his vehicle and said the victim was pulled from his vehicle and pounded on for no apparent reason. The victim was an older smaller meek type of guy and the perp was described as six feet four over two hundred pounds with long wild hair and beard.

There was a bar called The Cadillac Room that was less than a mile away on Van Dyke just south of E. 8 Mile Road that was pretty tough. Locals and people of color stayed the heck out of there as this place was well known as not a friendly place. I had worked the bar a couple of times when I worked undercover and had been physically challenged by patrons just because they didn't know me as a regular. Luckily we knew the bars reputation and I had a couple of big backup officers in the bar with me, but there had been a lot of other people who were assaulted there over the years. On occasion we would give this bar and other tough guy bars a walk through to let them know we were still around. We decided to sit in the parking lot next door as the suspects pickup truck was parked there. After a while the suspect and a few of his friends came out and walked over to his truck talking and laughing while he was showing them punching and kicking motions apparently reliving the attack. All four of us approached from different directions and distances. As my uniform driver approached getting his attention, one of my other plain clothes partners had arrived right next to the suspect unnoticed. The suspect ignored the uniform officer's order to "Hold it there" and as the uniform officer sped up next to him, the suspect turned away and then suddenly turned back attempting to strike the officer and shouting, "I am going to sue you." My plain clothes partner struck him with one quick blow to the mouth with his Kel-lite which immediately stopped his attack. Teeth and blood flew as the plain clothes officer said, "Now you got something to sue for." We quickly handcuffed him as his friends and a crowd had formed. They then realized it wasn't just one uniform officer's attempt to arrest, but it was a Cruiser crew who were ready to do battle. Another of my partners asked the crowd, "Does anybody else want a law suit?" They all just backed off and went back into the bar. Normally, I didn't condone hitting anybody in the head or face as that area bleeds easily and it looks worse than it is, but that was the only option available to keep his partner from being assaulted. We were pissed at what he had done to the little old guy and were already expecting trouble from the bars violent crowd. I think the crowd realized we really wanted a piece of them after years of trouble and wouldn't back down if provoked.

Right or wrong cops are human and we hold our feelings in most of the time but sometimes those that earn an attitude adjustment will get one. Most of the time when a cop is physically attacked it's by ambush, sucker punched, or when outnumbered and in my case usually being the smallest one, I was always on the alert as all my partners were over 6ft., 200 lbs.

Sometimes, when we were in the middle of an unruly mob and one of us had enough of somebody's antics, we had a code to let each other know we were going to make an arrest. When one of the crew loudly said, "That's about as disorderly as you can get," the rest of us got into position to quickly affect the arrest which usually worked well. We had gotten to know what each other was going to do in chaotic situations and worked together like a well trained and experienced team. We had white complainants who didn't want to talk to black crew members and black complainants who only wanted to talk to the "brother". Both types of complainants were quickly put in their places if they wanted our services and if not they were ignored. No doubt in my mind this was one good Cruiser Crew and I was proud to be a part of it.

Lucky / Abused Trust

Our station inside personnel got a call from a bank Repo-man asking for help on a repo of a Cadillac from a man who he was told to be very dangerous and a possible pimp on Woodward Ave. We didn't normally get involved with civil matters unless there was a strong potential of violence. In this particular situation, when we heard the name, it was one of our most violent pimps who had set a hooker on fire with lighter fluid and had shot up an officer's private residence in the past. His nick name was Lucky and he was on our radar for a while, but he avoided us like the plague and everybody on Woodward, hookers, pimps, and business owners, were afraid of him. Whenever we could catch him in a minor traffic violation we shook him down to let him know we hadn't forgotten about him hoping to legally catch him on a felony. He was street smart, polite, and unable to be baited, so any inconvenience or embarrassment we could legally cause him to go through, we were for. We told the Repo-man to stay by his phone and we will call him when we had him stopped.

It didn't take long before we spotted Lucky pulling on to the Chrysler freeway service drive just south of East 7 Mile Road without completely stopping at the cross walk. We notified dispatch to let our station know we had the subject detained and they called the Repo-man and gave him our location. Lucky was smiling knowing he was clean and we had nothing on him except a minor traffic violation. We had him in the back of our Cruiser after patting him down when the Repo-man came up, showed us the legal paper work, and drove off in his Cadillac. That immediately took the smile off his face and he said you know what happens to cops who fuck with me, alluding to the cop's house that got shot up. We were ready for his thinly veiled threat with one of our own. We simply asked him if his Momma still lived at so & so address, that he thought no one knew about. By the silence and look on his face, with his car just being repossessed you could see he was worried about us and what he thought we might do if he acted on his threat. Threatening a cop wasn't very smart; threatening a Cruiser crew was just plain stupid. We were hardened cops for hardened criminals!

With so many years in the worst area dealing with the most violent on a day to day basis, we had to be smarter, tougher and keep our emotions in check in order to stay legal, but we knew when we could push the limits. Normal people, who were just making a mistake or bad judgment, were dealt with in an easier manner. It was hard, even for us who had seen it all over and over, to go by the book instead of retaliating so as not to mess up the court case.

We had a 90-year old widow who was raped and viciously beaten for hours and was a physical and emotional mess. The 6ft. tall, 13-year old neighbor boy who she had befriended and trusted attacked her. She had given him small jobs raking her leaves, going to the corner store, or just helping her around her house since he was about 7-years old. Then at 13, he attacks her. I have seen the worst in people more than the good over and over and it was a daily struggle not to be negative and angry in the world I lived in. Rape was rampant and the community frowned on those that reported it. It was thought by some that it was just taking sex like anything else and they just took what wasn't theirs. The saying, "Snitches get Stitches" was a code some lived by in the seventies, as well as today. Almost 50 years later it's still that way and even more hate exists for outsiders who make the mistake of entering their world whether cop or civilian.

Slow Response

We had a few officers who suddenly got beer muscles when they saw us responding to a situation they were involved in and they would get aggressive. We had one who did it more than others and actually started physical confrontations that weren't necessary and could be avoided.

One day, as we were coming down the street to back him up on a family trouble call, I saw him looking our way and saw us coming. At the time everything was calm until he started poking a very large man in the chest until the man shoved him back and the fight was on. My driver saw the fight start and stepped on the gas to hurry and get there. I told him to slow down and let him learn a lesson. When we got there we slowly pulled the guy off of him while he was yelling about us taking our time. I told him if he was going to start fights he better learn how to win them or get off of the street. We were tired of fighting his battles. He was a decent guy otherwise and did eventually transfer downtown. There were plenty of violent people who needed attitude adjustments and you didn't have to egg anyone on that might have a reason to be angry but hadn't gotten violent. I had been in a lot of fights on the job by just being there, but I calmed a lot more of them down. Most inner City street cops had to learn how to show and get respect without looking for unnecessary trouble.

Rapists Arrested

We had responded to a Police run, "A gang rape in progress in a vacant lot." It was between two houses near our location. We had pulled into the alley with our lights out and without street lights it was pitch black. We were 2 or 3 houses north and just west of the only vacant lot on the block. We were facing the vacant lot and a marked unit had parked just south of the lot and quietly approached on foot from the south east. They notified radio that it was a good rape in progress and the victim was being assaulted by five men. We advised the uniform officers of our position and to approach the group from the east driving them toward us. When the uniformed crew approached the group, they attempted to escape on foot right across the alley as we drove slowly in the dark alley toward them.

I told my driver to "Hit it" to which he floored the engine and in the dark alley our black cruiser lurched forward with the loud sound of our four-barrel carb opening up and surprising them. It was so dark they couldn't see us and instead of turning back into the oncoming pursuing officers they made the mistake of attempting to cross the alley in front of and alongside of us. They all ran into the car bouncing off with one ending up jammed under our vehicle and another up under our wheel well. We immediately stopped and pulled them out from under the vehicle, handcuffed them and advised them of their rights as none were seriously injured. They were shocked and amazed as to what just happened. They thought they were getting away in the dark alley and then all of a sudden they were being pulled out from under and next to the Big Four's black Chrysler Cruiser. My favorite affirmative action Sergeant who tried to give me an almost perfect service rating showed up and was trying to get me to change my story as she was worried I might be in trouble for telling my driver to "Hit it" and running into the suspects. I wasn't going to lie or perjure myself, the chips were going to lie where they fell and I told her, "Sarge, rape is a capital crime and I could have shot all five of them as they were escaping, right?" She said, "Yes." I then told her, "What is the difference then, by running into them to stop them from escaping?" When we sped up we couldn't see any better than they could and we just wanted to block their escape, but if they believed we hit them on purpose we let them. For the Sergeant who jumped to the conclusion we did hit them on purpose, I decided to let her believe that, even though it was impossible to hit someone with the side of your car while travelling forward. The Sergeant and scout car crew conveyed our prisoners' downtown to the Sex Crime Division and verbally told the investigators, the Big Four ran them all over, getting all five. Of course, with the Big Four's long reputation of doing things nobody else did, and by doing the almost impossible feat of catching all five rapists while they were running through a dark alley, they believed them. When we entered the Sex Crime Divisions offices, some of the officers started clapping and congratulating us on our catch by running the perps down and smiling and winking. We were trying to tell them they ran into us but they wouldn't listen. I had made a joke and now no one believed us and thought our truthful report was to avoid lawsuits. So be it, another rumor of the Big Four's tough love on educating violent felons. We found out the five perps had punched, kicked and violently raped the 11-year old mentally challenged girl for hours; she was a Canadian Ward of the State. I heard no more about the case or even if she could testify or not. In the 70's there was no DNA evidence test and I, like a lot of my cohorts, were totally burnt out on the court system being more in favor of their constituents than real victims and dismissed whatever cases they could for any reason they could find.

We had real activist judges bordering on radical in the seventies. I saw murderers, rapist and burglars let go or minimum let plea to misdemeanors over and over. We just kept arresting them until they were killed or moved on. When you caught a B&E man and asked him how many times he was arrested for burglary, he would tell us. When we looked up his convictions, you would never have known he was a burglar. His burglary charges, one after another, were all lowered to entering without owner's permission or worse yet, disorderly conduct. No wonder crime was rampant and business was good for us because crime did pay in the Motor City. Victims needed to be aware because the media wasn't going to report those facts. In their eyes it was the Comeback City. We knew better and history proved it and now almost 50 years later it is still called the Comeback City.

Raiding Party

One of our officers received a phone tip from an informant of his while he was working in our detective bureau about a suspicious vehicle driving around in the McNichols and St. Louis area. He was in the process of running the license plate number when we received a police run to the McDonalds Restaurant in that location of a hold up in progress. The perps had escaped and the vehicle and license plate matched the informant's information. The Detective Bureau immediately sent our B&E Crew (11-31) to the address that was in the area and they arrested one of the suspects. Our old Special Operations Lieutenant was now a floating Lieutenant since they broke up the Special Operations Units and he was one of the best. He immediately put together a raiding party with the Cruiser, 11-31, and himself just like we did when we all worked together as a team. With the consideration of a lesser charge, he talked the suspect into taking us to where the other holdup perps were.

We raided 3 locations making numerous arrest and confiscating weapons, money and evidence pertaining to numerous McDonald Restaurants that were previously held up. We solved over 20 armed robbery cases and I received my 11th Commendation/Certificate but the best award was working with a fantastic Lieutenant as a team again like we had done many times in the past while in Precinct Special Operations.

His group of Special Operation crews had more arrest and lost more officers than all three shifts combined over the years he ran it. We all knew how he hurt for us young hot dogs and was proud of us and this raiding party reminded me of how it was working with a group of real pros who really cared from the boss on down. There were still a lot of cops doing more than asked, but we saw more and more of the younger officers with the lower standards being accepted by superiors taking their sweet old time responding to priority runs. We would be running full speed from one call to another, while driving past the same units that received the calls and weren't in any hurry. They technically did their job, but nothing extra, or any more than they had to. In the old days that kind of response wasn't acceptable by supervisors, or the rest of the troops. It was almost like two separate police departments and we were looked down upon by some supervisors and respected by others. The older bosses, who paid their dues, knew somebody had to be the warrior guardians.

Hold-up Man Shot

It was a little before midnight on December 21, 1979 as we were traveling south on Conant Avenue, I was thinking about my old 80-Series coworker who had been killed on this day five years before at Conant and Nevada. We had just passed that location and I was pushing it out of my mind as I still couldn't let myself go there mentally.

Christmas time and driving by that location on the same day made my heart race thinking about him and my other partner who was there and was never the same after. Since then, Christmas time had been a tough time for me since being divorced and burying him on Christmas Eve. I had always felt guilty it was him and not me, and guilty that it affected me to where I was usually out of sorts during the holidays. The only thing that helped was not thinking about it and my girlfriend who I had moved in with who understood me. I was quiet and troubled during those times and she kept my mind off of my memories of the past.

I was snapped back into the present when my driver said don't look now, but check out those two in front of Buddy's Pizzeria. I looked out of the corner of my eye and saw that two men were roaming around suspiciously. I thought it looked like they were looking for a good victim to snatch a purse. As soon as we were out of sight, my driver hurriedly headed back to the area of McNichols and Conant through the side streets. We parked in an alley near Alpha & Conant as they had crossed the street and were hiding in the alley behind the bar called Club Polski. It was raining and cold as we exited our vehicle. We wanted to get closer to them on foot figuring they surely were going to do something as no one would be just meandering around in this weather for that long. After about 15 minutes or so a young couple came out the front door of the Club and turned down Alpha Street on foot apparently heading to their vehicle. The couple walked past the two men who then followed behind them for a few feet.

Suddenly, one pulled out a hand gun and stuck it in the males back while the other jerked the female around roughly while holding a large hunting knife. I quickly scurried over to our car as my driver was also on foot with our prep radio turned off. I grabbed the radio mic on our still running vehicle and told dispatch, "Priority 11 Cruiser - We have a hold up in progress on Alpha just east of Conant." I then tossed the mic back on the car seat, turned the car off and hurriedly returned to my partners who were creeping closer, but stayed out of sight of the holdup men. It seemed like forever because we couldn't move in while it was in progress without putting the victims between us and them and possibly getting them shot or stabbed. Especially now that we knew it was not just a purse snatching. We also couldn't change our locations to surround or block their escape if they ran in any other direction except straight at us. Luckily for us, and the victims, after terrorizing the couple, they turned and ran directly toward us instead of the other escape routes. I was excitedly relieved. When they got close enough to us and the victims were no longer behind them, and our range of fire was clear, we jumped up from our hidden locations and ran toward them yelling, "Police, give it up mother fuckers." The male victim was running toward us yelling, "Shoot them." We knew then we had good complainants who would prosecute as he was mad as hell. My driver was to my right when the first perp started to turn and point his gun in our direction as he was running. As I was coming up with my .357 Magnum and about to pull the trigger, I heard the loud crack of my drivers .44 Magnum who fired from the hip. The perp flipped over as he was hit knocking him down and his revolver went sliding down the sidewalk. Immediately after, I heard three shots to my left in the alley behind the bar where my other partner had chased the other perp. I changed course as my driver had perp #1 in control and hurried into the alley and started searching the bar's parking lot where we found the second perp hiding under a car and arrested him. I was pleased that we got both of them and the victims were ok and was especially thankful I didn't lose another partner in that alley when the three shots rang out when he was out of my sight.

I didn't say anything to my partners about losing a co-worker on that same date and street years before and burying him on Christmas Eve. Normally I just wouldn't let myself think about our losses or what I had seen people do to each other over the last nine years, but certain things or actions brought the memories back. I received my 12th Citation/Commendation Award for "Keen observations, recovered stolen property and arresting two subjects for robbery armed."

I had become anxious when things slowed down and I had too much time to think whether on or off duty, so I spent most of my off duty time out in the same area I worked in. I had lost my off button and was getting involved too much when off duty by hanging out in rough areas. I had made friends with a lot of the bar owners and their patrons over the years and got protective of them.

Sergeants Test

My longtime partner (The Character) had been studying for the Sergeants exam for almost a year and knew the General Order Manual well. We all had top rated service ratings, but as white males we knew we would have to write in the upper 90's to even have a chance of promotion with a couple of thousand taking the day long test. Most of us didn't bother to take the test because of the affirmative action rules that weighted the promotions against us and only every other one would be a white male no matter how high we wrote on the test.

To my surprise my partner (The Character) wrote in the upper 90's which meant he was actually going to get promoted to Sergeant and leave the Cruiser Crew. I hadn't thought about my hand picked crew who were working so well together being changed. Usually the few white males that had a chance for promotion worked inside where they had time to study, but not very many street guys.

I found out if you took the test you could leave after 3 hours and get a full day's pay, so I decided to take the test with my partners even though I hadn't studied at all. I was surprised to find out that I wrote in the 80's and could have had a good chance of promotion if it wasn't for the affirmative action policy favoring minorities who got promoted while writing lower. I was happy working the Cruiser and didn't really want to be a Sergeant and have to be a supervisor especially under the Administration's new rules. Crew Chief on the Cruiser was as high as I wanted to go. I did however understand why the white male officers, who put everything into their careers, were upset because they were passed over numerous times while watching less qualified officers being promoted over them. They had to keep working the dangerous streets with no hope of moving up, while being supervised by some who shouldn't even have been hired as a police officer in the first place. It was the same getting into a Bureau like, Homicide, Vice or Armed Robbery because those positions also went to less seniority, less experienced minorities. Although it didn't impact me, I was proud of senior officers who no more had the hope of being promoted but still worked and took their chances on shift cars. They were getting burnt out doing the dirty work far too long without hope of advancement. It used to be if you worked hard and paid your dues working the street, you had options to improve your lot but that changed; everything became political!

The Character Promoted / Crew Changes

There was good news and bad news, the good news was my friend and longtime partner (The Character) beat the odds and was promoted to Sergeant and assigned to my old Precinct, the Seventh. He was my first pick for the new Cruiser and helped build and run the crew as the alternate crew chief. We were usually on the same page on decisions that formed the crews working habits. We had developed an honest, hard-working and fair crew that took to protect and serve seriously. I truly believe we were respected by our peers and citizens alike. We upped the number of felony arrest to 15 to 20 a month and totally eliminated citizen complaints by treating people with respect while still being tough and living up to the Precinct Cruisers (Big Four) reputation of no-nonsense enforcement. As a crew, I know we all liked and respected each other as we all had the same agenda to take the violent predators off the street and that is what we did.

The bad news was our original crew was about to change and we would be losing one of the main parts of our well running machine. He would be missed. Each and every member of our crew was the best of the best in my book. We all faced danger and hardships together and it hurt to see any of them go, even to a promotion.

The natural order would dictate that each of the crew would move up one notch as they all were capable and the third in line would make a good alternate crew chief. We would then pick up a new younger replacement that deserved to have the opportunity to join the Cruiser. We had done even more than we were asked to from our Commander and in my humble opinion a reward was in order for them.

Instead, we got a surprise that wasn't close to a reward as we learned our new replacement was a higher seniority re-hire who had quit the job and spent a couple of years working in a large Southern City. It was known that he had connections downtown and was re-hired through the Chief of Police Hart's office recommendation. With his higher seniority he automatically became the new Crew Chief on the Cruiser and I became the alternate Crew Chief with the rest of the crew remaining in their original order.

The crew didn't take the change well. We had a good crew and worked together doing good work and they did not like the change. When the Crew complained to me, I encouraged them to give him a chance. I was of the mindset that I wanted to help the new Crew Chief and not turn the crew against him. I became just another part of a good crew which was fine with me, so when they had a complaint, I told them to talk to the new Crew Chief.

The new Crew Chief tried to win them over and invited the crew and their wives to his house for dinner to help get to know everybody. My girlfriend and I were the only ones to show up. I felt bad for him and let the crew know the next day. They had to give him a chance as I heard he was a good street cop and would most likely adjust to his new position.

The problem was, when he had a day off, with the next highest seniority, I was the alternate Crew Chief and we worked the shift as a team as we had before and the crew liked to work that way. The new Crew Chief had a different style, he ran the crew as a boss rather than a team leader. I was hoping at some point he would realize the crew knew their jobs and he would treat them as experienced Cruiser crew members instead of underlings. I purposely kept my feelings to myself hoping everything would work out and I really didn't mind not being in charge and responsible for the crew's actions anymore. I didn't like the way I was replaced with politics from downtown being a part of it and my Commander letting it happen without warning, but I've always thought my Commander was caught in the middle.

Through my career I had mostly been senior man on the cars that I worked in Special Operations. I spent the last 10 years from rookie in an inner City Precinct to Cruiser Crew Chief working with officers who worked at only one speed, and that was all out full speed. I was proud of all of them as that was who I wanted to work with when I signed up for this. I was getting tired and burnt out, but didn't know anything else or how to slow down physically or mentally, I wasn't upset for myself when I was forced to let go of my crew and just be one of them. It was harder for the crew not moving up a notch. Times change, but this crew from day one, worked at full speed and weren't used to taking coffee breaks, long lunches or visiting people while they worked. It was an adjustment to working at a different speed.

I believe I made some mistakes during the transition: 1) Not relaying the crew's complaints to the new Crew Chief so he was aware. I wanted to help him take over an existing crew to work his way and not interfere. 2) Not following the new Crew Chief's work style when he was off and I was in charge. I would let the crew work like we used to which resulted in more arrests and court time for the crew members. 3) As his style became apparent, I started taking a lot of sick days off, burning them up, rather than working with the new Crew Chief and trying harder to adjust to the change and work his way.

The new Crew Chief didn't ask for advice or about how things were done in the past and seemed uninterested in checking daily teletypes, or talking to Detectives to see if anyone was wanted, or using and keeping up the Want Book. We didn't start our shift hunting felons as a team like we were used to doing. Instead we started our shift at the Clock Restaurant with a cup of coffee. There was nothing wrong with that, but we weren't used to slowing down or taking breaks especially at the start of a shift. In fact, after 10 years of running full speed, I thought it might even be good for me. Most smart officers after a few years of being cowboys out there adjusted their pace and did their jobs above and beyond what was required, but learned overdoing could and would cause problems within this Administration. Good felony arrests, or awards for risk taking, no longer got you respect or advancement.

It was ticket writing and avoidance of complaints or lawsuits and going along to get along that gave you rewards which were totally opposite of how we worked in the early 70's. The senior officers who continued to work the street at a fast pace, were openly called "Dinosaurs" meaning we were still working like it used to be before this Administration slowed everything down for political purposes. In the last five or so years it was increasingly feeling like swimming upstream, while watching the working units getting disbanded or watered down with the politically accepted new work ethics. I hadn't adjusted to the changes on or off duty and naively thought that crime had to be controlled and someone had to do it assertively. I was still naïve enough politically to be confused about why in the world they would change a working crew's makeup that could slow crime down and had proven results.

Crime Up / Layoffs

Crime was up, white flight was in full force and they were still laying off police officers in the beginning of the 80's. The Precincts were almost emptied leaving the neighborhood residents to be protected and served by fewer and fewer officers as Precinct units that knew the local area predators were moved downtown or eliminated. The officers that were left were put on shifts and ran from one call to another and started each shift with dispatch giving each car a dozen old calls to start with. That meant less and less patrolling and arrests and more writing reports of already long over crimes, if the victim couldn't be talked out of the report since they usually didn't have insurance anyway. The officers were pushed to keep up traffic ticket writing, but never counseled for not taking crime reports; that would have got you in a lot of trouble in the early 70's. More tickets meant more money and less crime reports meant less crime stats and that made the Administration very happy. The problem was without reports and stats, there was no accurate way of knowing where crime was happening in the neighborhoods. Some citizens insisted on making a report and some officers did take reports, but not all. With or without reports, crime still was going higher and higher even as it was being skewed to look like it was less. All that was left with time to actually proactively work felonies were the 31 Series Cars (B&E crews) and us on the Cruisers (Big Four) and we would be kept busy with the in-progress priority 1 and 2 runs like shooting's, hold up's, burglaries, and violent crimes.

The few cars that were out there usually were out of service on other calls. There were 12 scout car area's and usually, even on weekend nights, there were only 2 to 4 cars to cover all 12 areas. There were 4 mini-stations that didn't respond to police calls and further drained man power from the shifts mostly for public relations. The public was led to believe they were being served and protected; which they weren't. The cars on the street were not able to back each other up when out-numbered or in trouble which put the officers and the public both at risk.

Downtown Traffic Enforcement (ticket funds), Community Relations and Crime Prevention sections (public relations) were enlarged and given awards, while crime and services were forgotten in the rest of the City.

Organized Crime Enforcement was eliminated as the Italian Mafia gave way to Black Organized Crime and gangs who had City connections. The outer Precincts like #11 had caught up to the high crime inner City Precincts like #7 and #10 where I used to work in the mid 70's. I saw firsthand how it morphed into a dangerous, dirty and neglected area with those that could leave did and those that couldn't had to put up with more and more violent predators with less and less protection. Within the Precinct there was one Sergeant for every 2.6 police officers because of mass promotions by affirmative action of minorities to even up the races with Sergeants who weren't supposed to answer police runs. It was kind of like way too many chiefs and not enough Indians.

When I transferred into #11 in 1973 it was a busy Precinct vice wise with Woodward Ave. hookers and a lot of bars and clubs throughout the Precinct, but the neighborhoods were safe and clean unlike the inner City neighborhoods. It was mostly Polish and full of successful small businesses.

In 1980, I moved into a quiet little neighborhood with manicured lawns where my older Polish widowed neighbors would bring me fresh vegetables from their backyard gardens. They happily welcomed a cop in their neighborhood at 8 Mile and Van Dyke. Sadly, in just a few years, it had changed and the local parks were garbage dumps full of drug users with used needles and empty broken bottles. The Van Dyke small businesses had been robbed and harassed out of business. The hookers had spread all the way from Woodward Ave. to 8 Mile and Van Dyke and the Big Imperial burger restaurant on the corner was full of pimps watching out for their girls. My neighbors eventually moved out and the homes and lawns weren't kept up anymore. We could hear gun fire at night and smell the garbage rotting in the alley. Next door to me the yard was full of dog shit as my new neighbor was raising mean inbreed Bouvier dogs and usually had about 6 or so pups at any one time. The new neighbor who moved behind me across the alley had a bunch of unsupervised kids who liked to throw rocks against the back of our houses denting the siding. Cars and garages started getting broken into and it wasn't safe to bank, shop, or even go around the corner to Van Dyke Ave. anymore. I knew the next step would be home burglaries, robberies, dope houses and shootings as this was the 4th neighborhood that I lived in that changed over my short career and that's exactly what happened. I lost money on every house that I bought while watching the suburban home prices go up.

The department started a fully manned unit that's only job was to follow and make sure cops really lived in Detroit as residency was required then or they would be fired. It was called the Residency Unit and even your family had to live in the City, not just you.

A lot of police officers who loved the City were heartbroken watching and risking all to see the Administration take special care of downtown and their friends while ignoring the neighborhoods, street cops, and residents who were actually suffering and dying daily. The media didn't help because they were either too lazy to check what was happening or were in the Administrations pocket. They reported some things like homicide numbers committed in the City that usually was 500 to 700 a year. They didn't report the stats. of Detroit's predators as violent crime had reached to the suburbs with Oakland and Macomb County's jails being filled with a majority of Detroit's predators. Listening to the media parrot the Administrations false propaganda of how safe this come back City was becoming, was a sick joke to us and the neighborhood residents who suffered and knew better. The mid 70's were just the rapid start of Detroit's demise, as nothing has changed in the last 40+ years and won't until the problems are admitted, faced, and changed.

Those of us who loved this City and gave their all, are still heart sick about what has been done to this once great City. We were proud to have protected and served, while also fighting an uphill battle with those who had political agendas'. We were on the front lines and knew firsthand what was happening, but one of the first things the Administration had done was put a gag order on individual police officers from talking to the press. They made it very clear that anybody not going along with them would be punished, while others rewarded. We Dinosaurs were abandoned with the neighborhood tax paying, law-abiding citizens.

Inkster Murder

We received information from a connection of ours from the Inkster Police Department that one of our fine residents was wanted by them for murder. Like normal, we put the wanted subject's information in our Want Book. We periodically checked his known residence and hangouts while actively hunting him, exactly like what the Precinct Cruiser (Big Four) was designed for 50 years ago in 1930. Months later while we drove by his last known residence, unbelievably, he drove by in the victim's brown 1977 Cougar. After a short chase, he stopped and we placed him under arrest and recovered the victim's vehicle. A few weeks later I received a Commendation letter from the Inkster Chief of Police, my 5th Letter of Recognition for "Good police work". A few weeks later, I received my 6th Letter from Chief Hart for "Dedication and professionalism and an asset to the department" and thanking me for doing good work.

Old Partner Shot

A few years later my old 80-Series partner and friend who was then working a shift car, got into a chase with a subject wanted for shooting at other officers. They chased the subject into Hamtramck. He fled on foot into the front door of a bar and my old partner was right on his heels going into the front door as his partner ran around to the back door to cut him off. The armed wanted subject immediately turned back around after entering the bar and starting to come back out the front door firing shots. He hit my old partner in a main artery in his thigh and then turned back into the bar. He then ran through it and came out the rear door firing at the officer in the rear who shot and killed him with a M1 carbine. My old partner who was seriously wounded and was bleeding profusely was holding back a group of people at gun point not knowing if they were friendly or not.

Over the years, we had learned that a large group or crowd in a chaotic time usually wasn't friendly, especially during a police shooting. We had worked with an officer, years before in the 10th Precinct, who told us the story of a hostile crowd trying to get to him when he was wounded.

He had to hold them off until help arrived and this situation was very similar.

The officer in the rear of the building heard his partner in the front of the building very calmly on the police radio calling in, "Officer shot, EMS needed" and giving out the location and description of the perp. The officer in the rear of the building later said his partner was so calm on the radio he couldn't figure out who was shot as he thought only the two of them were there. He hurriedly ran back to the front to help whoever needed help and surprisingly saw his partner down against a tree and bleeding out. My old partner, who was seriously wounded, but still had his old cop sense of humor, told me his partner who just shot and killed a man was turning white and seeing him wounded and bleeding, was worried about him. So when he asked him if there was anything he could do, the wounded officer decided to lighten up the situation and said, "You can give me a blow job before I go," and they both laughed as help arrived. Most people might not understand cops and chaotic situations, but those of us that have been there know and smile at a crazy calming joke like that. My old partner survived, but was retired as they couldn't remove the bullet. It was too close to his spine and his leg would give out on him periodically.

Those who know or have met a Detroit Police Officer, who lived his life on the edge, now know why we have a strange sense of humor. It's one of our survival modes, kind of like laughing so you won't shed a tear and it allows you to do what most people can't or won't do when needed.

Bar Owner Shot / Police Chase

I had a bar owner friend who owned a rough biker type go-go bar some of us hung around once in a while. The bikers knew who we were and we all pretty much left each other alone. One day he called me and asked if I could come in and be a manager of his bar that night because one of his employees shot a biker the night before. He needed time to work it out with them. He was scared and told me he was told they were going to come in and tear up his bar and shoot him. He normally had a good relationship with his biker clientele and no one wanted cops involved or to prosecute each other. It was going to be street justice and he wanted time for them to cool down. I had arrested a few of the bikers before and had their respect because I treated them fair. For years, I spent a lot of off and on duty time in their world and partied with some of the same people they did. So in a way I was kind of accepted by them even if I was a cop. He was good to me and I liked him and I was goofy enough to like the challenge so I told him I would be his bar manager for one night. He paid me $100 and assigned a bouncer to watch my back.

The bouncer was right off of the boat and couldn't speak English, only Italian. I was told by the head bouncer that he was a professional wrestler in Italy and was being sponsored here by the owner. He was as wide as he was tall and followed close behind me wherever I went, even to the john. I sat at the corner of the bar facing the front door and he stood behind me. I had no doubt in my mind if the shit hit the fan that he would go down with me, if necessary. Everybody was on edge, but for some strange reason I was enjoying the attention I was getting from everyone. I had often taken action while off duty in the world I lived in, but that was usually something happening suddenly when someone needed help. This was different and real crazy, I was putting myself purposely in harm's way because I was either too confident in my ability and enjoyed street creds or I thought I was immortal and I was willing to push the life or death envelope one notch further than ever before. Whatever it was, somebody was watching out for me again and my luck held. About half a dozen bikers came in after midnight looking for the owner and they were directed back to me, the new manager. A couple of them recognized me and seemed to crack a smile as I smiled back and calmly told them there wasn't going to be any trouble under my watch and they quietly turned around and left. Everybody seemed to relax and go about their business apparently thinking I had shown them I was nuts enough to take them on, but they didn't see the mutual respect smiles we gave each other.

I recognized one of them who we helped previously when he had been jumped by a group of guys in the alley behind the bar. I am sure that had something to do with the respect I received. We had roughed up his attackers and then sent them on their way while letting him decide if he wanted them arrested or given a break. Little things like that gave you street creds with these groups. Still I kept watching the front door concerned that they might come in shooting until the evening was over. The bar owner and bikers ended up working out their differences and I was totally accepted by all of them.

I used to joke that the only difference between a Detroit Cop and bikers were we had badges and a bigger club, meaning some of us, when off duty, were just as nuts and apparently I was proving it. I sold my .357 Magnum revolver to the owner of the bar who spoke broken English. After not being there for a while, I had heard he was in a shootout and had killed an attacker. When I stopped in to visit him he was all excited and telling me proudly, "I shoot him with your gun; you no shoot anybody with it," over and over to the delight of himself and his buddies. I laughed and joked with him about it. He was in another shooting later. I again hadn't seen him in months and when I stopped in he quietly asked me, "Did you hear I get shot; I get shot my stomach?" He and his buddies waited for my comment. When I asked him if he had my gun with him, he said, "Yes," and I replied, "Wow, I never get shot with my gun," and we all had a good laugh.

I used to stop in the bar about once or twice a year and one of my old co-workers who had been retired early on a disability would also stop in periodically. We would leave messages with the bar owner for each other on how and what we were doing. He had moved to the Philippine Islands and was running a large whore house and wanted me to come and work with him. Apparently he thought I was as crazy as he was. After a few years the messages stopped coming and no one heard any more from him. I can't help wondering what happened to him as not much physically scared us anymore and the Philippines had a violent Coo during those times.

I first realized he was determined, or a little bit nuts years before when he was working with another co-worker and got in a car chase when he was driving. He had just passed 7 Mile on the Chrysler Freeway Service Drive travelling south bound at a high rate of speed right on the tail of the car they were chasing. It suddenly veered to the right then left down the freeway ramp and they thought they lost him as they passed the ramp. Just as suddenly, he drove down the grassy side of the freeway just past the entrance ramp and he said later it felt like they were going to roll over. On they went, until they finally stopped him a few miles down the freeway. It was the kind of ride that would put your heart in your throat. It's hard to explain how the passenger officer feels as the officer driving goes all out to catch whoever their chasing and a lot of officers are seriously injured or killed in accidents. I once saw a movie called "Freebie and the Bean" and after a wild chase scaring the passenger officer almost to death, he reached over and started choking his partner who was driving after it ended. It was funny in the movie, but in real life and many times, I wanted to choke my partners who put my heart in my throat.

Hunting Vacation

I had worked with an officer who was a good officer but was starting to lose it like a lot of us who had been on the street too long. Some stayed out of trouble, did their job and kept a low profile, but off duty started to show signs and act out with strange behavior. The City chose to ignore this because they didn't want to give out disability retirements for PTSD for on duty related mental conditions or even acknowledge the problem. The conditions would be ignored until they got out of control. This officer somehow obtained a Federal Firearms License that allowed him to possess and sell explosives and weapons most of us couldn't touch. One day he asked me if I wanted to go and fight as a mercenary with him in one of Africa's civil wars, as we both had a 3-week furlough (vacation) at the same time. He told me the government paid $125 per rebel ear. I told him I had other plans thinking he must be kidding, but his response was, "Maybe another time." I had seen and worked with many officers who did their job well but snapped when off duty. He didn't abuse alcohol, wasn't divorced that I knew of, or suicidal; so our so called personal affairs section didn't do anything with him. They usually only got involved if you had drug or alcohol problems and were suicidal and requested help. Then you would be put on what was called 'The Rubber Gun Squad' where they took away your weapon and put you on desk duty which would basically be career ending. There was no help for the officers who just burnt out from too many years of working the streets. There was no psychiatrist or even a psychologist in the medical sections psychiatric section. All they had was a social worker and a social worker's assistant. Both were from the suburbs with no education, training or experience with inner City police officers or their unique situations. Usually what happened was nobody, even supervisors, requested an officer who was losing it be sent to the psychiatric section because the City didn't take any responsibility. The officer was left to take the burden of what he was going through himself. Some were put on sick leave until sick days ran out and then carried sick with no-pay. So in effect, the officers burning out just kept working until they did something illegal, quit, retired early with less pay, or acted out and were fired which basically solved the City's problem about having to pay for their disability retirements.

In my co-worker's case, he went from mercenary combat, to playing with plastic explosives in the park next to the police station after the park closed. The explosions were big enough to shake the station windows. Everybody knew it was him and the desk Sergeant or Lieutenant would tell somebody to go over to the park and tell him to knock it off. When he was on duty he did his job without complaints or problems like most officers who were burnt out and on the brink. Everybody, including supervisors, knew what officers had been under fire for too long, but didn't want to wreck a good officer's career because the City didn't offer any real assistance or duty retirements. They basically were saying, not our problem; they would have to get help on their own, or worse they would just ignore it until the explosion. In his situation, he had shot and killed a suspect who had shot at him years before and it was deemed self-defense, but as usual the family was suing.

One night as I watched the local news I saw a story about an off duty Detroit Police Officer who was caught wearing army type fatigues, black stocking cap with his face blacked out, digging up a grave in a suburban cemetery in the middle of the night. I wasn't surprised when I heard who it was. A few weeks later he showed up at my house and I asked him "What the hell were you thinking?" He calmly replied that he was at court that day and relatives of the man who he had shot where putting on an emotional show and kept saying, "We don't want money, we just want our baby back." So, I was going to give them their baby back. It was very apparent that he had hit the wall and should have been retired or treated long before. The City with a lot of like cases, didn't want to set a precedent and acknowledge officers who had been through too much and cracked up was also their responsibility. What he did was wrong, but he, like so many others, started off complete and now with what he went through on the job, was damaged and being thrown away because the City he served didn't care to treat him.

We had another officer who was a good street officer who had carried a Bible in a special leather pouch on his gun belt and passed out religious pamphlets instead of tickets. Naturally there were no complaints and it didn't harm anyone so nobody paid attention to it. By this time in my career, I had seen a lot and had been affected by our world of daily violence and danger. I didn't think anything negative about what he was doing, just curious. He had received numerous awards and had been under fire and shot and killed his assailant. I asked my friend Reverend Lund the Police Chaplin how he could be so religious when he had taken a life and there was a good chance it could happen again. The Rev told me he was alright and a newly born again Christian and would eventually settle down his enthusiasm on sharing the word to everyone he encountered.

I believe in God, but never had a Christian education and was conflicted on how I would handle it if I had to kill someone. I knew I would if I really had to, but so far by waiting to the last moment before pulling my trigger and maybe taking more personal risk, I had avoided it. Like most cops, when we were put into positions where we could legally kill and most likely even receive an award for it, we didn't. There is a bigger law inside human beings that was against killing and the officers I knew who had to kill were sickened by it and never the same after.

So the Rev's explanation that "God knows our heart" and "Blessed are the peacekeeper's for they are sons of God," helped me to understand that I was here to protect, even to kill if it was a last resort. In my career I worked with, and was friends with, a lot of officers who were wounded or killed, and some that had killed in the line of duty. All that survived were changed. Those of us that were lucky enough not to have been killed, wounded, or have had to kill another, were also affected by surviving it. Usually when a cop is killed, his partners, coworkers and friends are also severely damaged and us that survived that time after time were sometimes broken survivors.

Weak Awards

Apparently the City decided it was too hard for some of their new lower-standard hired officers to gain ribbons and awards. So they decided to add categories and give some out for less than what was required in the past to make some officers look good. The problem with that was it diluted the awards given to the officers who really went above and beyond while volunteering to take great risk for the public they were protecting and serving. Most awards were earned and lots of award winning actions weren't awarded as that was the norm for those officers. Medals and ribbons in the early 70's were awarded only for Meritorious service and they had only 6-7 categories and it took being in great danger to receive them. They also had letters of commendation and commendation certificates for service above and beyond that was required and those were limited too.

In 1980 we were all given blue and white ribbons for working the 1980 Republican convention held in Detroit and most of us laughed thinking how silly that was. We joked about next they are going to give out awards and ribbons for attendance. Then they started giving out lifesaving awards for those who actually had a supervisor write them up for it. That sounds ok, but the problem with that is most working officers saved lives often. If there were more serious risk taken you would have been written up for a higher award while lifesaving.

It turned out the amount and type of awards sky rocked as time went on to around 30 uniform ribbons instead of only 6 or 7. They were given for attendance, lifesaving, perfect driving, working the all-star game, the super bowl and other special events. In the early 70's those duties were considered get out of danger assignments that serious street cops didn't volunteer for until their street dues were paid. All those ribbons on the chest looked good to civilians who didn't know any better, so some wore them, but the serious police officers didn't want to have to explain to someone what each one was for. Imagine saying, I got this for perfect attendance or this one for working the baseball all-star game, or this one for answering a police run and making an arrest. I understand it started with the convention ribbons and went out of control. I feel sorry for the hard working officers who really earned their awards and I salute them. In the early 70's we respected and looked up to our senior officers and were proud when we earned their respect as peers. We won awards because of our experienced street Sergeants who put us in for them when deserved and not by asking or political reasons.

Thin Blue Line/Brotherhood

Civilians talk about it "The Thin Blue Line" but they and the media don't really know what it is about. I think Marines might understand because there are no ex-Marines or ex-cops. It is said, once a Marine always a Marine; same for cops, once a cop always a cop. It is always there in your blood, the brotherhood, willing to go in harm's way with each other or give your life or limb for another. We don't enter with caution when an officer needs us; we go full speed into the fray no matter the odds or danger time after time without concern for our own safety. You can't ask anymore of anybody ever and that's what we share that most people never have the privilege to know. It's a brotherhood that goes past race, sex, or even location. It is shared throughout the world by police officers in all cities as we know unlike anyone else what officers go through. It's totally unacceptable for an off duty officer to give an on duty officer a hard time. We don't always agree or even personally like each other, but we respect the job and the officers doing it. Yes, the thin blue line also means it's only a few of us keeping the violent predators from the masses while being second guessed by everyone all the time. Once a cop your civilian identity is gone you live a totally different life and grow closer and closer to each other like real brothers and farther away from old friends and a normal life. There is no going back even after retirement; being a cop stays with you until death. Yes, cops do stick together and feel a very special bond forever. My civilian friends, relatives and even my parents before their passing always introduced me as "My son the Detroit cop" or "My friend the Detroit cop". Some think we protect bad cops; we don't. We don't want our deceased friend's badges dirtied by bad cops and they discredit our brotherhood. To make a comparison think about how many civilians would trade their life to save yours. I have known a lot of cops who would, and did.

Hit Man In-route

We received a call from Lieutenant Gill Hill of the movie fame "Beverly Hills Cop" when he was then a homicide Detective Lieutenant. He had in the past given us good information on suspects wanted for homicide and we were very pleased and proud that he used our cruiser crew instead of their own downtown cruiser units. He received a tip on a hit man who was hired to kill a Southfield business man's wife and that he would be on his way in a stolen Lincoln Versailles. He further said that the tipster said the hit man would be in the area of East 7 Mile and Buffalo Street at approximately 7pm that night on the way to make the hit at an unknown Southfield location. He was also told that he was armed with a cocked 9mm automatic that he kept on the seat next to him and usually wore a bullet proof vest. Time was of the essence as we were just coming on duty for our 7pm - 3am shift. So with our given information we hurried out to the 7 Mile and Buffalo location just in time to spot the vehicle heading east on 7 Mile from Buffalo Street. It had been snowing and the roads were slippery as we pulled behind. Our Cruiser was brand new and its only police markings were on the doors, so he had no idea he had the police Cruiser following him. We had armed ourselves with 12-gage shot guns loaded with 00-buck shot and knew we had to get to his car quickly as possible and take a head shot because he was reported to be wearing a vest. We further knew he had been just released from prison after serving 8 years of a 20-year sentence for murder. Most likely this wasn't his first contract hit and we were dealing with a pro who wasn't about to be taken alive. With that in mind, as he slowed to make a turn off of 7 Mile Road, I told the driver to hit him in the ass and drive him into the pole, which he immediately did. Both vehicles had slowed as we were on snow covered streets and we pushed his vehicle into the pole. I had hoped he would think it was a minor accident with a citizen on a slippery street and that would give us enough time to get the drop on him. Luckily it worked perfectly and as he turned angrily to look back out of his driver's side window to see who and what had hit him, we hurriedly, even before our car came to a stop, ran to his passenger windows pointing our shotguns directly at his face. His fully loaded 9mm automatic had slipped off of the front seat next to him and onto the floor board. I saw his facial expression change when he reached for his gun while looking directly down the barrel of my shotgun and found the gun wasn't there anymore. I was sure if it was, he was going to go for it and I would have had to shoot him. He then looked around seeing he was had, and raised his hands in surrender.

We conveyed him straight downtown to homicide where Lieutenant Gill Hill talked him into setting up the business man who hired him. He was co-operative partially because he thought surely we could have killed him. Since we didn't, he told Lieutenant Hill that we were straight up with him and he was willing to cooperate. Lieutenant Hill sent an undercover police woman to collect the remainder of the murder fee from the business man, telling him the hit was completed, and he paid her. He was then arrested for inducing another to commit murder in the first degree. Commander of Homicide, Robert A. Hislop then sent my Commander a Letter for a Meritorious Citation/ Commendation, my 14th for "Competent and professional work on the arrest of two felons and directly saving the life of the proposed victim." He further stated he was sure that, "If we had been anything other than professional and efficient that this plot would have been completed."

CHAPTER 10

New Shift

Surprising Move/Cruiser Career Ends

Shortly after the hit man's arrest, I was surprised when a shift Lieutenant pulled me aside and told me I was being assigned to his shift and would be working in uniform with the inside shift until a position on a shift car opened up. I was shocked and asked him, as he was a good Lieutenant and boss, why this was suddenly happening and he said the Cruiser can't have two Crew Chiefs at the same time because the crew was second guessing the new Crew Chief. I was disappointed on how this was happening, but knew my hand picked crew would have to adjust to a new leader, and I would have to adjust to my changing circumstances. Heartbroken as I was, I understood I had done things my way throughout my career and times were changing. You had to be politically correct and go along with the PC agenda and that was not me. Yes, this dinosaur was finally being put in his place as my way was no longer the City's way. I wasn't alone, as the shifts now were shorthanded, but full of great cops. The old dinosaurs that I used to work with in Precinct Special Ops that hadn't transferred, quit, been disabled, burnt out, or killed were there, but not many had been promoted, as we weren't in the correct ethnic class. We were returned to where we started as rookies to the rotating shifts and were supposed to write tickets, answer police runs and stay out of trouble until retirement. That was our reward for many years of good police work.

Injury - Beginning of the End

After the shock wore off I got my uniforms in order and showed up to the afternoon shift for inside duty as the new report clerk. I never had worked inside and didn't know anything about the clerk, computer, doorman or operator positions. Heck, it had been so many years since I had even done reports like, Accident, Missing Persons, or the other miscellaneous duties of a report clerk. I also helped with answering the phones and advising callers on their problems and transferring priority calls to 911 operators. I was so bored and fidgety that I helped everyone I could and learned the computer data entry, which I shouldn't have been doing because I wasn't authorized, so I had to use the desk clerk's authorization code. I gave everyone I could a little help so they could take a break or when they were being slammed with excessive work, but mostly because I was going nuts and feeling trapped working inside. I learned enough to be more than just a report clerk and unknowingly became helpful to the inside crew. A lot of officers had asked me what happened as I went from being Crew Chief of the Cruiser to a regular shift working inside that I hadn't done since being a rookie at #7. I didn't know how to answer them. I know I didn't screw up, get in any trouble, crack up or piss anybody off. I think some assumed I was tired and wanted off the street and others had a good idea I was there due to politics because it was happening to a lot of the good hard working and longtime street officers that worked Precinct Special Operations. I just told them it wasn't my choice, it was politics and they seemed to understand.

The inside crew was a great bunch of guys who worked hard and totally accepted me, but it wasn't what I signed on for. I was a street cop and wanted back on the street even if I was starting over. There were perks to working inside like a TV in the print room that you could catch some of the sports and you were out of Michigan's nasty weather. For me though the quiet time, when it was slow or when all the work was caught up, gave me too much down time to think and remember things I didn't want to remember. I had to keep going forward to mentally survive and this wasn't what I wanted. It should have actually been good for me to be off of the battle line for a while, but it wasn't for me, not now! I had hope because the shift Lieutenant said

I would be back on the street as soon as there was an opening on a scout car and a lot of the guys on the street wanted to work inside. Working inside wasn't punishment, it was a preferred position that you needed seniority to get. I hadn't thought about what I would do after the Cruiser and didn't pay enough attention to the changes all around me, so I was caught off guard. It bothered and worried me watching my old Cruiser Crew and ex-Special Operations co-workers out on the street while I was safe inside and not out there with them. I had come to think, whether luck or skill, bad things could happen when I wasn't with them and I just had to get back out. I was also using up my sick days as fast as I got them and spent a lot of time off duty in the precinct out on the street in the bars like when I was working morality. Months went by and still no opening on a regular scout car and then things got worse. One day on the way into the station I did a flip on black ice on the scout car ramp injuring my left elbow. The Medical Section put me on light duty status which meant even if there was an opening on a shift car I would still have to work inside until I was fully healed. After numerous tests, it was determined that I damaged my ulnar nerve, the large nerve that runs through the elbow; known as the funny bone. Anyone that has hit their funny bone knows it's like a very painful electric shock type feeling that runs all the way down your arm to your hand. In my case, anytime I tried to use my left hand or arm I would have severe pain and drop whatever was in my hand. I had to use my right arm for everything or pay the price. For over 6 months I went for treatment almost weekly at our Medical Section and then the Maybury Clinic. They shot my elbow up with cortisone using large painful needles over and over. They also treated me with wet heat 3 times a week all on my own time off duty while I worked midnights and afternoons. The doctors just kept carrying me on light duty work. Nothing they did seemed to help, one doctor would have me wear a brace and a sling on my arm immobilizing it and then another doctor would reverse the immobilization. It went on like that, back and forth, over and over with no improvement on the elbow or the pain. It was the same results with the cortisone shots, one doctor even told me I was most likely allergic to the cortisone because I was experiencing periodic dizziness and hyperventilating often after getting the shots. Finally, they sent me to a specialist after more than 6 months of pain and aggravation with treatments that the doctors couldn't even agree on and with no improvement.

The specialist then put me through some painful tests where they put needles with wires that transmitted electronic pulses from the top of my neck, down my arm all the way to my hand and fingers and back up my back. The test started out with light pulses of electricity that increased in power and speed that made me sick to my stomach and had me flopping around like a fish out of water. The specialist told me not much was known about the ulnar nerve and as damaged as mine was it was dangerous to have surgery because there was a possibility I could lose complete use of my hand, but that would be my choice. He continued to tell me that it was a type of injury that could and most likely would take years to recover from, if ever.

After months and months of suffering, I now find out they don't know much about the ulnar nerve or how to treat it. The news didn't sit well with me, as it seemed time and being careful was the only real solution. I had been through enough physical pain and suffering and didn't know how much more I could take. Mentally I was between a rock and a hard place, working inside and remembering past losses and traumatic experiences that I couldn't ignore anymore kept coming to the surface with too much time to think. The Medical Section put me back on full duty status saying I would heal in time. I was totally torn, I wanted street duty and off inside duty so I could move on and stop reliving the past that had been mentally buried. On the other hand, I knew I couldn't trust the use of my left hand and arm and that could be dangerous to my partners and me on the street. I now had mixed feelings about my future and questioned myself as to whether I could make good decisions and do my job safely.

During this last year, I hadn't slept well with nightmares, flashbacks, night sweats and constantly worrying about my world being turned upside down. For the first time in my life I was lost, confused and everything felt out of my control. This tough little cop had been through too much and couldn't handle the pressure anymore. I decided to put one foot in front of the other and say to myself, like I always did in difficult situations, "Just do it." Whatever the department ordered, I would do.

Decision made, I put on my uniform and reported for duty on Scout car 11-5 at 3:45pm Roll Call on the afternoon shift on September 11, 1981. I had especially been through hell mentally the last year inside and going through all the botched up medical experimentations had taken its toll. On my first day on the street on full duty in almost a year, we were halfway through my first shift and were called into the station busy to replace some of the inside help who were conveyed to the hospital after a large fight in the station. I don't know what happened and to this day don't remember much, but I was standing at the end of the stations long desk as my partner was notifying dispatch that our car was shutting down. I suddenly collapsed and went into convulsions and everything happening from that moment on became a blur. I was later told that my shift guys immediately removed my Sam Brown and gun then picked me up and rushed me to Holy Cross Hospital in a scout car. They later said from the way I looked, they couldn't wait for EMS because they didn't think I would make it. I have vague memories of them driving at an extremely high speed to the hospital. They said I was all white, clammy, disoriented, out of it, and couldn't speak or communicate. At the hospital it took most of the night before they had stabilized and medicated me.

At 4am, eight hours later, my girlfriend, who I lived with, was picked up by a scout car and brought to the hospital. She said before they would let her see me, a Sergeant took her into a small dark room at the hospital to explain what happened. She said there was a lot of confusion as no one really knew what happened. She was just told by the Sergeant, "He was on duty patrolling when his car was called back into the station, he fell to the floor, went into convulsions and lost consciousness." She was then taken to see me in the emergency room. They wouldn't tell her much because she wasn't a relative, but at that point what happened was still a mystery. When she came into the room she said I was pure white, weak and unable to speak. She held back tears as she looked in my eyes trying to understand what happened. She remembers that I tried to let her know I was ok and not to cry, but said it just confirmed how bad my condition was.

The next day my girlfriend took me home heavily medicated, still confused, disoriented and unable to communicate clearly and only staring straight ahead. They gave her medication for me to take and instructed her to have me see my personal physician right away. She took care of me for months as my hair fell out and I had constant dizzy spells. As time went on I was finally able to speak with a stutter and slowly improved over the years. It was one hell of a crash and burn!

Those were my last days as a working police officer and the start of years recovering as my worst fears came true of being retired on a disability and that story is a book in itself!

THE END

Officers who gave their all to Protect and Serve in the Seventies
"The Best of the Best"

13 Greater love has no one than this: to lay down one's life for one's friends.

John 15:13

Richard P. Woyshner
End of Watch: 1/24/1970

William Slappey
End of Watch: 3/11/1970

Glenn E. Smith
End of Watch: 10/24/1970

Joseph M. Soulliere
End of Watch: 12/3/1970.

Danny Lee Watson
End of Watch: 1/14/1971

William G. Wortmann
End of Watch: 1/15/1971

Joseph K. Siepak
End of Watch: 1/26/1971

Daniel G. Ellis
End of Watch: 2/3/1971

Ulysses Brown
End of Watch: 8/20/1971

Robert Dooley
Shot Critically Wounded: 12/27/1972
End of Watch: 9/15/2012

Harold E. Carlson
End of Watch: 1/27/1973

Robert T. Moore
End of Watch: 11/8/1973

Alvis P. Morris Jr.
End of Watch: 11/12/1973

Leonard M. Todd
End of Watch: 1/16/1974

Edward Pakula, Jr.
End of Watch: 1/16/1974

Gerald A. Morrison
End of Watch: 3/11/1974

Brendt L. Stephens
End of Watch: 5/25/1974

Jon A. Ryckman
End of Watch: 6/28/1974

Frederick D. Hunter, Jr.
End of Watch: 8/26/1971

Alonzo Marshall
End of Watch: 9/1/1971

Marta Shanaman
End of Watch: 12/12/1971

William Schmedding
End of Watch: 12/31/1971

Gilbert T. Stocker
End of Watch: 7/31/1972

Gerald James Riley
End of Watch: 12/8/1972

Robert P. Bradford, Jr.
End of Watch: 12/27/1972

Byron B. Soule, Jr.
End of Watch: 6/28/1974

Robert John Hogue
End of Watch: 12/21/1974

James B. Watts
End of Watch: 3/15/1975

Chaplin William Paris
End of Watch: 3/3/1976

Johnnie Shoates
Shot Critically Wounded: 10/16/1976
End of Watch: 12/7/1986

EPILOGUE

I WROTE THIS BOOK TO let people know the price cops pay to protect and serve them and to try and face my own monsters that I had buried as I couldn't bring myself to remember. I have no regrets of serving and I am still proud of my time on the job and the men who I served with during my years on the job. I, like most cops or combat veterans, try to forget the unpleasant things that happen to say the least. It was just the way of the times, the deadly decade of the 70's in Detroit and I went through it with a great bunch of guys!

CPSIA information can be obtained
at www.ICGtesting.com
Printed in the USA
BVOW06s1436170717
489503BV00011B/118/P

9 780692 760949